John Grundy's

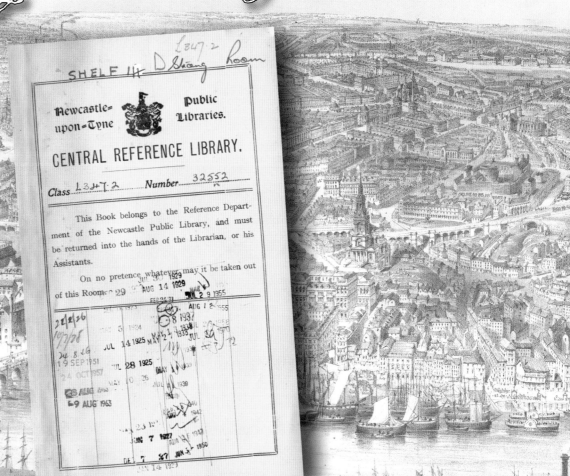

History of Newcastle

Illustrations and photography from the collection of Newcastle Libraries, unless otherwise stated.

Modern photographs by Steve Brock Photography.

Published by:
City of Newcastle Upon Tyne
Newcastle Libraries
Tyne Bridge Publishing, 2016
www.tynebridgepublishing.co.uk

Design: David Hepworth

Editor: Vanessa Histon

Image research: Shawn Fairless and Sarah Mulligan, Newcastle Libraries

Front cover, clockwise from top right: 1) *A 'Perspective View of Newcastle upon Tyne' c.1771 from* The Complete English Traveller. 2) *Newcastle in the time of Elizabeth I.* 3) Grey's *Monument and the Central Exchange, 1900.* 4) *Construction of the Tyne Bridge, 1926.*

Title Page: *Newcastle Upon Tyne during the reign of Queen Victoria, John Storey.*

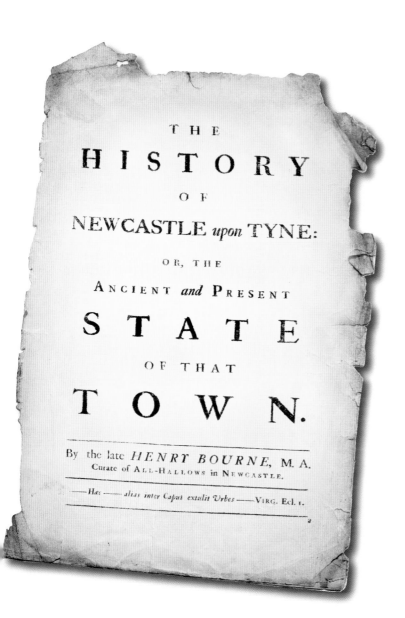

THE

HISTORY

OF

NEWCASTLE *upon* TYNE:

OR, THE

ANCIENT *and* PRESENT

STATE

OF THAT

TOWN.

By the late *HENRY BOURNE*, M.A.
Curate of ALL-HALLOWS in NEWCASTLE.

—— *Hæc* —— *alias inter Caput extulit Urbes* —— VIRG. Ecl. 1.

Contents

Thanks and acknowledgements:

City of Newcastle Upon Tyne
Lord Mayor of Newcastle, Councillor Hazel Stephenson
Steve Brock Photography
Newcastle City Guides
Newcastle Libraries
Tyne & Wear Museums and Archives
The Master and Brethren of Trinty House
Patrick Tracey, Civic Officer for Newcastle

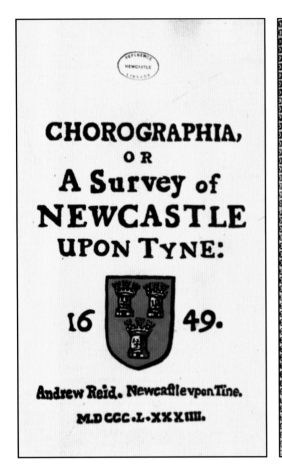
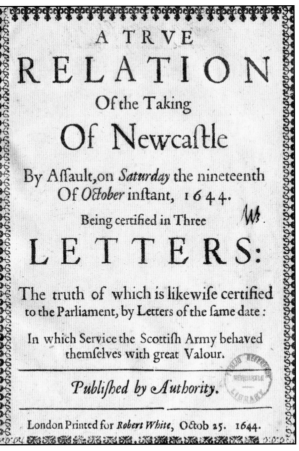

Texts showing various times in Newcastle's history.

FOREWORD

To try and capture Newcastle's history in one volume is a difficult task, the City has such a rich, diverse and complicated past. However, John Grundy – one of Newcastle's most popular local historians, has managed to tell the whole story from the Roman occupation to the modern day. He tells the story in his unique, accessible style – with plenty of tongue-in-cheek asides along the way!

My favourite chapter has to be the last one on the Mayors and Lord Mayors of Newcastle. 2016 is the 800th anniversary of the creation of Newcastle's Mayoralty and of Newcastle's Burgesses (Freemen). King John granted Newcastle to the Freemen at an annual payment of £100 which until quite recently appeared in the City's annual accounts. This Charter and its successors were then repeatedly confirmed by successive Sovereigns.

Few cities in Europe have had the same office handed down over so many years in an unbroken chain. This reflects the history of Newcastle which is one where we have enjoyed the benefit of stability; social cohesion; systems of law, justice and administration along with a strong trading base; innovative businesses and strong communities which have enabled Newcastle to become the great city it is.

I was made Lord Mayor in May 2016. I'm really proud of the Office of Lord Mayor and my role in it. Local politics must run in my blood, my mother Alderman Isobel Cooney, was a Councillor for Fenham ward for twenty years, and my late father, Terry Cooney, was a Councillor for thirty-eight years and Lord Mayor

in 1989/1990. This means that I am proud to be the first ever second-generation Lord Mayor.

The modern role is very different from some of the Mayors that John talks about in this book. Unlike some previous Mayors down the ages I don't have any plans to try and murder a Prior at Tynemouth Priory, or be involved in a plot to kill a King, or sail down the Tyne to burn down North Shields, or in the case of John Marley, organise and lead the defence of the City against the Scots!

My roles are largely ceremonial. The Lord Mayor of the City of Newcastle upon Tyne is the first citizen of the City and speaks on behalf of the area and its community. As First Citizen, the Lord Mayor has a diplomatic role and offers an official welcome to visitors to the City by hosting Civic Receptions and other functions. The Lord Mayor is involved in promoting the City, forging links with business and commerce, attending events organised by local and regional societies, and attending official openings and presentations.

Close links exist between the Lord Mayor and local community groups and a range of organisations such as schools, hospitals and residential homes. The Lord Mayor attends many functions in support of voluntary and charitable organisations as well as supporting many good causes throughout the city – this is something that's really important to me, my theme as Lord Mayor being 'working together'. As part of the diverse duties there are a number of religious annual events which each Lord Mayor attends during their year of office. The Lord Mayor is also responsible for chairing the City Council

Top right: *A print of the Tyne from Gateshead.*
Above: *The Castle Garth near the top of Dog Leap St*
Left: *The Bigg Market, early 1900s.*

meetings, conferring Honorary Freedom of the City status and celebrating and recognising the contribution which individuals make to life in the city via the Lord Mayor's Award scheme.

In the very short time I have been Lord Mayor of Newcastle, I have been involved in many and diverse events and activities. These have included the Newcastle Pride Festival; welcoming tourists when the *Disney Magic* cruise ship docked in the Tyne; local Flower Festivals; the making of honorary freeman of the City; entertaining the Crufts' Champion – the little West Highland Terrier 'Geordie Girl'; riding in the Lord Mayor's Carriage to open the 'Picnic in the Park' event; I used the ceremonial sword to cut cakes at the Queen's 90th birthday celebrations and at the inauguration of the Bishop of Newcastle; I was the first Lord Mayor to attend and address the Eid celebrations in Newcastle; I opened the Hoppings and went on one of the rides with the 5th Battalion of Fusiliers Band while they played their instruments. You can tell the Office of Lord Mayor is a very busy one, but I've loved every minute of the last three months and aim to make my year in the Office of Lord Mayor as open and as accessible to as many people as possible.

I love being able to sing the praises of Newcastle, it's such a beautiful and vibrant city. People love to see the Lord Mayor in the Civic Regalia – especially when I attend school assemblies. The Lord Mayor's robe is scarlet, trimmed with synthetic fur. The Lord Mayor also wears a tri-cornered black hat complete with ostrich feathers and a jabot – a kind of frilled and ruffled lace tie worn around the neck. To complete the regalia, the Lord Mayor wears the Chains of Office which are two eighteen-carat gold chains, each sixty inches long. Suspended from one chain is a gold medallion - on one side are the Arms of the City and on the reverse the Royal Arms inscribed with *Georgious IV Coronatus Julius 19th 1821*. Suspended from the second chain is a gold button with embossed flowers and leaves. The Lord Mayor carries the Great Mace on ceremonial occasions. The Great Mace dates back to 1687, is four foot eleven inches long and is believed to be the largest post-Restoration Mace in the United Kingdom. This is displayed at Council meetings with one of the Swords of State.

What strikes me when I leaf through the book, is that Newcastle is a City of both constant change yet with unbroken links to the past. The Victorians removed many of the older buildings to make way for their new shops and houses, just like T Dan Smith made way for new infrastructure in the 60s and 70s – his activities are reviewed here, many people think he was a vandal but John acknowledges that without him we might not have easy road access to the City, Eldon Square Shopping Centre or such a vibrant learning sector.

Many of the places and buildings discussed in the book are easy to visit and enjoy. Whether you're a visitor to Newcastle or have lived here all your life. How many residents of Newcastle can say they've been to the top of the Castle and looked down across the bridges to the river? Or stood on top of Monument to look down Grey Street the 'best street in England'? Many of these places come alive on special occasions such as 'The Late Shows' or during Local History Month or on Heritage Open Days. Did you know you can get married at the Mansion House in Jesmond? Or visit the perfect, tiny chapel at Trinity House? Or walk around some of the most complete medieval walls in Europe?

Many of the buildings have found new uses and purposes, I hope that this book will help you appreciate and understand their wonderful and intriguing stories.

Lord Mayor of Newcastle, Councillor Hazel Stephenson

THE ROMANS

What we know about Newcastle starts when the Roman Emperor Hadrian decided to build a wall 'to separate the Romans from the Barbarians' as his biographer Aelius Spartianus put it. Hadrian arrived in Britain in July 122 AD on an inspection of the northern edges of empire. (He definitely wasn't on his hols if we are to believe his contemporary, the Roman poet Florus, who wrote, rather wittily I believe, 'Ego nolo Caesar esse ambulare per Britannos' which seems to me to say something like 'I'm glad I'm not Caesar because I don't fancy touring Britain' and he goes on to add some rather cutting remarks about the awful weather – the 'Scythian winters' is the way he puts it - to be experienced up north).

As far as we know there wasn't a lot at the place now known as Newcastle when Hadrian arrived but some clues suggest that it wasn't just an unpopulated wilderness. The river that flows along the southern edge of the place, the Tyne, is still known by its ancient Celtic name and so, apparently, are most of the other local rivers and streams – the Ouse Burn and the Lort Burn, for example. A stone axe was revealed during excavations at the Castle in 1992, so presumably there were people here in Neolithic times. When the Romans arrived the land all around was occupied by Iron Age British tribes and some of them probably lived here or fished here or hunted here – indeed plough marks were found in the soil underneath the foundations of the Roman fort so the Romans seem to have muscled in on some sort of earlier settlement.

The Romans themselves had arrived in the north fifty years earlier when the Governor of Britain, Agricola, had made a push to conquer the whole island and by 79 AD they appeared to have gained control of everything right up to the River Tay in northern Scotland. Ten years later, by AD 90, they'd abandoned the Highlands (probably a

Previous page: Top) *An image showing Pons Aelius by Newcastle artist John Storey, painted in 1853.* Bottom) *Now in the middle of a housing estate in Benwell off the West Road - the Temple of Antenociticus, the image on the right shows a tinted postcard of the Temple made in the late 19th century.*

combination of the midges, the rain and the whisky-flavoured marmalade favoured by Scottish landladies) and fallen back to a line between the Forth and the Clyde. Ten years after that, by 100 AD, they had given up Scotland altogether and pulled back to the Tyne-Solway gap. You might have thought that would have been the start of Newcastle but with a callous disregard for the feelings of future Geordies they had entirely ignored the place and focused instead on Corbridge and Carlisle, which had been built beside the roads that had led the legions north into Scotland. Both towns had bridges over their respective rivers and they were connected with each other by a road (the Stanegate) but here, on the east side of the country, everything from Corbridge to the sea appears to have been out of the frame … until the arrival of Hadrian in the year 122.

Hadrian decided to build a wall from Newcastle in the east to Bowness-on-Solway in the west. It's not entirely clear why he chose to do this but there seems to have been a number of main reasons. The Romans, as I've already said, had experienced difficulty holding land on the edge of their Empire. There'd been trouble on the frontier just before Hadrian's arrival (they'd had similar difficulties in northern Germany as well) so he decided not to try and expand the empire any further. In fact he went the other way and gave up some of the land won by his predecessors. He also felt it was important to give soldiers plenty to do, to encourage good discipline by busy-ness, so he instructed them to build a wall – eighty miles long …five or six metres high … three metres wide, awash with turrets and milecastles and things … oh, and by the way, out of stone! It was an extraordinary thing to do – by far the most impressive frontier works in the whole of the Roman Empire and by far the biggest project in the province of Britain; but as David Breeze has written, it was in fact 'a monument to failure' – the failure to hold on to Scotland.

The original plan for Hadrian's Wall as agreed on in 122 AD was to end it at Newcastle. They started to build immediately in fact, and in 122 and 123 AD the first seven (Roman) miles were built from the river bank at Newcastle and off towards the west. It's now known that the wall went through the site of the present castle, down The Side and so presumably reached the

An artist's impression of 'Newcastle' and 'Gateshead' (some time around the beginning of the 3rd century. The Roman bridge, Pons Aelius spans the broad river linking the fort on the 'Newcastle' side and what would be Bottle Bank, in 'Gateshead' (picture by Judith Dobie).

Tyne beside the Lort Burn, a tributary that still runs under Grey Street and Dene Street and joins the Tyne round about the foot of Dene Street and Sandgate and just downstream from the present Swing Bridge. The reason they ended it at that particular spot was that Newcastle turned out to be the lowest practical bridging point on the river and so they built a bridge pretty well exactly where the Swing Bridge now stands and the Wall provided the bridgehead with some protection. The bridge was called Pons Aelius, in honour of Hadrian himself because Aelius was his family name.

It seems to me entirely extraordinary that the Romans should have been able to build a bridge over the River Tyne at Newcastle; it looks such a difficult feat of engineering. I myself would not know where to start, but then I'm not even capable of putting up a shelf. Of course the river was wider then. It has been channelled and deepened (as we will see later) by the construction of the Quayside in the Middle Ages, so presumably, given the same amount of water coming down, it would have been shallower and less formidable in Roman times. But still!

It had stone piers and a wooden superstructure. It also had two altars and a dedication stone that stood on each one and they are dedicated to two sea gods – to Oceanus, represented by an anchor, and to Neptune with his trident entwined by a fish. They were rescued from the river bed during the building of the Swing Bridge and they're currently on display in the Great North Museum.

It's possible that these two dedications seemed appropriate to the bridge builders because this was the lowest bridging point on the river and the Tyne was still tidal here, but there are other explanations. It has been suggested (by Birley) that these two altars were put there to reproduce the altars that Alexander the Great used to mark the end of his mighty campaign across Asia and into the heart of India. If this was true it would suggest that someone was trying to make the bridge seem pretty important, to associate it with momentous achievements and there's another piece of evidence to go with this – its

name. This is one of only two bridges in the Roman Empire to bear the name of an emperor. The other one was called Pons Aelius as well; it was built in Rome ten years after Newcastle's and it led across the Tiber to Hadrian's mausoleum.

It would seem that this bridge was seen to be a pretty important monument in Hadrian's life – as if his plan in building the Wall and bringing a permanent settlement to the problem of the northern edge of the Empire was regarded as his great achievement. So that's a nice plus for Newcastle.

But why was the bridge built at all? Nowadays we take it for granted that the Tyne Bridge and all the other bridges over the Tyne are gateways to the south – we're so used to the Great North Road bounding off down to London. But there was no great north road in Roman times. As far as is known so far, all the roads from further south were channelled towards the north through Corbridge and Carlisle. So where did the old Aelian pons lead to?...South Shields!!!

It's a rather humbling thing to say but it seems that in Roman Newcastle, all roads led to South Shields. Now, I myself live in Newcastle and worked for many years in South Shields so the notion of crossing the Tyne every day and heading east should not come as a surprise, but the notion that Newcastle more or less started because it was created to service South Shields takes a bit of swallowing. That seems to have been the case, though. In 122 AD, Hadrian, not content with a wall eighty miles long, also started to build a fort at South Shields to act as a point of arrival for troops coming to the Wall by sea. From Shields there was a road (later called the Wrekendyke) along the south bank of the river to…well, initially to Gateshead, I'm sorry to have to say, because there's increasing evidence (Roman pottery and stuff) that the bridge might initially have been protected by a fort on the south side of the river, making Gateshead older than Newcastle. It's a bitter pill to swallow.

Eventually Newcastle was to get a fort of its own but

that wasn't to happen for some time. Initially in fact, the Romans didn't plan to have any forts at all on the line of the wall itself. The forts were to be further back with troops available to charge up to any bit of the wall where they were needed but almost immediately after they started building this plan was changed. As early as 123 AD they made two big new decisions – to build forts into the line of the wall and to extend the wall further east to Wallsend instead of stopping at Newcastle.

Big snub for The Toon – it didn't get a fort and it was no longer the end of the line – just a bridge under the protection of Gateshead. It's a worry.

Eventually, though, as I say, Newcastle did get a fort. It was built seventy or eighty years later and has at least the distinction of being the only fort added to the line of the wall after the death of Hadrian. It's not known exactly when it was built but coins found within it prove that it was in existence by 213 AD and some of the pottery found on the site suggests that it may have been built a little bit earlier than that – at the end of the 2nd century AD during the reign of the Emperor Severus.

It was built on top of the cliff immediately above the bridge, on the site where the Castle is nowadays. It must have been a fearsome approach to the fort from the bridge – especially if you were hauling a cart up to it. I have never tried to do this but I have hauled a considerable amount of personal weight up the steps that still connect the same points and barely lived to tell the tale so it's not clear to me how they did it. I imagine they used one of the other gateways into the fort and wound their way up the hill in a slightly more roundabout and gentle way than the full frontal assault but whichever way you use to try to get from the bridge to the fort it's a challenge.

You would have to say that it's an odd place to find a Roman fort. It is, as we'll see later, a great place to find a medieval castle, high on a cliff with terrific natural defences all around, but that wasn't what the Romans usually looked for in their forts – it wasn't the way that usually suited their military tactics. For the Romans, used to being tough eggs and having an army that, over the centuries, had duffed up any opposition, forts weren't intended to be places where you could defend yourself against attack. They were barracks for soldiers to live in and they were launching pads with gates on all four sides through which well-trained troops could pour out and bop any intruders. At Newcastle, because of the lie of the land, only the gate on the west side could have been used in that way, which would have limited the army's options in what you might see as rather a dangerous way.

Newcastle's fort was unusual in other ways. It was small (one of my history books rather insultingly calls it 'tiny'). Research in the 1990s revealed that it was less than two acres in size and about half the size of Carrawburgh and Great Chesters, the next smallest forts on the wall (and two other forts, incidentally, which were added rather late to the whole scheme of the wall). Because of the shape of the hill top, it wasn't the usual playing-card shape, either, but roughly triangular. So why was it built?...Don't know.

Presumably it was to beef up the defences of the bridge head and to control the roads into the military zone. There would have been a great view from it, along the line of the wall both to the east and to the west. Perhaps (heaven forfend) they'd got sick of living in Gateshead. It isn't clear, as far as I know, why they felt the need to build this rather odd little fort. But they did and Newcastle got going even if quite a number of books on the Roman Wall don't give it much of a mention, as if it was just a minor incident in the whole scheme of things.

Inset: *Part of the Roman Wall, Denton Turret is near the A1/A69 roundabout.*(Dr Tom Yellowley)

If you do attempt the full frontal approach by climbing up those stairs that caused me such pain (The Castle Stairs) you will come upon a curious thing. Finally, after much heavy breathing, you reach the curtain walls of Newcastle's medieval castle and through them, a postern into the castle, a narrow doorway with a semicircular arch. It looks to have been built in the 12th century when the Norman Castle was built, but it is set in a much larger, blocked arch, also semicircular. To the right of it, rather hidden behind bushes, is a second identical blocked arch. You appear to be approaching a sort of double gateway. The Normans, as far as I am aware, never built twin arched entrances into their castles; the Romans often did and I have been wondering for decades now whether this stretch of wall with its twin arched gateway, might not be a stretch of surviving Roman fort. Probably not, forget I mentioned it – it's worth going for a look though.

Nowadays Newcastle people are pretty used to thinking of themselves as the centre of things North Eastern and certainly the place where all right-minded people come to shop, which makes a trip to the Great North Museum to see the city's Roman remains a slightly disturbing experience for a Newcastle patriot because most of the posh stuff on display comes from places that locals now have a tendency to look on as less important than themselves. The museum, for example, is awash with beautiful and expensively made bits and pieces from South Shields – jewellery and domestic items – there are beautiful things from Wallsend and from Corbridge. The centre of Roman Newcastle on the other hand is represented most memorably by a child's stone coffin. It hardly seems a fitting start to our future status (come to Pons Aelius for all your coffin needs).

There must have been more to it than that. 4th century coins were found in considerable numbers when the fort was being excavated, which is apparently evidence that quite a substantial market was being held there by that time. The child's coffin in the Museum of Antiquities implies the presence of children and therefore families at the settlement and that implies the existence of a town round about the fort. The coffin was found in a Roman cemetery in Clavering Place behind Central Station, which is a reasonable distance away from the fort and suggests that there was a village (or *vicus*) of reasonable size beyond the fort walls.

The settlement was also south of the Wall. If you come north from Clavering Place, back under the railway arches towards the bottom of Westgate Road, you reach the Mining Institute – a splendid Victorian Gothic building with railings outside, and on the wall within those railings is a plaque recording the fact that Hadrian's Wall runs beneath this spot.

I love that plaque. I love the fact that as the modern city roars on past, the Roman Wall lurks still beneath our feet. Its route is well enough known. It came along the Fosseway from Wallsend, over Byker Hill (Shields Road follows the line of the Vallum). It went underneath where All Saints Church is now, towards the fort and then on, up Westgate road and away towards Carlisle and all points West. Only once within the city boundaries is at visible and that is at West Denton where a few relatively manky bits of stone lie on the grass verge of the A69.

Which is not to say there are no other visible Roman bits and pieces. My goodness no. At Benwell, well within the boundaries of the modern town, there was another fort called Condercum, which was one of the original forts on the wall. The Great North Museum is thoroughly replete with enthralling artefacts from Benwell – silver spoons, a bronze head, a swastika brooch (a sun symbol I was surprised to discover), lots and lots of altars and assorted carvings but most remarkably the Altar to the Witches Three, a bizarre little threesome of Celtic supernatural beings, wrapped in stone capes and standing under a row of stone arches. It was found, the card told me, when the Military Road (now West Road) was being built along the line of the Wall and through the ruins of the fort in 1751.

Of Condercum fort itself, nothing remains visible. It is buried under 1930s housing and modern roads. But in the middle of that housing there are two terrific survivals. On Broomridge Avenue there are the footings of a tiny temple to a Celtic God called Antenocitus whose head … at least a carving of whose head is in the Great North Museum and I can reveal that he is rather an attractive looking god with a slightly enigmatic Mona-Lisa-like smile, bug eyes and a Beatle hairdo. Altars to him (or replicas of them at least) still stand guarding the apse of his little Benwell temple. A few yards from the temple, at the bottom of Denhill Park there's a bit of the Vallum exposed and a crossing over it that led into the fort. The Vallum is only about six feet deep now as against its original twelve feet but it still looks pretty daunting and the crossing is fab! There are just a few yards of original Roman road and one stump of a pier that held the gate, which is carved in the most careful smoothly worked stonework – wonderfully worn Roman textures and all surrounded by the un-exotic comfort of rows of 30s semis.

The merest glance at a map will reveal that everything I have mentioned in this summary of things Roman lies on the extreme southern edge of the town we now call Newcastle. North of that line, as far as we can tell, was wildness. When I'm standing on Westgate Road, for example, I like to think that once it must have seemed like the view still is today when you gaze north from places like Houseseads – an unconquered land beyond the edge of empire. That's what most of Newcastle was in those days. As I said before, the Emperor Hadrian's biographer wrote that he had built the wall to separate the Romans from the barbarians; presumably he was thinking of the Kentonites or those nasty rough people from Gosforth.

Top) *This statue was in the Temple of Antenociticus, only the head and parts of the limbs were found.*
Far right) *An altar to Neptune (God of water, rivers and the sea) was found in the Tyne with an altar to Oceanus in the 19th Century.*
Right) *A plaque showing the location of the roman wall near the Mining Institute. The foundations of the wall were recently found while a new access ramp was being installed at the neighbouring Lit & Phil.*

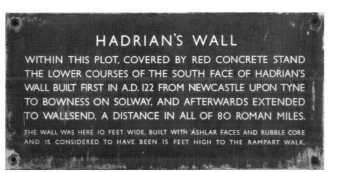

HADRIAN'S WALL

WITHIN THIS PLOT, COVERED BY RED CONCRETE STAND THE LOWER COURSES OF THE SOUTH FACE OF HADRIAN'S WALL BUILT FIRST IN A.D. 122 FROM NEWCASTLE UPON TYNE TO BOWNESS ON SOLWAY, AND AFTERWARDS EXTENDED TO WALLSEND. A DISTANCE IN ALL OF 80 ROMAN MILES.

THE WALL WAS HERE 10 FEET WIDE, BUILT WITH ASHLAR FACES AND RUBBLE CORE AND IS CONSIDERED TO HAVE BEEN 15 FEET HIGH TO THE RAMPART WALK.

ThE SAXONS (rather a short chapter!)

This is just a little bit irritating. The Saxon years, after the departure of the Romans, were one of the greatest high spots of North Eastern history, a flowering of religion, philosophy, art, literature and civilisation, which placed the region in a most unusual position – not on the further edges of somewhere as it has been for much of its history, but firmly at the heart of Europe. In nearby Jarrow, the Venerable Bede, the greatest of all North Easterners (except Peter Beardsley obviously) produced the greatest writing of the age. At Bewcastle away to the west, someone carved the Bewcastle Cross, the most wonderfully civilised of all the stone crosses. At Hexham, St Wilfrid built a church that was described as the greatest in Europe north of the Alps. Born in York in 782, Alcuin became the greatest poet and teacher in Europe, the greatest Latin scholar of his age. From Holy Island came the Lindisfarne Gospels – a miracle of artistic synthesis … you see what all of these places have in common? They're not Newcastle. After its early burst, history goes curiously quiet at Newcastle. Indeed some writers have assumed that nothing happened here at all for several hundred years. Middlebrook, writing in 1950, said 'So far as we know, however, there was no Saxon village on or near the site of Pons Aelius'.

This is odd for a number of reasons. Pons Aelius lay almost in the heart of the kingdom of Northumbria, which stretched from the Humber to the Firth of Forth. Along with Wessex and Mercia in southern England, Northumbria was one of the greatest kingdoms of Anglo Saxon times. Ruled by a succession of highly competent kings, it achieved, in the 7th and 8th centuries, a golden age, which led to all of those extraordinary achievements that I have just been describing. It had been formed by the joining together of a number of smaller kingdoms, especially one called Bernicia, which had stretched from the Forth to the Tyne, and another called Deira which went from the Tyne to the Humber. Pons Aelius had been a border town therefore and it seems very likely that its Roman bridge still existed. It has been claimed that King Athelstan used the bridge early in the 10th century on his way north to fight against the Scots. That would make Newcastle still the lowest bridging point on the river that sliced the kingdom of Northumbria in two, so you might have expected it to have achieved at least some sort of commercial importance.

The evidence is slight but there are some suggestions that Newcastle did maintain a presence in these times.

All around the town, and in fact well within the boundaries of the modern city, there are places with Saxon names: Heaton, Kenton, Fenham, Jesmond. At Benwell, among the Roman remains, at least one splendid piece of Saxon jewellery has been discovered – an elaborate brooch from the seventh century. The Venerable Bede wrote that twelve miles from the sea (and he was usually extraordinarily accurate about such matters) there was a Royal Manor called Ad Murum (or *on the wall*). Later chroniclers such as the 12th century Simeon of Durham recorded that Newcastle's pre-Norman name was Monkchester – the castle of the monks – which would seem to suggest the existence of a Saxon monastery somewhere in the area.

None of these things have ever been found - but in the late 20th century, archaeologists explored the site of a Saxon cemetery beside and partly underneath the Norman castle, in an area that was almost certainly part of the Roman fort. So there were Saxons dying here, even if nobody has yet proved that they were living close by.

Some of the graves were relatively posh with carved stone grave markers, which would suggest that the locals included people of some status.

One possibility for the church they may have used is the church of St Andrew.

St Andrew's lies right in the heart of the modern city just three or four hundred yards north-west of the site of the Roman town. It's on a slight hillside and at the foot of the hill there was originally a small stream – a classic site for an ancient church and St Andrew's is indeed jolly old. But how old? Including ours in Newcastle, there are thirteen other really old 'St Andrew' churches in Northumberland and Durham. Every one of them contains Saxon remains. Some (Corbridge, Bywell, Heddon-on-the-Wall, Hexham and Aycliffe) are among our most important Saxon Churches. The dedications to this particular saint probably started at Hexham, which was founded in c.675 AD when St Wilfrid went to Rome on his hols, or a pilgrimage or something, and was hugely impressed by a visit to Andrew's tomb. When he came back from Rome he brought with him a few mementoes (as you do) including the Saint's knee bone, which he put on display in his new and purpose-built crypt at Hexham. It was eventually nicked from there by William 'Braveheart' Wallace and taken to Scotland where Andrew subsequently became venerated as the country's patron saint.

Our Newcastle St Andrew's contains no visible remains that are Saxon, though it is the city's oldest church with lots of Norman bits and pieces. However, in 2002 the church was 'dowsed' – it was investigated by dowsers using the same techniques as water dowsers use to look for water. Church dowsers don't look for water but for buried stone and they have suggested that the foundations of a typical Saxon church lies underneath the Norman nave. They've left a nice diagram of what they think they found on the wall at the back of the nave and though I don't think that anyone has yet dug down to test their findings, these dowsers have a pretty convincing record from other churches and the whole thing feels … well, it feels possible.

So there may well have been a Saxon town following the departure of the Romans but the evidence is scanty and there's no knowledge at all about what happened here when the Vikings sailed up the Tyne and sacked Jarrow in 879 AD. Whether there was anything to attack on the site of Newcastle, whether they destroyed it or settled in it like they did at York and Carlisle, no evidence has yet come to light – except for two oddities. Byker and Walker are both Viking names. The 'ker' part refers to a bog or marsh, so Byker means the village by the marsh while Walker was the marsh beside the wall, the Roman Wall presumably.

St Paul's Church and a bit of the monastery in this 1938 photo (not Newcastle...).

THE NORMANS

Everybody says this, all the history books. They say that modern Newcastle was founded when Robert Curthose, the eldest son of William the Conqueror, built a new castle beside the Tyne, which gave the place its name. He did this in the year 1080 AD.

It's a funny name, Curthose. 'Curt' means short, 'hose' of course means stockings. So Newcastle was founded by someone called 'shortstockings' (or *short-arse* we might say in these rougher days) – a nickname of course, which referred apparently to his diminutive stature. His dad used to take the mickey out of him. The name still exists in the modern form of Curthoys and I happen to know that there is at least one person with this name still living in Newcastle, though I have no information at all as to that person's height, or indeed their propensity for founding castles though I suspect that castle-founding is a lost art nowadays.

Not only did Robert Curthose have an amusing name (and who is a man called 'Grundy' to laugh at amusing surnames?) but he had an odd history. He was, as I said, his father's eldest son but he didn't do very well out of it. He got on well with his mum (Matilda of Flanders) but he was constantly falling out with his brothers and with his father. In 1077 AD, when he was about twenty-four years old, he rebelled against his father, a rebellion that went on for several years; in fact in January 1079 he fought a battle against his dad and even got involved in one-to-one combat with him. He managed to pull his father out of the saddle and only backed off from doing serious damage when he recognised his voice and realised who he was fighting with. Understandably William the Almost Conquered was humiliated by this, not to

mention feeling pretty disgruntled, and he cursed his son and the two of them only achieved a reconciliation (of sorts) the following year - at Easter 1080 - the very same year that Robert built his father the new castle upon the River Tyne that started our city. Isn't that odd?

The decision to build a castle here at all isn't exactly odd but it does require a bit of explanation because it doesn't seem to have been a natural or even the first choice of place to build. As we saw in the previous (short) chapter, there isn't a lot of evidence that Newcastle (or Monkchester) amounted to a great deal in Anglo-Saxon times and the evidence from the beginning of the Norman Conquest rather backs the view that Newcastle wasn't especially noteworthy on anybody's map. Until 1080 nearly everything that happened in the area, happened somewhere else.

For example, William himself came north, as your medieval kings liked to do, on a pillaging mission in 1069. He came because he'd chucked out the Saxon Earl of Northumbria and appointed one of his own Norman followers, Robert de Commines, as Earl instead. De Commines didn't hold down the job for very long, in fact on his first day at work the locals revolted against the appointment and he was murdered in Durham, along with about seven-hundred of his followers. So William came north in a spirit of some irritation to do a spot of pillaging. The worst impact was in Yorkshire, which was laid waste in an outburst of savagery that has been known ever since as 'the harrying of the North'. But William came further north as well and interestingly what he pillaged was not Newcastle, no mention is made of Newcastle - instead he is recorded as attacking Jarrow

The wooden castle under construction in around 1080. Warehouses are starting to appear along the river's bank . Within the Castle Garth a small church and graveyard are still in use on the ground where the stone Keep will be built. (Picture by Judith Dobie).

and the Tyne Valley, presumably because they were the places that were the important centres of population and local power.

Three years later, in 1072, William came north again on his way to control the Scots. He seems to have crossed the Tyne at Newcastle over the old Roman bridge, but on the way back there had been floods and the bridge was impassable so he had to make other arrangements. On the same trip the Conqueror built his first castle in the North East.

The whole business of building castles was a very important part of William's strategy in becoming a Conqueror. You built a castle; you put somebody important and loyal to yourself into it and that person controlled the natives round about for you. That's pretty well what feudalism is all about. There weren't many roads around the country in those days so if you put your castle in the right place where it dominated a main road, stuffed it full of well-armed friends … well, the country was yours.

In 1072 William built his first north-eastern Castle. He built it at Durham, which he clearly intended to make the centre of his power base in the area. He appointed Walcher of Lorraine, another of his Norman followers, as Bishop of Durham and gave him all of the powers of the old Earl of Northumberland and a lot more beside so that his job was not just to look after the spiritual welfare of his flock but to lick them into shape at the same time.

Now I don't know what your expectations of Bishops are. I have to say that all the bishops I've ever met (just the one actually – he tripped over in front of me when I was in a choir and I caught him before he fell – he was a Bishop of Durham, too, now I come to think of it) have seemed to be pleasant chaps. Walcher doesn't seem to have been at all like that. You get the impression he was a tough egg. His followers murdered a Saxon leader called Liulf Lumley, which annoyed the locals, so in a bid to placate them Walcher came to meet them at Gateshead with a hundred of his knights. Why Gateshead? Well, the south bank of the Tyne was the realistic limit of his territory as Bishop of Durham. North of the river was the old earldom of Northumbria centred on Bamburgh and the Tyne Valley, and it was still evidently a hotbed of Saxon resistance to Norman rule, so he presumably thought he would be safer meeting the opposition in his own back yard, on the northern edge of his lands. A mistake. Those of us from north of the river would have shaken our heads knowingly and warned him not to go. Think very carefully, Walcher, we would have said, before you venture into Gateshead; but he went and was massacred along with his knights. They were locked in a burning church.

William was cross. He sent his half brother Odo, another tough egg of a Bishop (of Bayeux) who, in a sort of North Eastern reprise of the harrying of the north, virtually wiped out the land between the Tees and the Tweed in retribution for Walcher's murder – to the extent that in the Domesday Book the only record of most of the manors in these northern lands simply and rather chillingly says, 'It is waste'.

All of this happened in 1080 AD, the year that Robert Curthose came and built a castle at Newcastle for his newly befriended dad.

You can see why he built it, what with the locals being revolting and all. It was absolutely clear that the King needed a bit more of a presence in the area, that the castle at Durham hadn't turned out to be enough of a deterrent; but why build his second castle at Newcastle when the place had apparently been ignored up to this moment?

To be honest, I don't know, not for certain; but there seem to be a number of likely reasons. By 1080, with Durham already firmly established as a power base south of the Tyne, the King's remaining problem was mainly to be found north of the river in the old Earldom of Northumberland, which was clearly still awash with unruly Saxon barons. A castle on the edge of that territory would be likely to send clear messages.

Above: *An engraving by Collard of the Castle dating from the early 19th century. The Castle seems to have deveoped a more domestic than defensive purpose, judging by the washing line.*
Top right: *Early 1900s.*
Right: *The Castle Keep shown in the early 19th Century before it was embellised with the four corner towers and crennellations we see today.*

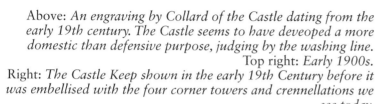

The entrance to the Castle is on the second floor.

Beyond Northumberland, of course, there were also the Scots who were already a threat to William's northern border. Building a castle at Newcastle would help strengthen that border but it would also let him guard both ends of the bridge over the Tyne to provide a sure route north. It has been suggested that Robert Curthose repaired the old bridge in 1080 as well as building the castle and I would have thought it very likely that the bridge was the starting point. Just like in Roman times, the bridge would have come first and the castle would have been built to protect it.

Finally, Mr Curthose did, of course, already have the Roman precedent to follow. The ruins of the Roman fort must still have existed and the Norman castle was built entirely on top of it. The Romans chose the location because the site was superb with tremendous sight-lines and cliff-like sides that were easily defensible; the same qualities must have appealed to the Normans as well, surrounded as they were by a load of hairy Saxons who didn't like them. Another thing that might well have appealed to him is that there was a Saxon cemetery on the site and he partly at least dumped his new castle on top of it. It's difficult not to see that as an act of deliberate conqueror's arrogance – a firm statement about who had the power now.

Robert presumably built a typical early Norman castle. I say 'presumably' because I don't think it has ever been proved by excavation exactly what he built. What we see now was a rebuilding done about ninety years later and I'll come to that in a minute but what he probably built was a timber palisade. There seems to have been at least one stone tower as part of the defences and there may have been more but nobody's really sure. The footings of the one known tower are visible under one of the railway arches just north of the keep. Some books assume, on the basis of what happened everywhere else, that there must have been an artificial mound or motte at the heart of the original castle as a last line of defence, but as far as I know no sign of it has ever been proved and it strikes me as quite possible that in this place with its wonderful natural defences, such a thing would not have been deemed necessary.

But whatever the castle was like, it wasn't good enough. Within a few years, despite its remarkable position, it had been besieged and captured. Northumberland was still a semi-independent earldom and a huge problem to the Norman kings and in 1095 the Earl of

Northumberland, Robert de Mowbray, rebelled against William Rufus and, among other things, took Newcastle. It did him no good though, because William besieged it and got it back again. I would like to tell you a little more about this story not because it has a lot say about Newcastle itself but because I want to mention Robert's steward who was called Arkle Moreal, which I think is a remarkable name. It sounds like a horse's name. While he was off rebelling, Robert had left his wife and Arkle in charge of his castle at Bamburgh and when Robert had been captured at Tynemouth, William paraded him in front of Bamburgh and threatened to put his eyes out if Arkle didn't surrender. He did, because he was a nice ~~horse~~ steward, and William regained control of the north. He abolished the earldom and made Northumberland a county ruled by a sheriff, the king's officer and answerable directly to the king. Newcastle was part of that county, ruled by royal administrators, subject to royal justice and with a royal castle as its focus.

You'd think it would all be over then, that thirty-odd years after the Battle of Hastings and the supposed date of the Norman Conquest the north and Newcastle would finally have been won and become a settled part of England at last...but it was not to be, not for a long time.

The problem...I think it's a problem but I'm not entirely sure...was David I, King of Scotland. He was a great early king of Scotland; in fact he's sometimes called 'The King who made Scotland'. He was also a Norman who had been brought up in England and was a great chum of King Henry I. Henry named his daughter Matilda as heir and she was in fact crowned in 1127 but her cousin, Henry's nephew Stephen, muscled in and claimed the throne as well. There was a civil war which went on for donkeys' years and during it King David ended up in control of Newcastle and Northumberland.

There are two possible reasons why this happened. Firstly, because Henry had been his buddy, David supported Matilda in the war and so got involved; but also he seems to have had an eye for the main chance and used the Civil War to follow up a wheeze of his own. Lots of historians believe that he wanted to recreate the old Saxon Kingdom of Northumbria, which had stretched, until it was destroyed by William the Conqueror, from Lothian in modern-day Scotland, down to the Humber. So, in 1136 he invaded. He captured the castles at Carlisle, Wark, Norham, Alnwick and Newcastle before being halted in his advances and signing the First Treaty of Durham in which he handed everything back except Carlisle which he liked (sensible man) and decided to live in and make his capital.

In 1138 he invaded again. The same castles were besieged and some of them taken. There was a battle at Clitheroe in Lancashire at which David's troops (if reports are to be believed) behaved with excessive ferocity and finally there was a battle called the Battle of the Standard, just outside Northallerton in North Yorkshire. Against all the odds apparently David was defeated but not so convincingly that he had to give up all of his ambitions and at the subsequent treaty (Durham again – the English negotiators were led by Stephen's wife, Matilda of Boulogne, which is an interesting sidelight on the role of women) he kept quite a bit of the North. He kept hold of Carlisle and his son Henry was made Earl of Northumberland. The only places that the Treaty specifically excluded him from were the royal castle at Bamburgh and the royal town of Newcastle but he paid no attention to that and by 1139 Newcastle belonged to David. It stayed that way until he died in 1153 and in fact didn't revert to being part of England until 1157, when his successor Malcolm was made to abandon the north and the border was finally established where it is today.

Did it matter to the people of Newcastle that they were ruled by a Scottish king? Would they have preferred to be part of the Kingdom of England? The answer isn't clear. The Northern Kingdom that David seems to have been trying to create had been a reality for hundreds of years before William the Conqueror invaded and destroyed it. It had been a period of glory for the north and the attempt to prevent it happening again seems to have been led by knights in Yorkshire not those in the North East. The North East had in fact fought tooth and nail against being taken over by the Norman invasion from the south so it might well have seemed a reasonable thing that they were once again part of a different rule. There are still plenty of people even today who feel that the North East should be a bit more detached from London and there might well have been more in the 12th century.

At the end of the Civil War Henry II was the new king who had to bring the country back under control and the things he did in Newcastle were typical of his approach throughout the land. Once he'd chucked the Scots out and established the border on the river Tweed he used a mixed approach to dealing with the town. He was tough – but he was generous.

The first thing he did was to grant Newcastle a charter; he made the town a Chartered Borough and granted it a whole mass of freedoms. The burgesses were allowed to run their own courts, and they had jurisdiction over merchant shipping. They could buy and sell their own land and pass it onto their children. They were exempt from trial by combat (what a relief that must have been) and if they happened to strike someone with a stick, they didn't have to pay the fine called 'strengesdint'. These were tremendous freedoms and there were lots of others which Henry granted to towns all over the country. They were examples of his charm offensive – he bound people to him by making them grateful.

But he was tough too and he showed that by rebuilding the castle as a symbol of his power and control.

The castle was rebuilt between 1168 and 1178 and the work cost £1,144 5s 6d which is roughly the amount I have just spent on getting a few minor repairs done to my car. Presumably £1,144 (not to mention five and sixpence) was worth a bit more in those days because what Henry got for his money was a pretty substantial and pretty impressive castle.

It had stone walls around the outside - quite a lot of which are still standing and in the middle it had a keep which is one of the great Norman keeps of England and one of the main surviving monuments of early Newcastle.

It was designed by a man called Mauricius Caementarius who was paid twenty shillings for his efforts. He built the keep at Dover Castle at about the same time. At both he created a formidable entrance into the tower. Dover and Newcastle were the only keeps in England where the entrance is not on the ground floor, not even on the first floor but right up on the second floor. An extraordinary flight of steps leads to the door and fortified doorways on the stairs made the approach even more difficult.

The Keep was one of the last of the great Norman keeps and it is one of the most elaborate. Each floor has one huge room with a whole host of smaller, ancillary rooms built into the turrets and the thickness of the walls all around. There is a beautiful and richly decorated chapel on the ground floor built into the base of the stairs that lead to the entrance so there isn't a lot of room for it and as a result it's an amazing shape. It's L-shaped, the only L-shaped church I can think of. Because of the position of the Keep, the nave faces north-south but the chancel goes off at a right angle so that the altar can face east in the expected manner. Above the ground floor the Keep is just as packed with architectural interest but it becomes also an object of the most intense romantic fascination – a warren of tunnels and arches, staircases and sudden glimpses...and from the roof....well, a terrific view which includes the Black Gate.

The Black Gate seems to have been the last major addition made to the castle's fortifications in the middle ages. It was built in 1247, by which time castle building had become a great deal more sophisticated. It was built to give added strength to the original north entrance to the castle and it does so by having a remarkable number of different defensive features.

Right: R.J. Johnson restored and rebuilt some of the Black Gate in 1883 (he could have hired a skip) - the Cathedral and the old Town Hall in the background.

It has an outer ditch, protected in those days by a drawbridge, which leads you to the stone vaulted passageway through the gatehouse. This was not only strong in itself but also had a portcullis and at least one set of doors. On either side of the passageway guardrooms gave shelter to defenders who could hamper your progress. Once you got through this first passage, the approach turned sharp right and came to another drawbridge entirely surrounded by high, blank walls from the top of which defenders could lob loathsome stuff on your head. Get through this and you came finally to the actual gatehouse of the castle. Indiana Jones would have had difficulty with that lot and to be honest I don't think the castle actually fell to attackers again.

In fact, to be even honester it didn't remain an important element in the defence of Newcastle for very long. Newcastle itself, as we will see later, was to be a positive hotbed of warfare in subsequent centuries but by the time that hppened the town had a set of mighty encircling walls which enclosed the castle as well and left it without a real function.

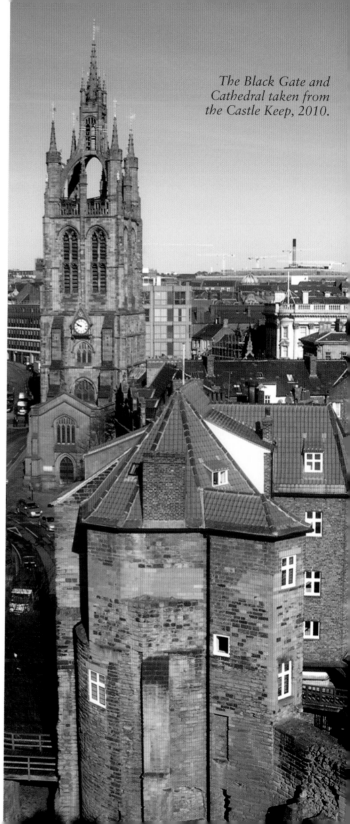

The Black Gate and Cathedral taken from the Castle Keep, 2010.

Clockwise from top left: 1) *An 1835 engraving of the Black Gate where shops and traders line the narrow lane. Some of the houses had four storeys, but were only ten feet deep. 2) By the latter half of the 19th century the houses outside the Black Gate had been cleared. 3) In 2016 the Black Gate and Castle form one of Newcastle's most popular tourist attractions. 4) Steam trains bisect the Black Gate and Castle Keep, late 1800s.*

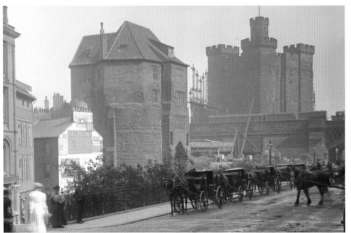

So that's the Norman castle, but what about the town itself? Do you know it's quite difficult to say exactly what there was and when it was built but the town's churches are quite a good way to start thinking about it. There are four medieval churches in Newcastle. Actually there are three now since All Saints was rebuilt in the 18th century but there were four originally and the interesting thing is that all four of them show or have shown evidence that they existed in Norman times.

St Andrew's is the most obvious example. It is still dripping with Norman bits and pieces including a beautiful high chancel arch richly carved with the same zigzag mouldings to be seen in the Castle's chapel. It was clearly designed in the late 1100s and the arches and piers of the nave were probably built at the same time. Lots of other interesting additions have been made over the centuries since then but this is basically a Norman church quite possibly rebuilt on the site of a much earlier Saxon one as we saw in the previous (utterly brief) chapter.

The evidence is less obvious in the other old churches but it is there. St John's was almost entirely rebuilt in the 14th and 15th centuries but above the vestry door there is a survival from a much older building – the head of a Norman window. All Saints has nothing older than its marvellous 18th century design now but at least one old drawing recording the building that was demolished to make way for it reveals ... a Norman doorway.

Left: *The chancel of St Andrew's drawn in 1825.* Below left: *The interior of St Andrews Church.* Below right: *St Andrew's churchyard is perhaps one of the most atmospheric places in Newcastle.*

This page - Left: *St John's at the bottom of a busy Grainger Street, 1900.* Below Left: *St John's in 1991 perhaps following some restoration and cleaning.* Below: *The nave of St John's in 1940.*

Next Page, clockwise from top left:
1) *A view down the Groat Market to the Cathedral. The painting is* The Lost Child *by James Ramsey (1786-1854). The chap on the left in the top hat is Thomas Bewick.* 2) *A view from the Cloth Market, the Town Hall on the left with the Castle in the background, around 1900.* 3) *With the Maddison Memorial.* 4) *From around 1766, a picture of the Cathedral's steeple.*

The Cathedral, St Nicholas's, is another wonderful 14th and 15th century building of which more later, but it too has a sneaky little Norman fragment, another blocked 12th century window in fact and there seem to have been a lot more Norman bits and pieces that were drawn in the 19th century but which have since disappeared.

The interesting thing about these four churches with their Norman stuff is that they are a long way apart. At a brisk jog it would still take you a good quarter of an hour to get from All Saint's to St Andrew's and so their evidence implies that a pretty fair size town was already in existence by the early 1100s and where they are located has some implications for the shape that the town was taking. St Nicholas's, first of all, forms a group with the castle, forming a sort of civic bastion at the heart of the town; the main road from the bridge curled up the deep-steep valley towards it. All Saint's was on the lower end of Pilgrim Street, the other main road up from the bridge and one of the roads that was to stay important throughout the Middle Ages and beyond. St John's is on the equally ancient Westgate Road – the street which headed (and still heads) west. And then there's St Andrew's, due north of the Castle, up the Bigg Market and the Groat Market, along Market Street, marking the end of the main shopping street of the medieval town

So, by 1200, Newcastle had already laid out the road patterns it was going to keep for hundreds of years. It might still have been an infant among the towns of England – but it was already a pretty big infant, extraordinarily well-developed for its age.

STEEPLE OF ST NICHOLAS' CHURC

Most respectfully inscribed to John Hedley Esq. Alderman of Newcastle upon Tyne.

The Middle Ages

In 1200 AD, Newcastle was still a little town – growing maybe but still a mere toddler among the strapping towns of England. By 1334 it had become the fourth wealthiest town in the kingdom (after London, Bristol and York!) It has been described in the following terms:

'*The great success story was the planted town of Newcastle upon Tyne, the boom town of 12th and 13th century England. The customs and franchises on which it was founded were a model for urban development throughout the north and beyond.* (Frank Musgrove, *The North of England*)'

That's the sort of stuff that Geordies need to hear – a bit of success, silverware in the trophy cabinet!

Towns grow in all sorts of ways. They grow economically, of course, they get richer and attract more people to live in them and so become bigger places. More money means posher buildings too and so growing towns develop a more impressive face. In one sense at least towns are like people; as they get older they grow more independent; they get extra rights, freedoms, privileges, they increasingly take control of their own affairs and manage their own destiny. They are like people in another way too; they develop character with age – they become individuals with unique personality traits and an identity all their own. All of these are things that happened to Newcastle in the three centuries after 1200.

Some of the changes that occurred in Newcastle in the middle ages were caused, in a sense, by accidents of geography and history. If there had been no wars against Scotland or if the North East had not turned out to be so rich in coal, or if there had been no great navigable river to export that coal, the town might never have achieved greatness. But other factors that drove Newcastle onwards and upwards came from the people themselves. If they hadn't been driven by a desire for increased personal freedom or had the commercial skill to use the opportunities that circumstances provided, the town might well have remained in obscurity. But whatever shortcomings they might have, Geordies aren't very good at obscurity. Much later in this story, in Victorian times, the North East became internationally famous for the technical and entrepreneurial geniuses it created, but way back in the middle ages the same determination seems to have been a driving force in the emerging success of the town.

Successful people don't like to be bossed around, they want control over their own destiny and by the beginning of the 13th century the people of Newcastle had already begun to achieve that. They had become (thanks to Henry II's charter) a Chartered Borough with a court of their own and a considerable number of freedoms from outside control. Henry's youngest son, King John, despite being portrayed as a BAD THING in so many history books extended the town's freedoms in the same way that he did to other towns all over the country. He provided a new charter, which confirmed everything that had been granted before and added a few of his own. He made the Fee Farm his father had granted a perpetual lease. He granted the town the right to hold a two-day fair at Lammas-tide (when the muir men win their hay, as the old border ballad says – early August to you and me) and he allowed the town the right to elect a mayor.

This was a big step, a GOOD THING, you might say, because until towns got mayors the power all belonged to the lord of the manor – in the case of Newcastle, the king. In mayor-free zones the king appointed a sheriff to collect the taxes and enforce any royal decrees and he appointed a number of bailiffs to help him. Even if he happened to be a local, the sheriff was first and foremost the king's man but the point about a mayor was that he was elected by the locals and (theoretically at least) he had the interests of the town in mind.

Newcastle didn't lose its bailiffs – local power was only granted a bit at a time and for at least another century the town was governed by a combination of a locally elected mayor and a number of bailiffs who acted as the administrative officers for the crown and ran the court system. It's known for certain that in 1300 there was a mayor and four bailiffs.

Still, the possession of a mayor was a big step. He might not have immediately assumed full control but he was part of the growth of local power – a way to pressurise the lord of the manor (the king) to cede more and more power to the town. According to Middlebrook the first mayor of Newcastle was Daniel son of Richard, or to put it another way, Daniel Richardson. And then there was Richard Emeldon who was the mayor on eighteen separate occasions between 1305 and 1333. He might have gone on to extend his run but in 1333 he led twenty-eight Geordie men at arms and thirty-one light horsemen to the battle of Homildon Hill near Berwick and got himself killed. William Bishopdale was another warrior-mayor. He is recorded as having fought bravely at the Battle of Otterburn in 1388. In his honour Richard II granted the right for the mayors of Newcastle to have a sword borne before them in ceremonies. It still happens though I don't suppose leading the chaps into battle is part of the mayoral job description nowadays, more a question of leading the charge to the canapés.

To say that the mayor was elected is a touch misleading. He *was* elected – but not by many people; he was elected by the members of Guilds.

Permission to have Guilds was another of the rights granted to Newcastle by the early charters. Guilds were closed shops, cartels of local businessmen, which were designed to promote their members' interests by protecting markets and regulating standards, keeping outsiders outside, suppressing the opposition. Guild members shared tools and looked after each other in old age. They were a system of self-regulation too, policing their own trade and overseeing the training of apprentices in order to keep standards up. They also acquired the right to elect the mayor, though the way they did it isn't at all clear.

The earliest Guild (in Newcastle like in most other towns in the country) was the Merchant Venturers. It was usually the Merchants' Guild which came into existence first and its members were among the most prominent and influential people in many communities so it often remained the most powerful of all the Guilds. Other smaller and less powerful Guilds developed out of it – each one dedicated to a particular craft or trade such as the Guild of Shipwrights, the Tanners and the Fullers and Dyers. There was a guild of Bakers and one of Brewers - twelve craft guilds in all and they were known as the twelve Mysteries from the French word 'metier', which means a trade.

Well, it seems that it was the oldest and most powerful guild, The Merchants' Guild, which did the electing and that clearly wasn't always popular. In 1340-41 there was an extraordinary situation. The sitting mayor was a man called John de Denton who had already been mayor on four earlier occasions. He was also one of the town's most successful merchants, a tax collector, and a customs official. In 1339 there had been allegations of misappropriation of funds against him and he had been accused by the king of wafting away huge quantities of wool without paying proper duty on it. Despite all this he was re-elected in the normal way in 1341 by the posh members of the Merchants' guild, the senior people of the town as they liked to think themselves – but he quite clearly wasn't everybody's choice. The members of the less important craft guilds were convinced he had an eye for the main chance so they wanted to elect Richard of Acton in his place. Riots ensued and indeed much violence so that the King (Ed II) felt the need to intervene. He fined the town a colossal £500 (remember that the year's taxes were only £100) and imposed a new and fiendishly complicated electoral system onto the government of the town. I can't even begin to tell you how it all worked. There were 'former electors' and 'lesser electors', several stages of ballots, people dropping out after different stages. There were phone-ins (much more expensive on most mobile networks). It was worse than *Strictly Come Dancing* but the effect was the same as was being imposed in towns all over the country in the 14th century – the mayor ended up ruling with a council of twenty-four members (the Mayor's Brethren) to support him and essentially the council had been elected by the same wealthy and prominent members of the merchant class who had possessed the power before. The crown, in the 14th century, was pretty conservative with a small c – it was interested in local democracy – but not too much. Power was to be held in comparatively few hands.

In the 13th century those hands were the Scott family and the Carliols whose name survives in Carliol House on the corner of Pilgrim Street and Market Street. The City Library is on the site of the old Carliol Tower and incorporates a few meagre bits of its stone on a window sill as a reminder. Thomas and Henry Carliol effectively ruled the town in the 1250s and 60s. Then the Scott family provided three Nicholases and a Peter as mayors, not to mention a Henry as a bailiff.

When these families waned, Richard Emeldon took over. He was mayor almost continuously from the 1290s through to the 1330s when he got himself killed at Homildon Hill and that led to the fracas of 1341 which we've just been talking about.

What all these people have in common is that they were rich. They were all merchants as well as customs officers and tax officials and whether they were scrupulous in their honesty or not, that combination of roles certainly provided them with lots of opportunities to get rich.

Which they did.

Newcastle's most memorable mayor of the Middle Ages was called Roger Thornton. He was a merchant (of course) and had made money from silver and lead mines in Weardale. He had arrived in the town virtually penniless but died, 'The richest merchant that ever was dwelling in Newcastle'. From nothing he became a bailiff, a customs official (probably a pretty secure way to raise a bob or two), an MP (from 1397) and ultimately many times a mayor (1402-5, 1416-17, 1423-25). You can still see him in the cathedral. The engraved brass to him and his wife now hangs on the south wall of the chancel. It is an extraordinary object – the largest brass in England and quite fabulously detailed in its engraving. Apart from the large figures of Mr and Mrs Thornton (no name for her, I'm afraid, she was only a woman and so remains anonymous in history books) there are ninety other figures including all fourteen of their children in a row along the bottom of the brass. In the buttresses that flank the main figures there are little figures only half visible, seen in profile on the sides of the buttresses and they are considered to be a remarkably early example of an artist using the trick of perspective.

Rog seems to have had a real impact on the development of the town. Before he even became mayor, while he was MP he seems to have gained some influence with the brand new king. In 1399 King Richard II was deposed and Henry IV (parts one and two) took his place. The following year, 1400, the town achieved the next great leap in its search for independence and local power – it was separated off from Northumberland and became a county in its own right. Only the castle was retained by the king as a royal enclave in the new county.

There are odd things about this story which I have never really understood. Henry IV owed his position largely to the Percy family, in particular the First Earl of Northumberland and his son Hotspur, whose revolt had deposed Richard and put him (Henry) on the throne. Why he should have repaid them by hiving off part of their county and making it independent is not easy to see. Perhaps Henry was conscious of the Percy's power and wanted to limit it. Perhaps Roger Thornton managed to persuade him that a strong independent Newcastle would act as a counterbalance to the Percys and add an extra layer of defence against the Scots. Perhaps he was just impressed by the power of the place, its wealth and potential and wanted to encourage it.

And to Geordies it must have seemed pretty encouraging. London, York and Bristol were other towns that achieved this distinction of becoming simultaneously town and county, so clearly the honour placed Newcastle in pretty rarefied company among the towns of medieval England. And presumably it was the honour that made it worth doing. As a richly chartered borough they already had more freedoms and privileges than their country (and county) cousins possessed but there were some new advantages to be had. They got more control of their own justice system. They got a sheriff of their own. They would get their own Assizes too and that was always a big deal – a big social and ceremonial deal when the King's Justices came to town. They were able to appoint their own JPs who would serve in the town's own courts and they were freed from the duty of serving on juries anywhere outside the town. There was also a requirement to hold their own prisoners. Perhaps most importantly they were freed from all the stuff that happened in on the Border, they were out of the clutches of the Warden of the Marches and technically separate therefore from the war zone. That must have seemed significant, made them feel a bit more like a normal place.

So there you are, 1200-1400, a period of growth from little mini-townlet to major town/county awash with strong local government structures and honoured with splendid titles ... but did this independent local government have any impact on the appearance of the city?

It did. There were public works in these years which changed the face of the city.

Perhaps most importantly there was the bridge.

We rather tend to take bridges for granted nowadays, there are so many of them about and we are able to ignore the barriers they cross. But it wasn't always like that; bridges were of the utmost importance. Newcastle owed its origins to a bridge in Roman times and its medieval rebirth came about because the bridge was there. So making sure the bridge was there and in reliable condition was of major concern to the community. The ancient bridge, still with its Roman piers and the wooden superstructure added by Robert Curthose in 1080 was more or less where the Swing Bridge is nowadays. The Norman bridge was partly destroyed by fire in 1248; its replacement re-used a couple of the original stone piers but added new ones. This one was also badly damaged, by flood this time, in 1339, but each time it was damaged the town's government put it right because the bridge was vital to the town. It is a clear indication of the turmoil the town was in around 1341 that the damage caused by the 1339 floods had not been fixed and the king had to step in and insist upon its repair. This medieval bridge had a gate at each end to act as a sort of customs post and for the control of undesirables from the south who might want to sully the town and almost inevitably for a medieval bridge it became lined with houses, or to use the historian Bourne's more elegant phrase, it became 'a pretty street beset with houses on both sides'. In the middle there was a tower that served as a mini prison or lock-up in which 'lewd and disorderly people' were held before trial – difficult to believe that they would manage to find many lewd and disorderly people on Newcastle Quayside ...

And speaking of the Quayside, this was the scene of the other great public work that exercised the infant borough of Newcastle.

Left: *From Gray's* Chorographia, *a depiction of the Medieval bridge.*
Above: *The Pandon Burn revealed near the Law Courts and Broad Chare, 1994.*

When Newcastle first became a town the river was broader than it is now and washed up close against the steep-sided banks of the Tyne gorge. Two substantial streams joined the river. There was the Pandon Burn, which roughly followed the line where Broad Chare is now, and there was the Lort Burn, which still flows in a culvert under Grey Street and Dene Street and in those days joined the Tyne at Sandhill just east of the Guildhall. There was no quay; boats were just beached in the shallows and unloaded onto the shore. They probably used the mouths of the two streams as little harbours, safe havens, in much the same way as the mouth of the Ouseburn is still used today. Nowadays, of course, there is a broad flat platform over fifty metres wide between the cliff face and a quay wall facing onto the river. It's an artificial platform, gradually built up over hundreds of years starting in the late 1100s. It didn't just happen, local government decisions must have been taken, council artisans appointed to carry out the work. How it developed has been revealed by excavation, for example by an excavation that was carried out in 1995 at Stockbridge, near Broad Chare, and a second excavation further west in The Close.

The area near Broad Chare where the Pandon Burn ran down to the river seems to have been the first to have been reclaimed from the river. Starting in the late 1100s (i.e. after the city got its Henry II charter) wattles were placed in the water to trap river-borne material and allow it to build up. Stuff was deliberately dumped there too, substantial loads of cobbles to build up the dry land. A lot of the new material wasn't local stone but ballast brought from ships trading up and down the east coast and dumped on the shore at Newcastle. Eventually, by the late 1200s a riverside wall was built and filled in behind creating a platform about thirty metres wide from the base of the cliff and very soon it had become inhabited; streets were built and metal-working industries had been established.

Further west, at the other end of the modern Quayside, a similar process was going on to create more new land – another broad platform over fifty metres wide between the cliff and the river. On this new land one of the medieval city's main streets, The Close, was laid out in the 13th and 14th centuries. Parts of it were certainly in existence as early as 1260.

This was big stuff, major works, and of course it had a dramatic effect on the town because in these years Newcastle became a major trading port.

You didn't need to be by the sea to be a port in the Middle Ages. Because land transport and the state of the roads was such rubbish, and because boats in general were small with a shallow draft most rivers were navigable for far more of their length than we would think possible nowadays. York was a major port even though it is almost fifty miles from the sea and on a smaller river than the Tyne. By comparison Newcastle was almost perfectly placed. The river was broad and tidal well beyond Newcastle, so boats could have the assistance of the tide as they came upstream. Newcastle also had stuff to export. Initially grindstones were a big seller apparently though it seems a limited market to me. I've heard it said that the trade developed partly to allow ships that had brought imports into Newcastle to have suitable ballast for the return trip but that seems dubious to me because there were all sorts of things that the town was eager to export. Hides, animal skins, leather were among the major products. There was a tanning industry (presumably exceedingly pongy) down by the riverside near the mouth of the Pandon Burn. And there was wool. Throughout the 13th century and later Newcastle was a major exporter of wool to the continent, indeed in 1353 it was named as one of the staple ports. Edward III, who was habitually and notoriously hard up because of the wars he kept fighting, was desperately keen to get all the taxes he could out of the export of wool so he limited the number of places from which it was legal to export it in a bid to keep tighter control on the trade. They were called the staple ports – Newcastle was one of them.

And then there was coal.

I haven't mentioned coal so far in this book but it's probable that I should have. The Romans probably dug it and the Saxons too, but whatever had happened before, by the 13th century it becomes a major part of the story.

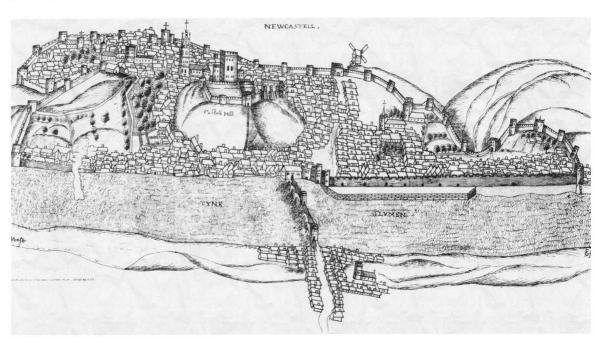

This 1590 drawing is one of the earliest depictions of Newcastle, it clearly shows the wall containing the City. (Reproduced from Mackenzies's History of Newcastle).

If you can't bring yourself to be interested in coal you'll be in a position to sneak off regularly to make a cup of tea while reading the rest of this book because coal and Newcastle go together like me and pies. Even today coal remains just as much a part of the story, though nowadays it's the lack of it that is the issue (come to think of it, in this new healthy world in which we live, that too is very much like me and pies).

Newcastle was (and probably remains) surrounded by coal. The sandstone that the city is built of and on is known by geologists as coal-measures sandstone, which is a bit of a clue. Early sources of coal were found in places that are now well within the city's modern boundaries – on Forth Banks just behind the station, and at Elswick, Fenham and Benwell and all over the Town Moor. Along the Tyne valley, upstream from Newcastle. the coal was at its most accessible – near the surface and near the river. Downstream from Newcastle the coal was less get-at-able, it was further away from the river, so those areas were only developed later in the region's mining history.

By the middle of the 13th century there were definitely ships exporting coal from the Tyne. At the beginning of the 14th century at least 7,000 tons a year were being exported and by the middle of the century this had increased to more than 14,000 tons. Some of it was going abroad but most of it was going to London. As early as 1306 London tried to ban it because rich people, who preferred wood which smells nice, felt it smelt nasty (of 'sulphurous fumes'), but the ban failed because coal was cheap and efficient and the poor, who couldn't afford wood, and the large scale industries, which needed lots of power – smiths and brewers and such like – insisted in buying it.

For a long time the boats that carried this coal were foreign. They came from all over – from the Baltic and the Netherlands, as far away as Italy. Even hundreds of years later locals were still complaining that the coal was being transported in 'French or Dutch bottoms' (no wonder there were sulphurous fumes).

The aim, the Newcastle aim, was to have as much of the trade as possible controlled by Newcastle merchants. The coal itself wasn't in Newcastle, except for the stuff on the Town Moor, which was the property of the burgesses of Newcastle, and it wasn't necessarily owned or mined by Newcastle people. Most of it belonged to the church – to the Bishop of Durham south of the river – it was the Bishop's mines who supplied most of the coal going to London - while on the north bank the Prior of Tynemouth owned lots of the mining rights including mines all round Newcastle - at Benwell for example, and at Elswick. And as we've seen it wasn't necessarily being carried by Newcastle boats.

Nevertheless, you'll be surprised to hear this, but it's clear that even in those days Newcastle people were absolutely determined to be top dog in the area and if the town didn't own the coal itself, it was absolutely determined to develop a monopoly of shipping on the river so it got a suitable slab of the action (and the dosh).

We tend now to think of Tyneside as a place which shares a common identity. People are even beginning to talk of *Newcastle-Gateshead* as if it were a single place. It wasn't like that in the Middle Ages. Newcastle was Newcastle and everywhere else wasn't. The city was ambitious, of course, eager to expand, and it snaffled up a few neighbouring districts – like the village of Pandon down on the Quayside near Broad Chare which had been a separate village but was incorporated into the city in the 1290s – but most places were still absolutely rivals and the rivalry showed most clearly in the control of the river. Middlebrook describes it well. He says that there was a 'perpetual struggle between Newcastle and its two ecclesiastical neighbours for the monopoly of shipping on the Tyne'.

Sometimes the struggle was physical. In 1267 the Prior of Tynemouth had started exporting coal and other stuff from North Shields. You can see why he would want to do it. It was his land, his coal, his stuff and the river above Shields was a notoriously difficult place, full of twists and turns and shifting shoals. It seems obvious that

that's where the coal should go from … but not to the merchants of Newcastle. Mayor Nicholas Scott led a band of marauding Geordies (local businessmen we might call them) to attack North Shields and set it alight. They were evidently not totally successful because in 1290 Newcastle's business community had to take political measures to support their more direct action, so they petitioned Edward I's parliament to stop the export of coal from North Shields. Parliament agreed and squashed the new port and gave Newcastle what someone has called 'unfettered control of trade on the tidal river'.

The Prior of Tynemouth wasn't the only enemy; the Bishop of Durham was another target. He owned the south bank of the river including the southern third of the bridge at Newcastle and he clearly didn't want Newcastle's merchants muscling in on his trade. But they did. They sent gangs to wreck his coal quays at Whickam and Gateshead (the richest coal mines in the country). In 1415 he had to complain to the king that Newcastle had seized his bit of the bridge as well.

It seems absolute cheek doesn't it, assuming a right over other people's property as well as their own. How did they get away with it? What gave them the right? Well, apart from Geordie arrogance (and lots of football supporters around the country are always eager to tell you about that), Henry II's original charter gave them the right and each subsequent coronation repeated it. I'm paraphrasing here but the charter said that all merchants, foreigners and others resorting to Newcastle shall stay and depart in peace, paying the accustomed dues. It also exempted the burgesses from having to pay any of the many dues that were normally demanded on any goods they could claim to be their own (this included, you may be impressed to know, 'toll, passage, pontage, hanse duty and every other impost of goods'). They had been given,

in effect, a right to everything that passed in and out of the river because they were the chartered port.

In the case of coal, the town council charged a toll for every chauldron of coal (25.5 cwt) that passed through the port but that was only one of the ways that Newcastle benefitted. In most parts of Europe trade was carried on directly between the merchants who wanted to buy stuff and the producers who wanted to sell it but Newcastle (and lots of other English ports such as Yarmouth, Ipswich, Norwich and Southampton) came up with a cunning additional wheeze. They introduced the process of HOSTING. They introduced a regulation that any visiting businessman had to be placed under the control of a local merchant who became his host, looked after him, and who alone could buy things off him or sell things to him. The Newcastle Merchants' Guild became known as The Company of Hostmen. It was obviously a marvellous situation for the merchants of Newcastle who, despite mining no coal themselves (unless they happened to own mines in a different and private capacity as some of them did), became the critical middlemen in the whole deal. Theoretically there were advantages to both sides in the arrangement. Supposedly the arrangement meant that the whole business was simplified and the visiting merchants were being looked after by locals who knew the ropes and they were being given hospitality. However, I say 'supposedly' because it is worth remembering that the word 'host' is closely connected to the word 'hostage' … I suspect that on the whole the balance of advantage in the process went to the merchants of Newcastle … who got rich, just as the whole town got increasingly rich.

The wealth generated by the river and the Quay led to other significant public works that changed the face of the town – in particular the building of the town walls.

Inset: *The seal of the Hostmen.*

THE TOWN WALLS

Not many visitors and possibly not many locals realise it, but Newcastle has more surviving medieval town walls than any towns in Britain other than York, Southampton and Chester. In recent years their extent has become a little more obvious as long stretches have emerged from demolitions and the clutter of surrounding buildings behind Central Station and on Bath Lane and behind Stowell Street. Even now they look relatively spiffing – high and powerful and built of beautiful big blocks of well-cut stone. They bristle with battlements and even today are punctuated by loads of towers and turrets. In the past they were even more impressive. The full statistics that everybody quotes are these:

- Two miles long
- Twenty to twenty-five feet high
- Seven to ten feet thick
- Six main gates and assorted minor gates and sallyports, none of which survive
- Seventeen towers of which six survive
- Oodles of turrets of which several survive

The walls, of course, surrounded the whole town. On the inside a narrow lane followed the line. At one place at least it can still be followed. Along the back of Stowell Street is a narrow lane; on one side lie the rear entrances of many restaurants, on the other is the wall, high and sheer. The lane itself is prettily decorated with wheelie bins bearing rubbish from the restaurants. To be honest they pong and there are those who think it's not a very nice place but it seems to me that there are probably few places in the whole of England where so much of the atmosphere of the medieval world is still to be found. It's a dark and rather oppressive street and it makes you realise what a formidable barrier the walls must have been and how tightly enclosed the town was inside the walls.

There is a statement about Newcastle's walls that everybody quotes, everybody that is who writes about the history of Newcastle. I don't suppose DJs on the Bigg Market find it on their tongues very often. It's from John Leland, who is one of my heroes. He was the first great English antiquary and was commissioned by Henry VIII in 1540 to record all the ancient buildings and other antiquities in England – he spent six years doing it (what a job!) and he said in the *itinerary* that he published afterwards that 'for strength and magnificence' Newcastle's walls ... '*far passith all the waulls of the cities of England and most of the cities of Europe*'.

That's saying something isn't it. I'll say it again. Newcastle, according to Leland had the most impressive town walls in England and among the finest in the whole of Europe. I almost feel like writing it for a third time in a glow of gently historic regional pride but it is a statement that needs to be examined. We need to ask *why* they were so splendid.

They were begun in 1265 when the town was granted *murage* by Henry III. Murage was a special right granted to a town to collect tolls in order to raise money to pay for the building of a town wall. It was usually a toll levied on all items being brought for sale in the town's markets. If you sold a cow for example, a halfpenny might go for murage, a hundred rabbit skins – another halfpenny. A horse's or cow's hide (raw salted or tanned) would knock you back a farthing. These examples are from the murage grant made at Northampton in 1301 but they give the general impression. The right to apply the tax didn't last for ever; it was granted for a number years to raise money for a specific purpose. In Newcastle the original grant was renewed on a number of occasions. So, for example, in 1327 Edward II granted the town murage for seven years but a few years later, in 1332 when the wars against the Scots had been renewed in earnest, he made a further ten-year grant in a bid to get the walls finished.

However, in 1265 when the walls were started, there was no war against Scotland nor even any threat of one. The North East had been thoroughly part of England since Henry II took over in 1157 and the Scots had finally and supposedly irrevocably abandoned any claim to lands in England at the Treaty of York in 1237. So why did Newcastle want walls?

It's a complicated question.

There had to have been a threat. You don't build massive defences unless you perceive some sort of threat. In Newcastle in 1265 as in many other towns in the country at that time, the threat was civil unrest. For the previous two years the spectre of civil war had returned to England in the form of Simon de Montfort's revolt against Henry III, so in the wake of that, Henry was eager to strengthen his kingdom and especially those bits of it near the frontiers so he was encouraging towns to apply for murage grants.

It wasn't just kings who got nervous though. People in the middle ages were used to war; it wasn't continuous, but it was common and people expected it. All over Europe at this time communities were affording themselves some protection behind new walls in much the same way as we nowadays counter the threat of crime by turning our houses into fortresses with reinforced glass windows, burglar alarms, multiple locks and attack dogs richly endowed with teeth.

That was the threat bit – not the Scots initially but internal conflict – but there were innumerable other reasons to build a town wall. For example there were good administrative arguments in favour of having a wall. Walls needed gates and gates meant places where incomers could be controlled and taxed, so the walls, though they cost a lot to build, also generated income in the form of tolls. They also meant that you could keep out people you didn't want to let in, vagabonds and undesirables. They provided a clear and conspicuous indication of the limits of the town's jurisdiction. This is us, the walls say; out there, that's them. Inside these walls our rules and privileges apply; outside ... you can dee what you like, pet.

The development of the Newcastle walls demonstrates this point clearly. In the 1290s, when the walls were largely built, Newcastle annexed the village of Pandon, on the east bank of the Pandon Burn at the east end of

Holding up an ancient monument.

39

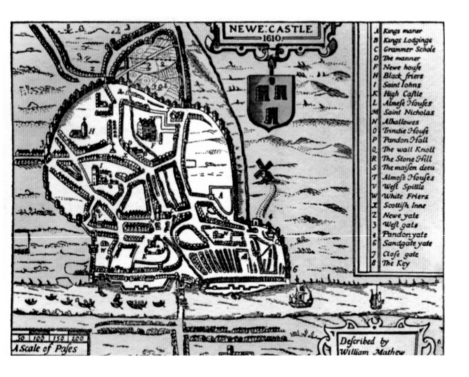

A	Kings maner
B	Kings Lodgings
C	Grammer Schole
D	The maner
F	Newe house
H	Black friers
I	Saint Iohns
K	High Castle
L	Almese Houses
M	Saint Nicholas
N	Alhallowes
O	Trinitie House
P	Pandon Hall
Q	The wall Knoll
R	The Stone Hill
S	The maisen deou
T	Almose Houses
V	West Spittle
W	White Friers
X	Scottish Inne
Z	Newe yate
3	West gate
4	Pandon yate
6	Sandgate yate
7	Close gate
8	The Key

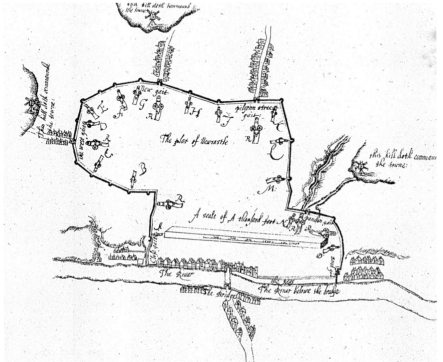

the present Quayside. Immediately the line of the wall was changed to wrap up the new acquisition and make it clear to everyone that Pandon was part of Newcastle now.

There were economic reasons to build a wall as well. Somebody had to build it and provide the stone so there was money to be made from it; merchants loved that. You also got to collect taxes from people and there's nothing a local government liked better than that. If you happened to be a cunning merchant, *and* a town councillor *and* a tax collector on the side, as many of the civic leaders of Newcastle were at that time ... well you were probably in seventh heaven ... or am I being a bit cynical?

On a less cynical note, the possession of walls had other economic advantages – you could use the spaces they provided in imaginative new ways. After 1400 for example, when Newcastle had become a county and was responsible for keeping its own prisoners, one of the gatehouses, the New Gate, was turned into the town gaol. Earlier in the middle ages there hadn't been much call for gaols. Apart from the odd 'lewd and disorderly' person sobering up overnight in the tower on the town bridge, imprisonment wasn't a common form of punishment. It was too expensive – far better to fine people, or demote them or leave them to languish in the stocks and throw a few loathsome droppings at them. But imprisonment gradually got commoner and in Newcastle, as at many places it was the walls that provided the necessary premises. Other rooms in the

Top: *A map showing Newcastle in 1610 surrounded by the wall.*
Bottom: *A 1639 map showing the locations along the wall where defensive guns were placed at the start of the Civil War when Newcastle was threatened by the Scots.*

walls could actually provide the town with an income by being rented out. Many of the towers on Newcastle's walls were let to craft guilds – the Ships Carpenters had a tower and The Company of Armourers, Furriers and Feltmakers, not to mention the one belonging to the Plumbers, Glaziers and Pewterers. The town band took a room and presumably paid rent as well. These administrative and economic advantages in having a wall were important but probably not as important as the final reason ...

Prestige ... identity ... local pride.

All over Europe at this time walls were status symbols, they were the outside image of the town. They gave newcomers and outsiders the impression that they were approaching a respectable, safe and well-run town. When important visitors arrived – if a king visited, for example, he was met in ceremonial manner outside the gates and formally led inside. The same thing happened when the king's justices arrived to conduct the assizes. When you look at medieval art you can see the pride in walls. Ideal towns are always shown with a ring of bright and splendid towers and towns themselves found ways to reveal their pride. Town seals all over Europe include depictions of the walls and Newcastle is no exception, the three little castles on the Newcastle seal are a representation of the town's fortifications.

So, let's go back to John Leland's comment for a moment...'*far passith all the waulls of the cities of England*'

It seems likely to me that Newcastle's walls were so great, not because they *needed* them to be great but because they *wanted* them to be – the walls were a physical manifestation of the town's ambition. Great town – great walls. There's another detail that backs up this view. When the walls down the west side of the town were being built, the intention was for them to angle in and join onto the walls of the castle but suddenly the plan was changed and the walls continued on towards the river bank and enclosed the whole of the Quay as

well. I interpret this in two ways. First of all the important people at the lower end of the town, in particular the wealthy merchants, didn't want to be left outside – they want to be part of this mighty thing. They would have wanted to be included for all the reasons discussed above – protection, administration and pride. But secondly, ignoring the castle is to leave it high and dry inside the town so that it no longer has any real function. They wouldn't have done that if their sole purpose was defence because the town walls, however grand they were, could never be as strong as the castle. They cut off the castle because it was yesterday's building. It had been built by a king to subordinate the local people. The new walls were being built by the local people as a symbol of their strength and independence ... they wanted not just their *waulls*, but the town itself to *far passith* all the cities of England.

I think that what I've just written is true enough of the years between 1265 and 1296 but as the walls grew it has to be said that the need for them changed also. From 1296 England was thoroughly and savagely at war with Scotland and Newcastle, if not exactly on the front line, was pretty damn close to it and the needs for defence began to loom large. Walls took a lot of time to build, often over a number of generations and they tended to be built in spurts in response to new reminders of threats. There was clearly a spurt after the start of the war in the 1290s when Pandon was included and the wall was started along the quayside. In 1315 a broad and deep ditch, water-filled in places, was added to the defences; it is still clearly and dramatically visible beside the section of wall between Bath Lane and Gallowgate though only half the depth that it was originally. Building started along the north side and simultaneously down the east and west sides of the town. Evidence of the speed of building is offered by the story of the Black Friars whose Friary in the north western corner of the town was cut off from its gardens by the wall. In 1280 the Friars applied successfully for permission to have a postern, a small gate through the wall to allow them access to their ground. In 1290 the Hospital of St Mary, which was further south on the west side, was in the same position and was also granted a postern. So there was no hanging around and by about 1318 it is likely that the walls were substantially complete except for the wall along the Quay, which was probably only finished a bit later in the 14th century. But apart from that, any further grants of murage throughout the 14th century and beyond were almost certainly to pay for repairs.

It has to be said, that for all their ceremonial significance, Newcastle's walls were also a formidable defence. Their height, their solidity, the number of towers lent them power. Inside the only access to them was by staircases within the towers so that attackers who scaled the walls still had the problem of getting down the other side. Wooden shutters between the battlements gave an added level of protection to the defenders. The additional turrets between the towers showed that defence and watchfulness was top of the agenda. These qualities meant that they worked. They were attacked regularly – for example in 1299 by William Wallace, in 1342 and in 1388 – but they never fell. Scottish armies camped outside but never got inside the town – indeed on one occasion at least the invading campers got a nasty surprise of their own when '300 valiant men issued and came suddenly upon a great army of Scots which lay in the west part of the town.' The Scots were put to flight and 'The Earl Murray' taken prisoner in his tent.

However, invaded or not, the conflict with Scotland must have changed everything in Newcastle. It probably started off OK when Edward I was in charge. He was out there busily hammering the Scots and the effect on Newcastle was probably pretty good. There were royal armies swilling about the town spending money, invading armies need to be equipped, clothed and fed and Newcastle was the closest large market that could do it. The king kept on coming to visit and must have generated a huge amount of business and prestige for the

town when he did. In 1292, for example, he insisted that John Balliol, the new king of Scotland, came to Newcastle to do homage to him – so suddenly the town housed two kings and their retinues. I bet they did a roaring trade in the pubs that day. In 1296 Edward ordered a ship from the town, the first we know about to have been built in Newcastle. It was 135 feet long and cost £205 – a substantial commission in those days. Those are just examples. Nowadays we're used to Newcastle being on the edge of things – last match on *Match of the Day*, only on the news when there's a strike or a story about single mums – but the war clearly put the town right in the heart of national affairs. Nor did it stop with Edward I. Edwards II and III were never away from the place. People probably got sick of sitting next to them on the buses. In 1309 Edward II even had to flee from the town. He was here with Piers Gaveston, but his army was restless and indeed revolting as so many armies can be and he had to escape to Tynemouth and all places south. On the whole, though, the presence of kings and soldiers, and the needs of war stimulated the growth of Newcastle.

But ... I have a but and it's a big but ... there was a downside, there were many downsides. The war led to real hardships, especially economic problems. In 1318 the people of Newcastle sent out a plaintive plea to the king *'The people of the community of Newcastle declare to our lord the king and his council that whereas they have protected that town at their own cost since the beginning of the war with Scotland and have enclosed the entire town with a ditch and most of the town with a wall ... the townspeople's lands outside the walls have been so utterly laid waste by the enemy that they can earn no income from them ... merchants have put so much effort into protecting the town that they are unable to carry on commerce because of those guard duties, while those cargoes they did send out have been captured at sea ... artisans can find no work...the community cannot sustain or bear its financial obligations...'*

It sounds like a sad tale and on that occasion the king was moved to let the town off from its taxes for two years. But the situation didn't get any better. More than a hundred years later, in 1433, the king had to help out again. He 'remitted to them all kinds of taxes' because of *'their grievous losses in shipping and merchandise on the sea, the desolation of the adjacent country, the dearness of corn in these parts, an approaching war with the Scots and the great scarcity of inhabitants occasioned by a pestilence in the previous year.'* You couldn't get much worse than that could you? And through it all the wall needed to be guarded and maintained. The town was divided into twenty-four wards and between them the wards had to maintain a nightly watch of 100 men – no mean feat in a population of less than 4,000. In Shakespeare's *Measure For Measure* the Duke discovers that all the men in one ward have tricked the pathetic Elbow to do the job on his own for ages and that's probably an example of the sort of tensions that existed. Can you imagine what a drag it would seem nowadays. Most of us can't even be bothered to get concerned with neighbourhood watch, let alone dressing up in uniform and parading the walls fully armed night and day and yet everybody had those military obligations, everybody was needed to defend the town if there was a *'clear and present danger'* and in Newcastle for more than two-hundred years there usually was.

And of course there was worse. Men were needed to go away to war as well as guard the walls. The king demanded a levy from all towns to help fight his wars, of which there were many. A town like Newcastle would be expected to provide, equip and pay for soldiers (at least until they arrived at the battle zone; the king was responsible for their upkeep once they were under his command). Newcastle would have to send mounted spearmen, archers, foot soldiers, men at arms - all of this at a time when there was no standing army so ordinary people had to give up their normal lives and go to war,

Robert Bertram, from the Walls of Newcastle, 1951.

Top: *The walls are particularly well preserved at Bath Lane.*
Above: *An artist's impression of the wall during the seige of Newcastle.*

supposedly for forty days at a time but in practice often for much longer. It's not clear who went or how many or what class or indeed how many of the richer sort paid for others to go in their place. When Edward II called for troops after 1322, for example, it seems that many wealthy people asked if they could fund a soldier instead of going themselves - but clearly that wasn't always the case and clearly there was suffering right across the board - the Newcastle men who died with Mayor Richard Emeldon at the Battle of Homildon hill are evidence of that. To be honest nobody knows how many Newcastle men died in the war against Scotland or how many merely got fed up with their military responsibilities but either way the burden must have been heavy.

And yet ... and yet, when you look at the story of Newcastle in the three-hundred years between 1200 and 1500 it's not only hardship that you see but also evidence of an expanding and successful town. Trade clearly went on and normal life. By 1400 there was a Guildhall where town government and justice were carried on. The streets that we still know today were already the core of the town and the street frontages lined with the houses of the posher people while the poor were relegated to the lanes behind. The really posh – the great land-owning families of the surrounding counties - each had their substantial town house. There would be gardens and orchards and animals everywhere. The town's substantial area held only three or four thousand people so there was loads of open space and every morning the town gates would be opened so people could lead their cattle and their geese out onto the Town Moor which had belonged to the townspeople since 'time immemorial'.

And between the houses - markets. In front of the Church of St Nicholas were the Bigg (or Barley) Market and the Cloth Market, indeed there still are if only as street names; and then there was Market Street where the livestock and the flesh markets could be found. Down by the river there was the Milk Market for all your dairy needs and the Cale Cross which specialised in nourishing bowls of cabbage soup – a tempting little delicacy and presumably one of your five-a-day. On Saturdays, which was market day, the town would be filled, as so many market towns still are once a week, with people from the surrounding villages – from Gosforth and Kenton, Jesmond, Heaton, Benwell and Byker. We modern day villagers still talk about 'going into town' as if it's a separate place from where we live and we still like to go there on a Saturday.

In August, King John's two-day fair had been expanded to a full month – clear evidence of commercial success

There was entertainment too. There was a town band and the town had its very own cycle of mystery plays performed by the members of the craft guilds each Corpus Christi Day. Middlebrook says that they were, 'by all accounts, vulgar, foul-mouthed and sensational, the leads often performing completely naked.' They sound great. I think we should have them re-enacted regularly ... on Northumberland Street.

But as well as applauding naked actors, Newcastle was also rich in good works. For a population of less than 4,000 there were four large churches, five friaries, a huge nunnery, twelve hospitals and loads and loads of chantries all concerned with helping people – helping their bodies as well as their souls. An indication of the importance of these establishments is that they took up an enormous area of the town. The nunnery of St Bartholomew, for example, covered the whole of what is now upper Grey Street, across to Pilgrim Street and as far as the Grainger Market. The White Friars, The Franciscans also had a huge precinct adjoining the nuns (I'm saying nowt!) on the opposite side of Pilgrim Street. The Dominicans or Black Friars had arrived in the town

Next page, clockwise from top left: 1) *The walkway along the top of the wall at Thornton Street showing Durham Tower, sixties Newcastle in the background.* 2) *Atop the hill, Sallyport Tower dominates the east of the town - shown in this 1880 photograph.* 3) *Heber Tower being used as a Blacksmith's shop in 1930.*

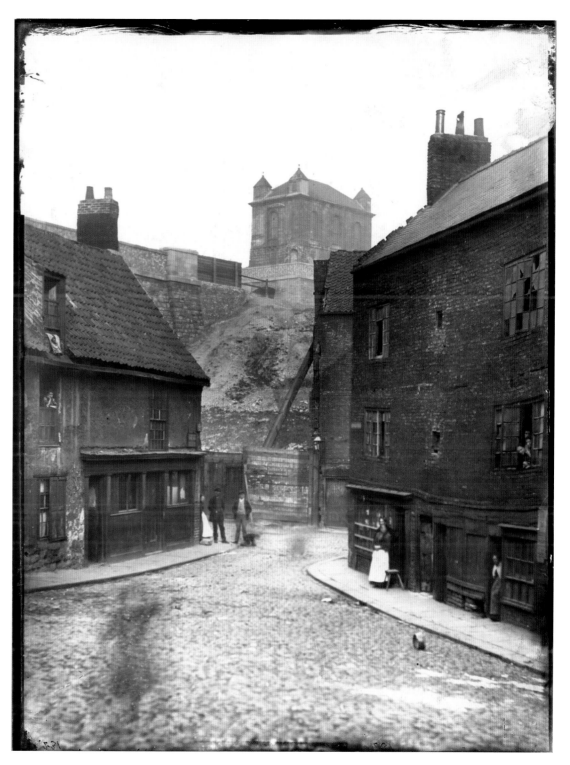

in 1239 and they built what was clearly a splendid place; in fact in 1250 the Prior got his knuckles rapped by the General Chapter of the Dominican Order for his architectural extravagance and what he built was clearly good enough to encourage royalty to stay. Edward II insisted that John Balliol, king of Scotland paid homage to him in the friary church and he stayed at Blackfriars himself with his Queen whenever he came to the town. He paid them a pittance for the privilege as well! In fact all the religious houses were paid a pittance whenever there was royalty in the town. Actually a pittance was 6/8d a day for each religious house, which was enough to buy you a cow or half a dozen sheep. I wish I could be paid a pittance.

So what was the point of such institutions? Well, chantries are an interesting example of the way that the medieval world did things. From our modern perspective they seem pretty pointless. Basically somebody left money in his will for a priest to pray for his soul in the hope that a few prayers wouldn't go amiss in shortening his stay in purgatory. Put like that, chantries seem entirely selfish establishments but in practice the chantry priests had other roles to perform. There was only so much time that you could spend on prayers for one dead soul so priests tended to diversify to fill their time. They helped parish priests with their duties, they did good works and they ran schools – so the practice was far more socially useful than it might seem.

Other charitable foundations were more obviously useful. The twelve hospitals, for example included one called the Maison Dieu down on the Quayside, attached to the Guildhall. It was paid for by that 'most opulent' Mayor/merchant Roger Thornton in 1412 to provide a home for 'nine poor men and four poor women' which is nice (except for the five women who got left out presumably) - but it had other functions too. Its hall and kitchens were available to the town '*for a couple when they are married to make their wedding dinner and receive the offering and gift of their friends*' – what a valuable role in a world where private houses were so small and where there were no church halls or dedicated wedding venues or even (and this is hard to contemplate) no John Lewis wedding lists.

The Hospital of St Mary the Virgin at Westgate also provided a mixture of services. It was there, according to the historian Brand, '*to serve God and the poor and to be a place of entertainment for the indigent clergy and such pilgrims as are passing this way*'. So it looked after the poor, provided accommodation for vicars on their uppers and it acted as a hostel for travellers and as if that wasn't enough it also had a leper hospital (or Lazar House) attached. This was at Barras Bridge where the Civic Centre is now – outside the walls of course to reduce the chances of infection. The hospital also provided a strip (or tongue) of hospital land (at Spital - or hospital - Tongues) to allow the lepers to remain self-sufficient.

The Nunnery and the Friaries were another part of the social and charitable jigsaw. The nuns might have led a gently pleasant and calmly isolated life but they also educated the daughters of the gentry, they acted as bankers for the rich of the town, they dispersed charity and cared for the sick, they provided sanctuary for those in trouble. The Friars also taught and preached, looked after the sick and the poor. It's clear isn't it, that in a world without government involvement or any sort of welfare state, charity and religion had to step in and pick up the pieces.

Of the Nunnery and the Friaries not a lot survives except at Blackfriars. The Nunnery has left us some street names - Nun Street and Nun's Lane - and it has left us the Nun's Moor which is now part of the Town Moor but was their pasture beyond the walls. A fragment of the house of the Austin Friars survives as part of the tower attached to the rear of the 17th century Holy Jesus Hospital beside the Pilgrim Street roundabout. But at Blackfriars lots survives – more in fact than is to be found of a friary in any of the towns in England, The Friars church has been demolished but extensive chunks of their buildings survive as a charming oasis in the heart of the city. They were taken over by the town corporation after the Dissolution of the Monasteries and leased out to the various craft guilds so the medieval buildings have been made picturesque by a pretty sprinkling of later doorways and windows but the core of the group is enriched by masses of original walls, doors and windows, most of them from that first building phase in the 13th century.

And then there are the churches, the four parish churches which, as we saw in the previous chapter, had all been in existence in Norman times. All Saints was rebuilt in the 18th century and of that more later, but the other three were all extended and beautified in the 14th and 15th centuries. This is interesting, very interesting I think, because in most of the rest of Northumberland the best church building comes, like at Blackfriars, from the 1200s, the 13th century, which was a time of comparative peace – after the Norman Conquest had settled down and before the wars against Scotland had got going. 14th and 15th century churches are rare in Northumberland because life was so savage at the time. As the people of Bamburgh (possessors of one of the great 13th century churches) wrote to the king in 1318 they had '...*once again been captured and laid waste so that they are utterly burned to the ground*'. A century later, in 1435, an Italian Papal Legate travelled through Northumberland. He was called Aeneas Silvius and he was later made Pope Pius II. He described the county as 'uninhabitable, uncultivatable and horrible.'

But Newcastle's churches are different from the rest of the county's and contain very little 13th century work. They are dominated by work done in the 14th and 15th centuries – right in the middle of the war. St Andrew's has lots of Norman work, of course, as we saw earlier but it also has massive 15th century windows and huge 15th century aisles. St John's, despite its one Norman fragment, was really built entirely in the hot flush of war. It has a slender and elegant tower of the late 15th century and beautiful stripped down arches in the nave. It really is a wonderful interior – noble and simple and intensely spiritual. And then there's St Nicholas's, a cathedral since 1882, but for most of its life one of the largest and greatest parish churches of England. It has the same utterly undecorated piers and arches as St John's, stripped bare of all decoration.

Each of the churches contains beautiful things made in the Middle Ages. All three have a wonderful, towering, intricately carved wooden font cover. Each one is suspended by a chain through the vault of the tower above it. St John's and the Cathedral both have their original fonts as well, elegantly octagonal. The Cathedral font has a brightly painted heraldic shield on ever face and looks the very picture of medieval chivalry. The cathedral also has one wonderful fragment of ancient stained glass. It shows a baby Jesus rather desperately sucking at his mother's breast. There's a slightly manic look in his eyes and if I were her I would be a touch worried about his teeth ...

What they seem to say, these three surviving medieval churches, is that despite the endless war that swirled around Newcastle for over 200 years, the town had other concerns as well – spiritual concerns, artistic concerns ... and business concerns. It is clear that despite the hardship of war Newcastle felt comparatively confident behind its cosily massive walls and its merchants continued to make money because they clearly had enough left over to pay for all the good things that happened in the middle ages - and none more so than the late 15th century merchant Robert Rhodes, whose initials

Centre: *A fragment of ancient stained glass in the Cathedral, showing a hungry infant Jesus* and coat of arms are to be found on everything. He paid for the tower at St John's and the transepts at St Andrew's. He put his coat of arms all over the font at St Nicholas's and it was he who paid for Newcastle's ultimate crowning glory.

The tower of the Church of St Nicholas with its extraordinary crown is one of medieval England's great architectural achievements. It is fifty-nine metres tall, which is just over 193 feet for those of you who prefer to think in old money. It's not a good tower, or a great tower ... it's an act of genius. It's daring, technologically brilliant and entirely beautiful and you can't get better than that. It was built in the late 1400s when Newcastle was still locked in a war zone. It was paid for by trade on the river in the same way that everything else in Newcastle had been paid for. By the time it was built Newcastle was the fourth most important town in the country. Its quay was among the longest in the country; its walls among the finest in Europe. We don't know a lot about its houses because none of them have survived, but there must have been splendour there if the people who lived in them could afford to produce works like the tower of St Nicholas.

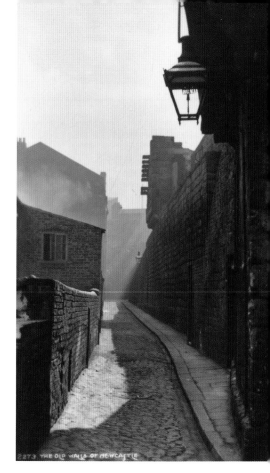

THE OLD WALLS OF NEWCASTLE

Compared to York, which was more or less on a par with it in terms of medieval greatness, Newcastle has fewer surviving monuments from those times but then it was never a cathedral town or the centre of a hugely rich hinterland like the one that surrounds York. Newcastle created its medieval greatness out of harder stuff than York – from coal and grindstones, shipping and war. And of course after the Middle Ages, Newcastle continued to grow and achieve until it became, in the 19th century, one of the powerhouses of the Industrial Revolution. But in my opinion, the amazing thing is that among all of that later expansion, so much of the town's medieval past still survives. I spent a few hours just before finishing this chapter walking around Newcastle with eyes only for the Middle Ages. It was September so the schools had gone back and lots of adults had come out to play; a ferry had clearly come in from Holland and the streets were filled with Dutch people clutching informative leaflets; freshers at the university had been sent off on exploratory town trails so I was far from alone on my little medieval tour; the castle and all of the churches were dotted with similar pilgrims. I suspect that we were all impressed with what we saw – mighty defences and delicate beauty – medieval walls, windows and doors; medieval glass, woodwork and metalwork. There was brash self confidence but there were tiny and tender moments as well and to see them all, I need to point out, required a substantial walk, much of it on extreme gradients. It was a two cup of coffee walk of more than three miles and it revealed a town that having emerged from its Norman origins had achieved greatness. I wonder what sort of Newcastle might be revealed by my blinkered walks through later centuries.

Clockwise from above. 1) *Plummer Tower finds alternative uses in 1915.* 2) *Heber Tower, used as a Blacksmith's shop in this 1903 image.* 3) *An illustration of the Wall betweem Gunner Tower and Pink Tower.* 4) *The City Walls behind Stowell Street sometimes smell like Medieval times.* 5) *Back Stowell Street from Morden Tower, 1890.*

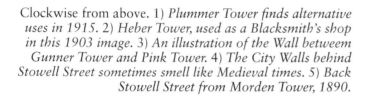

Tudor Times (1500-1600ish)

I ended the previous chapter walking around the town with an eye for the surviving riches of Medieval Newcastle. Well, I did it again before starting this chapter but this time I roamed about looking for stuff that had been made or built between 1500 and about 1600. I found nothing – well, virtually nothing, there were a couple of windows in the vestry of St John's Church that looked as if they might have been from the time of Henry VIII but that didn't seem enough to represent a whole century so I went home and did an armchair stroll through my guidebooks to see if I had missed anything but I didn't come up with a lot more - a few 16th century roof structures in buildings near the river, some timbers in the frames of houses and warehouses altered in the 17th century, just possibly one painted plaster ceiling down on the Quayside (though that was probably made after 1600 rather than in the 1500s) and that was it. There doesn't seem to be even one complete Tudor building or any decorative features, not even a Tudor monument in any of the churches; Newcastle today appears to be a largely 16th century-free zone.

I was surprised. I was surprised as you must be if you've seen some of the splendours that the town had been capable of producing in the war-torn medieval times – the castle, the quay, the town walls, the magnificent lantern tower of St Nicholas's Church. You would expect such endeavours to continue into a new century especially when you consider that in the nation as a whole, the Tudor period is generally advertised as a pretty impressive time and a bit of A GOLDEN AGE of English art and architecture when anybody who was anybody was littering the landscape with palaces and fine, mellow Elizabethan manor houses.

What surprised me most of all was that this shortage exists despite the fact that there were definitely reasons at that time why the people of Newcastle might have had the desire, the opportunity and even the money to change the face of the town. I intend to list some of them for you ... whether you want me to or not.

The first was that the wars against Scotland were gradually beginning to come to an end. After the Scots had been comprehensively defeated at the Battle of Flodden in 1513, full scale warfare gradually became a thing of the past. There were bits of flare ups in the middle of the century but even when they happened the fighting took place much further north so the only involvement Newcastle had was to watch occasional armies passing through on their way to Scotland. In the previous couple of centuries war had come much closer to home and there had been Scottish armies and raiders at the gates on numerous occasions; for the next hundred years there were none. In the past (as we saw) Newcastle had been awash with visiting kings, now, increasing stability meant that a whole century went by without a single royal visit, which might have seemed a bit sad if you liked your pageantry but at least was a clear sign that the town was gradually settling down to a more normal sort of life.

Further north though, in rural Northumberland, things were still decidedly rough. The 16th century was the time of the Border Reivers with cattle rustling, small-scale raiding and constant localised violence but Newcastle was clearly beginning to think itself beyond that sort of thing. In 1554 the members of the Merchant Venturers Guild made it absolutely clear that they wanted nothing to do with those nasty, rough country folk from rural Northumberland and especially those from the particularly violent valleys of Tynedale and Redesdale:

'No fre brother of this Fellysshype (they wrote in their regulations) shall, from hensfourthe, take non apprentice, to serve in this Fellysshype, of none suche as is or shal be borne or brought up in Tynedall, Ryddisdale or anye other suche lycke places; on payne of £200.'

You wouldn't get away with that sort of discrimination nowadays (not to mention that spelling) but it is certainly evidence that the people of Newcastle – well, at least the powers that be (since the Merchant Venturers were the richest and most powerful people in the town) were distancing themselves from the warlike past and keen to get on with the business of making money and you might have expected that that money would have left a visible legacy in the City today.

But no.

The second opportunity that was presented to the town was the Dissolution of the Monasteries. Though Newcastle was the only large town in the whole of England that didn't have a monastery within its walls it was rich in all sorts of other religious buildings. There were five friaries (two of them huge), a nunnery (even huger), twelve charitable hospitals and a whole host of chantries set up to pray for the souls of dead rich folk. All of these were closed down by Henry VIII over a ten-year period starting in 1536.

My impression of this process used to be that it seemed an extremely draconian thing to have done and that it must have caused a sense of tremendous shock at the time, but when you look at what the situation was in Newcastle (and I'm sure that the situation was no different in the rest of the country) there are clues that the Dissolution didn't quite come out of the blue. It is fairly clear, for example, that there had always been conflict between the town and the church; the old merchant Geordies with their insatiable desire to make money and keep complete control of their river had been in a constant state of opposition to the great potentates of the church. There had been hundreds of years of battles with the Bishop of Durham, for example, over his right (his cheek the Newcastle merchants would have said) to trade

Black Friars

on the Tyne and you might recall the literally inflammatory response when the Prior of Tynemouth had the temerity to attempt to create a new port at North Shields in 1267. Well those conflicts continued, to the extent that in the year that Henry VIII came to the throne there was (according to the historian Bourne) an attempt to murder the Prior of Tynemouth in Jesmond – not by some lone assassin but by 'a great number of the people of Newcastle headed by the Aldermen and the principal men of the town.'

The presence of the members of the Corporation and the rich folk (actually the same thing) makes it clear that this attack was not a religious outrage but a commercial conflict – the people of Newcastle in this instance were less concerned with the Prior's spiritual role than with his ownership of the local coal mines and the restrictions he was placing on their profits.

The Bishop, too, continued to be a target of their wrath. The Bishops had always been the lords of the manor of Gateshead and we heard in the last chapter about the battles that raged between them and the merchants of Newcastle throughout the medieval period. Newcastle had pinched the Bishops' bit of the bridge at one point and (as at North Shields) the merchants of Newcastle had burned down their shipping quays at Gateshead, but the conflict continued and the town's most audacious attack on the Bishop occurred just after the Dissolution of the Monasteries. Newcastle annexed Gateshead! They took it over in 1553, during the brief reign of the boy-king, Edward VI. Edward's regent was John Dudley, Duke of Newcastle and he was the one who encouraged the annexation. The Bishopric of Durham had been briefly suspended, so Newcastle nipped in and seized the opportunity. They were chucked out a year later but the incident reveals, yet again, that the people (or at least the merchants) of Newcastle had scant respect for the institution of the church.

It's clear that by the 16th century the medieval monastic ideal wasn't revered in the way that it had been. By the time that Henry closed down the Newcastle religious houses, there weren't very many religious people left in them. The figures given by different writers vary from about one-hundred and sixty to no more than sixty but neither of those extremes seems a lot when divided by the number of friaries and nunneries, hospitals, chantries, chapels and parish churches. One of the Friaries in fact, the Trinitarians, whose house was down by the river in the south-east corner of the town, was only occupied by a single Warden when the Dissolution took place and even the huge Franciscan friary only had a Prior and twelve brethren left – which I assume was less than would have lived there in the heyday of the medieval monastic world.

But however many priests there were, by the time the Dissolution was complete there were a lot fewer; there were only six religious officials left in the town. What a change. In Newcastle (as in the rest of the country) the focus had shifted away from the church; society had become much more secular and that secular society suddenly had a vast amount of real estate to play with - in fact I seem to remember reading that in Newcastle about a quarter of the town's area was suddenly available for purchase and redevelopment. You might expect that go-getting Geordies would have snapped it up and left us loads of Tudor goodies to enrich the town but in the event the use that it was all put to was rather patchy.

Some of it never went on the market at all. The hospitals were all spared because they had pretty clear and useful functions such as housing the elderly and providing medical care, so apart from St Katherine's down by the riverside, which became part of the town's new Guildhall, they were all allowed to continue their work. Three of the others were taken under the Corporation's direct control and one of those, St Mary Magdalene which used to be at Barras Bridge on the site of the modern Civic Centre, still survives today, though its buildings have moved to the edge of the Town Moor in Fenham.

The chantries were all closed down. The useful

educational work that their priests often undertook on the side was picked up by others. Each of the parish churches continued to have schools and choir schools. St Nicholas's and All Saints both employed two schoolmasters and Thomas Horsley, a mayor and one of the richest merchants in the town who died in 1544, left money in his will for the founding of the Newcastle Royal Grammar School (which still exists of course). If you do happen to have children or grandchildren, it is possibly worth pointing out to them that the school day started at 6am and in winter the pupils were expected to turn up with their own candles.

Of the major religious institutions two remained in public ownership. One of them was the Austin Friars, a little bit of which still survives as part of the 17th century Holy Jesus Hospital in a bizarre location on the edge of the Central Motorway, cowering beneath the traffic on the Pilgrim Street roundabout. It was taken over by the Government, by King Henry himself, as a sort of back-up HQ for the Council of the North, to be used whenever the Council wasn't in session at its main base in York. In some ways the Council of the North was rather a modern sort of institution, very recognisable to those of us who live our lives surrounded by debates about regional devolution. It was a bit like the 'Northern Powerhouse' that has been much trumpeted by governments in recent years – and probably just as effective. You see, the Tudors had almost entirely concentrated power in the South East of the country. In the area around London they built or acquired about eighty-six palaces, for example; in the whole North they had just two and one of them was this set of buildings in Newcastle. Clearly the north was in danger of being left out in the cold altogether and so the purpose of The Council was to make Northerners feel less isolated and hopefully dissuade them from being too revolting. So the intentions behind the formation of the Council were fairly good but in the event, like so many Governmental good ideas, the Newcastle branch of The Council of the North delivered very little and the friary building was barely ever used, so that by 1596 it was described as being 'much dilapidated'. Newcastle then (as now) was a step too far for the London establishment.

The Black Friars, the home of the Dominicans, fared quite a lot better because it was dealt with by local people who found a decent use for it. It was bought by the Corporation in 1544 and leased off in bits to nine of the town's guilds. The Butchers and the Bakers were there. There were no Candlestick Makers but there were Tanners, Cordwainers, Fullers and Dyers, Skinners, Glovers and Tailors. They didn't knock it down or pull it about too much. Well, they pulled the church down but the surrounding buildings were kept, The guilds just moved into them, got a room each and stayed there for centuries with the result that the Friary

The restored Black Friars provides a great atmosphere for small shops and a restaurant.

buildings still exist today to a greater extent than anywhere else in the country – not as Tudor buildings, mind you, but as a splendid survival from the Middle Ages.

Two of the other religious houses – The Nunnery and the Franciscan Friary which, you may remember, shared neighbouring sites inside the walls in the upper, northern part of the town, were bought in 1563 by a local man called Robert Anderson who knocked them down and built a vast house in a huge garden. It was called Newe Place initially though his Anderson descendants who continued to live in it for the next 250 years changed the name (rather modestly, you might think) to Anderson Place. It started life as the sort of great half-timbered house in the Tudor style that we expect but it was added to splendidly and adventurously with later classical additions in brick and it had the reputation (among Newcastle folk at least) of being the greatest house in the

kingdom to be found within any English town's medieval walls. It no longer exists, sadly, but its later history and its eventual demise was to have an enormous effect on the transformation of the town in the 19th century – but of that, more later.

Robert Anderson was a member of the town's ruling elite. He was also a merchant and a coal owner and his family and descendants, along with all their merchant buddies, were to go on and benefit from the Dissolution of the Monasteries in yet another strangely interesting way.

What happened was this. After the dissolution, all of the mines that had belonged to the church were effectively nationalised, they became the possession of the Crown (of Queen Elizabeth I, in fact) and at first, the Newcastle merchants (including the Andersons) continued to make money from them in the way they had before – by acting as middlemen in the coal trade. They

A fragment of the house of the Austin Friars survives as part of the tower attached to the rear of the 17th century Holy Jesus Hospital now beside the Pilgrim Street roundabout.

were, you will recall, the Hostmen, without whom no deal could take place and though they rarely owned the coalmines themselves they got a share in every bit of coal that was sold. It had been an extremely profitable business for ages, but things were soon to get even better for them.

In 1582 the Queen, who now owned all the pits on the south side of the river, leased the lot of them for ninety-nine years to a chap called Thomas Sutton, who was reputed to be the richest man in the country. He'd made his pile in the time-honoured way of combining the role of civil servant and businessman. His official title was Master of Ordnance in the North and he was responsible for all the military supplies and fortifications so he was all powerful – except that he wasn't a Geordie! A fatal flaw in his plan because, if you remember, it was only Newcastle merchants who had the right to make deals on the Tyne and so the Hostmen had him by the short and curlies. They challenged his legal right to trade on the Tyne and won. He had to sell his lease to the locals and the main buyers were two of the richest of the town's merchants – Robert Anderson's son, Henry Anderson and William Selby. They bought the lease of the mines from Thomas Sutton and shared it out between all of their richest chums, the top men in the hierarchy of merchants and guild members in the town who went on to form a sort of cartel which set about controlling the whole trade. They now owned the pits, they moved the coal, they owned the keel boats that transported it down to the more navigable bits of the river and they remained the Hostmen who took a bit of any remaining profit from the ships and traders who carried the stuff away to London or wherever. They made a fortune and by 1600 they had negotiated a deal with Queen Elizabeth known as 'The Grand Lease', which gave them absolute control over the whole caboodle. In return the Queen got a shilling for every chauldron (or wagon-load) of coal that was exported. The Government made a fortune out of it (about £8,000 a year, which was a huge amount of money in those days) and the people of Newcastle made a fortune out of it too.

I lie. I tell a lie. Of course the people of Newcastle didn't make a fortune out of it – just those few of them at the top did and they did it by starting a massive expansion in the amount of coal that was mined.

When the church owned the mines it kept a pretty tight control over the amount of coal that was dug up but the new owners weren't interested in that sort of restraint. They had a sort of 'dig it deep and pile it high' philosophy and the tonnage began to rise very rapidly.

Until the dissolution occurred the North's pits were just supplying about 15,000 tons of coal a year but very quickly after the closing of the monasteries that figure had more than doubled so that by 1565 the Tyne was exporting over 35,000 tons. And that was just the start. By the end of this chapter (1603) the figure had gone up to 162,000 tons. That is a lot of coal!!

The increase in volume came about because the new owners lacked the church's spiritual concerns. They were more interested in getting richer and they did that by expanding every part of the business. They opened new mines in Gateshead, Ryton, Whickham, Winlaton and Stella, and they pushed back the boundaries of what it was possible to mine. At least one of the new Gateshead pits, for example, was thirty-six fathoms deep. Now a fathom is equivalent to six feet which means that some of these new 16th century pits were 216 feet deep, which is a long way down in a world without engines and it gave access to new seams of coal. Bigger pits meant more workers so a single coal owner might employ as many as 500 men. There were improved transport systems too. Horse-drawn waggonways with wooden rails began to appear to get the coal to the river bank more easily; and on the river itself more and improved staithes were built – there were at least six of them stretched out along the south bank in the seven or eight miles to the west of Newcastle. It all adds up to a huge increase in scale, power … and wealth.

You'll have noticed that I have adopted a rather cynical stance so far when talking about the ability of the rich to get richer but I have to be honest and say that as soon as these North Eastern Tudor entrepreneurs got a bit of freedom to operate for themselves, they started to get increasingly innovative, finding new ways of doing things. They were the beginning of a process that would be part of the Newcastle story for the next 400 years. Newcastle was going to end up with a reputation for being brilliantly inventive and that was a quality that began in the 16th century with the revolutionary changes that were made in the coal trade.

The coal owners turned Tyneside into a land of coal. In the Middle Ages, Newcastle had been a port with a broad range of trading interests. It had looked beyond England towards the Baltic and southern Europe, but the dramatic rise in the growth of coal narrowed the focus of the town and turned it into a coal port – a big one, of course, but still a coal port. The great 16th century antiquarian, William Camden described Newcastle as 'the eye of the north, the hearth that warmeth the south part of the Kingdom with fire, an Egypt to all the shires in the north in times of famine for bread.'

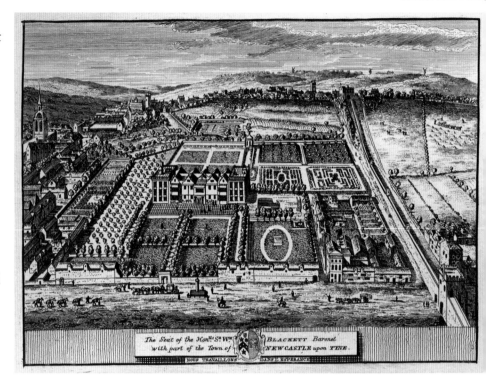

The Seat of the Hon.ble S.r W.m BLACKETT Baronet with part of the Town of NEWCASTLE upon TYNE.

So in the 1500s there was extraordinary wealth in Newcastle and it still seems a bit odd to me that it has left no visible legacy in the streets and buildings of the town today. What's happened, of course, is that there used to be Tudor buildings once, which have since disappeared, and in fact there's plenty of evidence that Newcastle had a pretty impressive face at that time though nothing survives on the ground from those days there are photographs in the City Library which were taken before the massive remodelling of Newcastle in the late 1800s and they show that streets like The Side used to have huge numbers of grand old timber-framed houses, beautiful buildings, four storeys high with each storey jutting out beyond the floors below. You can't tell from the photos exactly when they were built. Some of them were probably medieval, many, like the surviving Bessy Surtees House and the Red House, might have been built in the 17th century, but I think it's safe to assume that a lot of them must have been built in the 1500s and together they give an impression of the splendour in which the merchants of Newcastle lived at that time. That impression is reinforced when you read about their possessions from the wills they made.

There's William Jennison, for example, who was the mayor of the town in 1581 and went on to become an MP in 1584. His will reveals that he owned a house in Newcastle and another two in County Durham. He had farms at Benwell, just outside Newcastle, and others in Walworth, Thorpe and Haswell among other places in Durham. He owned a warehouse in The Close and a £1000 share in the Grand Lease (which was a vast amount of money). There were mines at Cross Moor, Fitburn Moor, Cocker, Newbiggin and Hollingside, piles of coal lying loose (or 'coal lying wrought' as the will actually puts it) at thirteen pits on the south side of the river. There were three keels, two lighters, a salt pan at Jarrow and a partridge in a pear tree …

I made that last bit up but I bet he wasn't short of a pear tree or two either.

The houses that such people lived in were clearly pretty comfy. John Wilkinson, who was the mayor in 1561, had a mansion on Middle Street that was just like any wealthy medieval house such as you would find in any volume on the history of English housing. It had a hall – not a narrow entrance hall like nowadays but a Great Hall where the public life of the house would be carried on. That was the core of the house and beside it on the ground floor there was a parlour. Parlours were quite new in the 1500s. In earlier centuries nobody really expected to have any privacy. Life was just lived in the Great Hall but a taste for a private life began to grow in the 1500s and parlours were invented to satisfy this new need. They were small, cosy sitting rooms with a fireplace where people could escape from the bustle of the Hall to have a bit of a chat ('parlour' comes from the French word parler, to talk).

At the other end of the Great Hall was the kitchen and the various rooms associated with it. There was a buttery where the beer butts were stored, and a brewhouse and a malthouse. They took their booze pretty seriously in the 1500s and they were wise to do so because you couldn't trust the water so what could you do? You had to drink

something. I have adopted the same approach myself.

That was downstairs. Upstairs there was a Great Chamber and a Little Chamber. In earlier centuries both of these would have doubled up as bedrooms and public rooms. The owner would have received important guests and held meetings in them but by the 1560s (with a nice cosy parlour downstairs) they were probably used just for sleeping. Above them, in the roof space, there were four lofts to provide storage and extra bedrooms for servants and anyone else in the household. Now that's big for a house in a town and there was more because the Wilkinsons had a barn and stables as well.

Inevitably these well-to-do blokes also owned plenty of stuff which also appears in their wills. All the usual things are there – jewellery and clothes, goblets and linen. There were feather beds and looking glasses. One will lists a bird cage, a pair of virginals and a cypress chest. These were all luxury items and suggest a nice comfy life style. You don't get cypress chests in Ikea and I bet the bird cage was a pretty impressive one too - suitably splendid and gilded for an exotic and melodious captive. And the virginals! A virginal was a sort of early harpsichord, an ancestor of the piano. If you look them up on Wikipedia they're gorgeous – made of beautiful wood enriched with inlaid patterns. You'd be pleased if you had one of them – but to own two! I bet they were really proud of them and invited the neighbours round to sit beside the fire in their snug little parlour singing all the latest madrigals while sucking back a few nice possets whipped up in the malthouse. Nice comfortable lives.

They weren't lords and ladies, though, these families who ran Newcastle, they were thoroughly middle class. There had always been some members of the aristocracy with a foothold in Newcastle. Great families like the Percys and the Nevilles (the Earls of Westmorland and the owners of Raby Castle) had houses in the town and even the king of Scotland had managed to hold on to his Newcastle pad over the years. But these great ones didn't hold the power any more – the baton had passed to the wealthy merchants who owned the industries and formed the government of the town.

When you read the books, you get the occasional bit of evidence that they were keen to separate themselves from the power of the great feudal families. The Newcastle common Council Accounts in 1597, for example, record a payment of '53/4d pde to officers called sergeants that they shoulde take no rewardes of no nobleman which come into the towne'. In the past this phrase has been interpreted as meaning that they were more worried by bribery than intimidation but it seems to me that the instruction is more to do with self-respect – they seem to be saying, 'We've got our own money. We'll pay you. You don't need their hand-outs any more.'

This independence from the old aristocratic powers outside the town showed itself most powerfully on those many occasions when there was unrest in the country. If this was a book about the North East as a whole instead of just being about Newcastle I would be writing loads about the religious conflicts that convulsed the whole country after Henry's break with Rome and in particular I would be writing about a series of revolts against the Crown. The first was in 1536. It was called the Pilgrimage of Grace and it was a backlash against the religious changes that Henry had introduced. It started in the north and was supported by monks who were losing their monasteries and by the Northern aristocrats who were sticking like glue to their catholic beliefs and who hated the political changes that were happening in London. The uprising was apparently successful initially and Henry made promises that seemed to satisfy the rebels, but the promises were never kept, so the revolt flared up again the following year and this time it was utterly and ruthlessly crushed by the king and thousands of people were executed in towns all over the North.

That was one major period of unrest but there were others. When Mary Tudor came to the throne in 1553 she was determined to bring back the Roman Catholic Religion that her father had outlawed and her reign was characterised by thousands of executions of those who refused to follow her. As it happens Bishop Ridley, who was one of the first and the most famous of her victims, was a North-Easterner, born in Tynedale to a family that has remained a force in the area ever since. Mary's half sister, Elizabeth took over in 1558 and went the other way – she started executing those who persisted in their Catholic beliefs, and that led to yet another uprising in our region. It's called the Rising of the Northern Earls and it too was a rebellion by the old aristocracy in defence of the old religion and it too was swept brutally aside by the Government.

So this was a time of the utmost religious chaos but what's interesting about all of these upheavals from a Newcastle point of view is how little the town got involved in them. The town ignored the Pilgrimage of Grace. During Mary's reign no protestant martyrs were put to death here. In Elizabeth's time there was a little bit more involvement. Two Catholic priests, John Lampton and Edward Watson, were executed at Newcastle while a third, James Watson, escaped and had the 'sleuth hounds' set upon him before he was recaptured and also executed. Those were horrible events but by comparison to what was happening elsewhere, Newcastle managed to stay well away from most of the anguish and during the revolts there was absolutely no involvement at all. The town just shut its gates and got on with its daily life. Some writers have seemed surprised by this. The Victorian local historian, Richard Welford, wrote,

'Through all changes of faith and government they were obsequiously loyal, boldly holding the town for their sovereign, they did not sway from this allegiance during the Pilgrimage of Grace nor during the Rebellion of the Earls'.

You would see why he might be a bit puzzled, what with Geordies normally being such a bolshie bunch as a whole, but it's clear that Newcastle didn't want to upset the nice new apple cart they had found themselves on. They had independence, they were fed up with war, they

Clockwise from top left: 1) *An image of The Side, 1870* 2) *A 1980s image of Bessie Surtees' House* 3) *Showing a rear view of a building on The Close while under restoration in 1987.* 4) *Inside the timber frames of No.25 The Side.*

were making money and they wanted to get on with it so they accepted the change in religion fairly quickly, smiled sweetly (even obsequiously) at the royal family and stuck to normal life as best they could.

Ah! But what was it like, normal life?

Well, in some ways it was probably getting better than it had been. One positive move was that the Corporation took responsibility for more than it had before. The water conduits that the nuns and friars had laid down in the past were kept and added to and by the end of the century it is probable that there were 'pants' or water sources in every street. The streets were all paved, which must have made a terrific difference to the cleanliness of the town, though there were huge problems with human waste. The council employed 'scavengers' to take it away to a vast dunghill that was so big that a few years later its mighty bulk was going to cause the castle walls to collapse. Now that is a load of … er … what do you call it … human refuse.

There was street lighting too, of a sort, but that was the express responsibility of the householders themselves. They were required by the council to hang lanterns outside their houses on moonless nights and it was their job to sweep the street outside their houses as well. Would that it were still so.

And then there was crime and punishment. Geordies, it seems – you'll

The Side, 1891.

be surprised to hear this – were not perfectly behaved; in fact on one occasion thieves stole the total revenue of the town from a locked chest in a locked room in the locked Guildhall and the council had to hire bloodhounds to follow their scent. For punishment, expensive prison sentences were still avoided whenever possible and cheaper alternatives were preferred. The town had a 'ducker', whose job was to duck people in the water to see if they floated or sank. If they floated they were guilty; if they sank they were innocent – but possibly dead. And there was the branks – a hideous iron contraption, which is still on display in the Castle and which fitted over the head and the face and had a metal tongue that went into the prisoner's mouth and flattened down her tongue. I say 'her' because it was intended for the punishment of women who talked too much. 'Scolds', 'shrews', all those words for women who had the temerity to have something to say and if they went beyond talking and committed adultery they would have their hair cut off ('powled') and be scourged round the town by the sergeant with a notice tied around their neck. And then there were the stocks and the pillory where prisoners had to sit, powerless, while people hoyed all sorts of nasty stuff at them. And of course there was the gallows, which were used often enough so that they wore out from time to time and had to be replaced. Normally the condemned were taken out of the town through Gallowgate and hanged on the Town Moor but in 1577, for some reason 'a newe paire of gallows was set up in the Market Place and a soldier hanged for quarrelling and fighting'.

If you were sick of quarrelling and fighting you could always go shopping because there were shops selling an extraordinary and unexpected range of stuff. In the National Archives there is an inventory of a Newcastle shop owned by a merchant called Richard Anderson whose business seems to have sold everything. There was clothing and bedding and food. There was cloth and lots of haberdashery items; there were pots and pans, kitchen scales and kettles – lots and lots of stuff but most

amazing of all is the range of places that it all came from. There were hats from Bruges and an extensive stock of French hats. There was aniseed from the Eastern Mediterranean and saffron from southern Europe. Rice and almonds were both southern crops as well but there were more exotic things on offer too. Sanders was a spice made from ground sandalwood which grew in India and lots of the other spices came from even further afield – mace, cloves and nutmeg had somehow made their way from the Molucca Islands (from modern day Indonesia that is) all the way across Asia to markets in the eastern Mediterranean and then across Europe to end up on the shelves of a shop on the Newcastle Quayside.

Isn't that a remarkable thing?

To be honest I don't know how many shops like this there might have been but there were a lot of merchants with things to sell and there were even more tradesmen

Puritan Punishments:
Left: *A 'brank' or 'Scold's Bridle'* Right: *The 'Newcastle Coat'. Both illustrations are from Ralph Gardiner's England's Grievance Discovered, first published in 1655. John Willis claimed to have travelled to Newcastle and witnessed* 'men drove up and down the streets, with a great tub, or barrel, opened in the sides, with a hole in one end, to put through their heads, and to cover their shoulders and bodies, down to the small of their legs, and then close the same, called the new fashioned cloak, and so make them march to the view of all beholders; and this is their punishment for drunkards, or the like.'

and craftsmen from the twelve licensed craft guilds, not to mention the other unlicensed trades like the cobblers, all of whom must have had workshops where they could sell their services and their wares…

…and then there were the markets – that whole range of specialised markets spreading north from the Church of St Nicholas and down by the Quay, which were described in the last chapter and which must have transformed the atmosphere of the town on Saturdays.

… and of course there was a whole range of other entertainment on offer.

The Mystery Plays which I mentioned in the previous chapter (naked actors – how could you forget?) survived the end of the Catholic world that had used them to educate the population about the bible and they seem to have become a piece of civic entertainment supported by the Corporation, quite unrelated to the church. In 1581 they were described by the Guild of Masons as '… the general plaies of the town, antiently called the Corpus Christi Plays …' and a few years later, in 1578, the regulations of the Guild of Millers express their willingness to do their bit '… whensoever the generall plaies of the town shall be commanded by the mayor'. They were no longer engines of religious instruction but had become secular entertainment.

All of the guilds seemed to have been involved. The Tailors performed *The Descent into Hell*, while The Barbers took on *The Baptising of Christ*. The Millers had a great title for their play; it was called *The Deliverance of the children of Isrell out of the Thraldome, bondage and Servitude of King Pharo*. The House Carpenters did *The Burial of Christ* while the Masons showed another burial, *The Burial of Our Lady, St Mary the Virgin*.

I found it impossible to read about these things without remembering Bottom (the Weaver) and his fellow Guildsmen planning their 'most lamentable comedy and tragedy' for King Theseus in *A Midsummer Night's Dream*. In 1536, for example, the Goldsmiths, Plumbers, Glaziers, Pewterers and Painters list their requirements

for the play they are due to perform. The play is called the *The Three Kings of Coleyn*. It goes like this:

Invoice:	*Bye beards to the kings three and for the messenger one with theyr head hayres*
Item:	*Three cappes and thre sceptres and thre crownes*
Item:	*One starre and twey crownes*
Item:	*Box with our ordenance and our playe book*

It wasn't cheap to take part either, especially if you had your reputation and your dignity to think of. So when the exalted Merchant Adventurers were to perform Hogmagog (or Hoggmaygowyk, as they put it) in 1554 it cost them £4 2s, which was a pretty princely sum.

On the whole it doesn't seem as if each Guild chose a play with a particular significance to itself except for the Shipwrights who almost inevitably got the story of Noah and his ark to re-enact and as it happens this seems to be the only play whose script survives in its entirely. It's great, really good. It starts with God in a bad mood:

God: *Vengeance now will I do*
Of them that have grieved me ill
Great floods shall over them go
And runne over hoope and hill

Everybody is going to be destroyed in this great flood except for 'Noah, my darling free' and God sends the Angel to warn Noah and 'Bid hime go make a ship of stiff board'. The angel goes and wakes Noah up who, like many of us, is not feeling his best first thing in the morning:

Noah: *What art thou for heaven's sake*
The wakens Noah off his sleeping
Away I would thou went

But the angel won't go and in typical shipwright style gives Noah a really detailed set of specifications for the boat he has to build – what its length should be and how

Right: *The Side, 1880.*
Below: *Milburn House now occupies this site.*

much draft it will need, how many portholes and so on. At first Noah is really reluctant to get involved. He says:

I am six hundred winters old
And unlusty am I to do such a deed

As if that wasn't enough he's never built a boat before and has no tools to do the job. He has neither 'ryff nor ruff, spyer, spurd, spront nor sprot'.

Eventually, of course, he is persuaded and sets about the task but the Devil gets involved and inevitably enlists the assistance of Noah's wife who, being a woman, is a soft touch for devils. He gives her a sort of Mickey Finn to slip to her husband and she goes home and schmoozes him into drinking the Devil's brew …

There are all sorts of twists and turns but of course it all ends happily as a good play should, with all the baddies dead, the devil outwitted and Noah and the other shipwrights all living happily ever after.

This curious survival from the old medieval, religious world only happened once a year it seems, but there were plenty of other more contemporary entertainments available. The theatre had taken off in England by the middle of the century and Newcastle was no exception. There was no actual theatre building but there were travelling bands of players such as The Earl of Leicester's Men or the Earl of Worcester's Men passing though the town. On another occasion (another occasion which brings Bottom and his 'rude mechanicals' to mind) a ship's crew danced 'at the commandment of the mayor and his brethren'. An actor was paid 3/4d for 'playing with his hobby horse upon the Forth' (would that be legal nowadays?) and there were live animal acts as well. I'm quite certain that the modern city council wouldn't be allowed to make payments 'to my Lord Monteagle's bearward' (i.e. Bear keeper) or 'to him that had the lion' (though we do still see circuses on the Town Moor from time to time, so perhaps nothing changes very much).

For the posh and the powerful there were banquets all the time. They were held in the new Guildhall or in 'the stately court of the Merchant Adventurers', which was attached to it. Every year after 1558 the banquet they held to celebrate the anniversary of Queen Elizabeth's accession was enhanced by flaming tar barrels outside the hall. There was a town band (the town 'waits') who would have performed at all the banquets and there would have been funny turns as well, not just because of the drink, but because the Mayor had his own jester who (if Shakespeare's clowns are anything to go by) would have had them rolling in the aisles.

And there were sports – archery practice on the Town Moor and … er … archery practice on the Town Moor … and erm … what was it?

So plenty of good stuff went on in the town and I'm sure that I have given the merest whiff of the pleasures on offer … but there was bad stuff too – bad stuff and sad stuff.

First of all, you won't be surprised to hear that it wasn't as good for the ordinary people as it was for the rich merchants. There was lots of poverty and had been for a very long time. The economy had collapsed in the middle of the 1300s during the worst times of the wars against Scotland and it seems to have been up and down ever since so that by the 1500s there were (as one recent

Right: *Arthur's Cooperage on The Close, 1879.*
Above: *The building now disused in 2016.*

writer puts it) 'extremes of wealth concentrated in remarkably few hands'. Another, talking about the North as a whole, talks about a 'pinched and penurious century' during which 'the living standards of ordinary people fell relentlessly.'

Some years were worse than others mainly because of the weather and perhaps unexpectedly, there was a sort of charitable safety net to help the worst affected. I hadn't expected the town government to be involved in moves to help the poor so long ago but in fact in 1563 the government gave local corporations the power to raise compulsory funds for the relief of the poor and in 1572 the first local poor law tax was imposed. There were elements of this which were probably an improvement on what had happened before. The town kept stocks of corn and coal to be handed out in times of real hardship and support was given to those who were too ill or too old to work. Other bits of the legislation were less ideal. In ways that were to remain a fixture of British life for the next 400 years, poor people tended to be punished for their misfortunes. The 'able-bodied poor' were set to work in a house of industry while the naughty old 'idle poor', who (then as now) were assumed to have achieved poverty deliberately were placed in a house of correction (and had all of their benefits taken away from them). And then there were those who fell beyond the system altogether – the beggars. Tomlinson mentions one especially interesting payment recorded in the Common Council Accounts in 1591 which says that John Hardcastle was paid 18/6d 'for making 137 badges … for the poor folk which shall be allowed to go into the town to ask for alms'. He says that 137 was two or three times more beggars than were provided for in other towns and he wonders whether the number of badges implies that Newcastle was more charitable than other towns or that there was just a greater need here.

Where the poor lived and what they lived in is quite hard to say and surprisingly there isn't any more hard evidence now than there was available to earlier writers on the subject. Perhaps they lived in the sort of one-room hovels, maybe with the room subdivided to allow space at the other end for any animal they might possess, such as have been shown to exist in the countryside at that time; or perhaps they lived in subdivided bits of larger houses that had come down in the world as became the norm for the poor in later centuries; or perhaps there were examples of both. There has always been an assumption that the better off lived in houses with a street frontage and the poor squeezed into the mean lanes behind – but whether that was a situation that was built into the town plan from the start or whether it happened gradually as the poor began to invade the lower end of the burgage plots that formed the original layout of the place is not entirely clear. A couple of hundred years later, the historian Eneas Mackenzie described exactly that situation in the chares along the Quayside. He said that the well-to-do lived facing the Quay while the lanes behind were 'the most crowded with buildings of any part of his majesty's dominions'. He is a touch dismissive of the poor who lived in these circumstances and says that 'Plumber Chare was noted as the receptacle of Cyprian Nymphs, whose blandishments were of the most coarse and vulgar description. Indeed most of these lanes were inhabited by very dangerous, though not very tempting females'.

It's not clear whether the situation that Mackenzie described was already the case in Tudor times but dangers were undoubtedly present among the poor and overcrowded population of the town and the worst danger of all was the plague.

Newcastle had suffered regularly and dreadfully from the plague in the 14th century. There was a terrible outbreak in 1369, and in 1379 it is said that a huge proportion of the population died. By Elizabethan times the situation had got no better. Two thousand people died of the plague in 1579. That's 2,000 out of a total population of about 10,000. So one in five of the people who lived in Newcastle died in that outbreak and a further 1700 died in the outbreak that struck Newcastle ten years later. I said it earlier in this chapter but I'll say it again – the Elizabethan age is often portrayed as a sort of golden age in English history but in Newcastle at least, the end of the 16th century was an absolutely dire time. In 1595, '96 and '97 there were plagues and terrible harvests; there was a dreadful dearth of corn and many were so fearful of the plague and so desperate that they left the town and camped in fields beyond the walls – at Barras Bridge and Spital Tongues to the north and west and at St Anne's to the east. The town provided water and food for them, paid for the funerals; the town's bellman called warnings to strangers and newcomers to leave. Infected houses were fumigated with all sorts of things that smelt as if they might do some good – pitch and resin, frankincense and sweet herbs. The town even appointed a physician, though whether he had any useful impact on the disease is hard to say, especially as the sickness was to return with even greater ferocity during the first half of the next century and for the sense of completeness I'll mention those outbreaks here as well. In 1635 five thousand people died of the plague in Newcastle and Colonel John Fenwick wrote that the town was 'almost desolate, the streets growing green with grass, the treasurie wasted, the trading departed'.

The suffering at the end of the 16th century led, as it so often does, to deep resentment and riots as the poor desperately lashed out against the horror of their fate – and the riots of the poor led, as they so often do as well, to the rich getting richer. In 1600 Elizabeth gave the town a new Charter, which guaranteed the wealthy Fraternity of Hostmen a monopoly on the control of Newcastle for the next one-hundred years.

So, there you are, Newcastle in the 16th century, a time that has left no physical reminders of its passing, as I said at the beginning of the chapter, but a time when the nature of Newcastle was profoundly changed. It stopped being medieval, it stopped being dominated by the church and became a much more secular society. It became less aristocratic too and was ruled by a small collection of wealthy and privileged, but entirely middle-class men. It became more successful as it was set free to exploit the massive potential of the coal with which it was surrounded and on which it was built. The ingenuity that became a marked characteristic of the town in all later centuries began to show its head and the rough edges emerged too – the awkward and rebellious working class. The 16th century turned Newcastle into the makings of a modern town.

Awaiting trial beneath the double-hammerbeam roof.

The Victorian artist, John Storey, painted this terrific view of the town as it must have looked in about 1600. He shows how the town was built on several hill separated by deep denes that were filled in later. Pilgrim Street, the main street of the early town, runs just right of centre, past the original building of All Saints church. Westgate road soars off to the west, towards the hills and the town is still protected by its splendid ring of walls and by the three towers on the bridge.

In 1852, when Storey painted this picture, many of the ancient buildings near the river were still standing but two years later, in 1854, most of them were destroyed in the catastrophic fire that followed the great Gateshead explosion.

The Seventeenth Century

You've been very good. You've put up with a lot of coal and wills and Hostmen and all of that sort of stuff so I think we should start this chapter with something a bit more dramatic. I think it's time we went to war!

In 1640 Newcastle was occupied by the Scots …

… Hmm … I have realised that you may need a couple of bits of information before you can absorb that last statement. You might need to be reminded that when Queen Elizabeth I died with no heirs in 1603 the crown passed to her cousin, James VI of Scotland, the son of Mary Queen of Scots, so from that moment Scotland and England were both ruled by the same King. By 1640 James had died and his son, Charles I, was on the throne.

That's the first bit of information; the second is less a fact than an observation about the irony of life because having spent about 300 years at war with Scotland and never having been captured once, Newcastle had to wait until the two countries were more or less united before it happened – but that's the way it was because …

… In 1640 Newcastle was occupied by the Scots – thousands of them, an army of them led by General Leslie occupied the town for a year. It was the principal action of a war called the Bishop's War and I have to admit that until recently I had either never heard of it or had forgotten about it entirely.

What happened was this. In 1639 Charles I was having bother with the Scots. He wanted them to be a bit more English and in particular he was determined to force them to accept a nice Church of England Prayer book, which had been devised by his religious advisor, Archbishop Laud. He was equally determined to insist that the Scottish Church should be ruled over by Bishops like it was in England and use the same sort of religious ritual that Laud was busy re-introducing in England. Well, the Scots determination to do none of those things

was implacable; the vast majority of them had become puritans and Presbyterians and they wanted none of that ritual which smacked of a return to the Popery that had been cast away almost a hundred years earlier by Henry VIII; so they said no and a rebellion ensued which is usually known as The First Bishops' War.

It didn't last long. There were a few skirmishes and a very few deaths but the two armies that faced each other across the Tweed near Berwick never came to battle and the whole thing seemed to have been settled by a treaty rather deliciously called The Pacification of Berwick.

If only it were that easy. Pacifications rarely are in my experience and on this occasion Charles continued to take an uncompromising stance, so a few months later, in 1640, the whole thing flared up again – except that this time there was no faffing around with armies facing each other across the Tweed. General Leslie led his troops across the river a few miles upstream from Berwick at Coldstream, bypassed the English army entirely and charged south through Northumberland like a bullet, heading straight for Newcastle.

Newcastle wasn't a random choice of target for the Scots. They came here because they wanted control of the coal, which they could use to finance their army and, perhaps even more importantly, to hold London hostage and cut off a major source of income to the king because by this time the king was used to getting two shillings tax for every chauldron of coal exported from the Tyne. If he lost that, the assumption was that he would have to give up on his demands on the Scots. So Newcastle was a natural target.

Now, as you know from earlier chapters, Newcastle had long been surrounded by a pretty impressive ring of defensive walls and in 1638 they had been strengthened. The Government had conducted a survey, which found that the medieval walls wouldn't be able to withstand modern artillery and needed beefing up. Recent archaeological evidence has shown that the recommended improvements were actually carried out; digs at the castle and at the Plummer Tower on the east side of the town have revealed that there were new bastions built, the walls were reinforced and deep ditches created in front of them – so the Scots should have been faced with a formidable problem – except that they were led by General Leslie who was pretty formidable himself.

He had been born in fairly humble circumstances and the evidence suggests that he never learnt to read or write. Instead he became a professional soldier on the continent – first of all fighting for the Dutch in their war against the Spanish. He then went to Sweden to fight for Gustavus Adolphus, the greatest of all Sweden's warrior kings. He did fantastically well and ended up a Field Marshall in the Swedish army before being tempted back home to lead Scotland's armies.

His cunning plan on this occasion was to avoid attacking Newcastle from the north, which was inevitably the most strongly defended section of the town since that was the direction that everybody expected an attack to come from. Instead he decided to cross the Tyne and attack from the south so he headed for the first available crossing point upstream from Newcastle, which was the ford at the village of Newburn.

Newburn was defended by an English army that had rushed out of Newcastle when it became clear what was happening so the two sides confronted each other across the Tyne. I have to say that it seems to have been no contest. The English army was massively outnumbered (3,500 against 20,000), they were out-gunned and the artillery that confronted them was brilliantly placed on high ground (and even on top of the church tower) so they were entirely exposed on the flat marshy land south of the river. They were also a rubbish army. The King had raised them hurriedly in the south of England and they had been neither paid nor trained. They were notoriously ill-disciplined and created havoc with violent disorder in

all of the towns they passed through on the way north. Lots of them deserted and others mutinied and two Roman Catholic officers were murdered by their own men. So it's not altogether a surprise that they were routed or that the English commander, Lord Conway, made the decision to abandon Newcastle altogether leaving it invitingly open to Leslie and his troops.

There's some evidence that the Scots were received reasonably well at the beginning. One historian (Frank Musgrove) states that there was a puritan element in the town, including the mayor, who actually invited the invaders in and it is true that on the first day Leslie and his officers were entertained by the Mayor, Robert Bewick. The soldiers were also relatively well behaved. They were all puritans and each group of men had a Presbyterian minister with them. Swearing and whoring were strictly forbidden and looting was punishable with death so things looked OK at the beginning but you can't expect an army of 20,000 men to occupy a town with a population of 10,000 without tensions rising.

There were lots of problems. It's all very well that the soldiers had to pay for stuff they needed and that looting was prohibited but there were still plenty of ways to offend the natives. The cavalry were allowed to commandeer fodder for their horses, for example, and soldiers were permitted to pillage any houses where the occupants had fled. And perhaps more importantly the demands of General Leslie himself were pretty imperious. He insisted that the corporation had to provide billets for 2,000 men and the town had to pay him £200 a day to cover the wages of his army. On top of that he demanded a loan of £40,000. These were vast sums of money in those days and he made it even worse by seizing control of any crown property in the town and (worst of all, I imagine, as far as the Corporation and the merchants who ran it were concerned) he confiscated all the mines and all the coal so nobody local could make any money any more.

Almost inevitably (given that the whole war was about Scottish freedom to worship in the way they wanted) the invaders instantly imposed their own religious beliefs on the defeated town. Scottish ritual was introduced into the town's four churches. Eneas Mackenzie, who wrote a history of Newcastle in 1827, described the invaders' attitude to religion with some bitterness. He said that St Nicholas's church was formerly filled with all sorts of ancient monuments and inscriptions but when the Scots arrived 'they plundered the church and broke down with axes and hammers the carved work and effigies that adorned these mournful but gratifying memorials'. Lieutenant-Colonel Fenwick, a fanatical puritan on the English side, described with undisguised glee what happened. '*The breath of the Scots Covenant in the Scottish soldiers,*' he wrote, '*did blow down (the Anglican churches) both root and branch with their altars and railings, service books and fonts, and all such fopperies'*.

So it's no surprise that the people disliked their occupiers. Their pride had been hurt by the ease with which they had been outsmarted at Newburn and even if the Scots avoided the worst excesses of invading armies they were still hated. One Alderman of Newcastle (who was a puritan himself and might have been expected to accept the puritan Scots on religious grounds) summed it up: '*The soldiers are intolerably insolent in their discourse, slighting the King's army and indeed the whole nation'*. He described them as '*a viperous brood so freely received into the belly of the country'* and worried that they were likely to '*eat through the bowels of their fosterers.'*

They stayed for a year and then left in August 1641 having achieved their aims. Their success went on to have really profound consequences for the country as a whole because by seizing Newcastle's coal and denying the King his usual tax from it they had put fantastic pressure on his finances and the only thing he could do was to recall Parliament and ask for more money, but he was denied. Instead of giving the king what he wanted, the members of the Parliament unanimously voted to control him and that led directly to the Civil War. The country divided between those Puritans who wanted a 'root and branch' reform of religion and those who supported the king and wanted to retain the bishops and the existing prayer book – the structures of the Church of England.

Rather surprisingly Newcastle chose to side with the king. I say 'surprisingly' partly because the character of the city nowadays seems to me to be rather bolshie and independent and partly because that seems to have been its

The passage of Newburn Ford.

quality in the centuries before the Civil War as well. The Newcastle merchants in particular had spent hundreds of years getting their own way as often as they could. They didn't even like the King all that much; they had argued for ages about taxes with him and lots of people in the city were puritans and disapproved of his religious policy … and yet Newcastle, along with Kings Lynn in Norfolk, became the only two major places in the country to declare their support for the King.

Isn't that an interesting thing?

Why did they do it? You earnestly ask. Well, there seem to have been lots of reasons. Newcastle had plenty of Puritans in it – I've already mentioned Robert Bewick, the Mayor, and that grumbling Alderman. Lt Colonel Fenwick was another - but there were fewer puritans than in most other places. More people had clung on to their Catholic faith than happened elsewhere and there had been complaints ever since Elizabeth's time that the town was a hotbed of popery. Tomlinson tells a story about a well known Roman Catholic lady called Dorothy Lawson who died in 1625 and was given what almost amounted to a state funeral. The mayor was there and all the Aldermen. Her body was carried up the river in the town's magnificent state barge and the funeral was carried out *'with a civility which astonished all'*.

An event like that would have been quite impossible in more puritan parts of the country and it offers a clue that the town genuinely held different opinions to other places – but more important than that was Newcastle's recent year of humiliation under the Scots. You have to remember that Newcastle had been part of a hostile border with Scotland for hundreds of years and all of those old antipathies were revived by General Leslie's occupation. Everybody knew that the puritan merchants in London and the south had encouraged and applauded the Scots in their attack because the invasion weakened the King, but in Newcastle the old enmities had been re-awakened and when the Civil War started the Scots were once again on the puritan side – so Newcastle went the other way.

Anyway the war started in 1643 and Newcastle (because of the strategic importance of its coal) became involved almost straight away. In January 1644, the Scots arrived again, with General Leslie (now elevated to the title of Earl of Leven) once again the commander. This time however the town had a new mayor who was a tougher egg than the man who had been in charge in 1640. He was an interesting chap called Sir John Marley, who had started his working life as a coal-fitter and alehouse keeper but worked his way up until he had become one of the leading Hostmen and worth about £4,500, which was a bob or two at the time. He was a royalist and ardent anti-Presbyterian and he had been knighted after the Bishop's War for his opposition to the Scots. When the Scots arrived this time he was resolute and despite only having about 1,500 defenders to hold the walls against an army of 30,000, he denied them access to the town. He had already strengthened the defences, built a couple of additional forts outside the walls, made the ditch more difficult to cross and cleared away all of the suburbs on the north side of the town so that any attackers would have no cover to help them. He had also sunk a series of ships in the river to prevent a parliamentary attack from that direction and when Leslie sent a message demanding that the town should surrender, Marley replied with a certain degree of arrogance and quite a bit of courage, *'His Majesty's general being at this time in the town we conceive all the power of government to be in him'* and he refused to open the gates.

For the time being, Leslie didn't faff around trying to force the issue. He left some of his men loosely besieging the town and clearing up pockets of local resistance in Northumberland and Durham while he set off south with the rest of his army where they took lots and lots of towns until, on 2 July, they took part in the crushing defeat of the the King at the Battle of Marston Moor.

Marston Moor left the whole northern half of the kingdom in Parliamentary hands … except for Newcastle, and Newcastle had to be taken quickly because no coal had reached London for ages and the city was desperate for it. There was a report that *'many poor have perished, being unable to buy fuell'* and others had taken to burning parts of their own houses.

So General Leslie came back and the second siege of Newcastle began. Initially it sounds more like a civil engineering job. The records reveal that 3,000 countrymen were *'summoned to bring mattocks, spades and shovels and labour in the trenches'*.

For me, the extraordinary thing about this siege was that it happened here, in our town – all the significant events occurred in places where we go for walks or sit and drink coffee. The Scots captured the fort at Shieldfield (just along from The Biscuit Factory); they dug mines under the walls near Pilgrim Street and beside Newgate, at White Friars (on the northern edge of the present city centre) and at Sandgate down near the river. They built bastions and temporary batteries and pounded the town with artillery fire. During Victorian restorations at St Andrew's church, cannon balls were found lodged in the walls of the tower. They're still there, resting on a window sill in the church – smaller than I had imagined they would be but no less lethal. At one point the town wall by the church was blown up and *'the defenders suffered dreadfully trying to block this up'*.

I have to admit that I have always had quite a specific image of sieges. I have imagined long periods of silence, hunger and tense waiting for the final attack to begin but the reporting of Newcastle's siege gives a very different picture. One Parliamentary correspondent with the attacking forces wrote *'The enemy from the castle doth mightily annoy us with their great artillery but the Scots are casting up with incessant labour what works they can … In the meantime our pioneers are as busie at works underground as our cannons are playing above it. The endeavours of both sides are indefatigable and in the thick clouds of smoke the thunder of the cannon are perpetually disputing …'*

There must have been sallies and attacks to repel; we know this because prisoners were taken who were to play a role in the final act. Propaganda played a part too; pamphlets purporting to be *'from a well wisher'* were thrown over the walls to try and tempt the defenders into surrender.

But there were also endless attempts to resolve the situation without any more violence. Letters flew between the attackers and the defenders. On the 7th September, for example, the Scots made a plea for surrender… *'we earnestly incite you to the end that further Effusions of Christian Blood may be prevented … acquit yourselves like rational men …'*

They didn't even get a reply to that one so Leslie wrote again saying *'we desire you to prevent those Evils which cannot longer be avoided …the citizens and soldiers'*, he said, *' may be safe and the town, being preserved from ruin, may enjoy the Fruits of settled peace'*. He finished the letter by telling them that if they failed to act, *'you then may expect the extremities of war.'*

This time Sir John Marley wrote back with extraordinary coolness. He said *'We have received your letter wherein you require and summon us to give up and surrender the town, alledging divers Reasons, mixed with Threats to move us, all of which we have well weighed and considered and so now return this answer, That we declare to the world that we keep this Town for the use of his Majesty.'*

That's quite impressive, isn't it, and his next letter, following a day of failed diplomacy, was perhaps more impressive still. It was a more emotional letter, sadder, a little petulant. It's clear that Marley knew that the time had come and there was no more room for negotiation and he ended bitterly by urging the Scots to *'...think of some other course to compose the Differences of these sad distracted Kingdoms and annoying us who never wronged any of you.'*

One curiously modern form of warfare is said to have emerged during the siege. According to Newcastle's 18th century historian, John Brand, General Leslie sent an ultimatum to the mayor, threatening to blow up the tower of St Nicholas' Church, if the gates weren't opened immediately; Marley's response was to set up a human shield. According to Brand he *'immediately ordered a certain number of the chiefest of the Scottish Prisoners to be carried up to the top of the old tower and placed below the Lanthorne and there confined'*. He said that the tower was indeed a beautiful object but that Leslie should know that *'the moment he destroyed the beautiful structure, he should bathe his hands in the blood of his countrymen'*.

The tactic might have saved the tower but it didn't hold back the inevitable. By now the mines were ready. Two of them had been detected and flooded by the defenders but two remained, packed with explosives and ready to go and at 3 o'clock on the 19th October the attack began simultaneously in a terrifying variety of places. Mines were blown up under Sandgate and White Friars causing the walls to collapse and there were further breaches of the gates all round the town - at Pilgrim Street on the east side, at Closegate (down by the river in the south west corner of the walled town) and at Westgate. The Scots poured in and for a couple of hours there was terrible carnage through all the streets we know today. The casualties were to be found on both sides and one Scottish source almost praised the defenders who *'left nothing unessay'd to repel the fury of the assault'*.

In fact the most vivid accounts of the fighting that I have found have come from the diaries of Scottish soldiers. One, called Lithgow, wrote about, *'the thousands of musket balls flying from our faces like to the driving hailstones from a Septentrian blast, the clanging and carving of naked unsheathed swords, the pushing of broughing pikes crying for blood, the carcases of foemen lying like dead dogs in the groaning streets'*.

Robert Bertram, from the Walls of Newcastle, 1951.

Top: *The defence of Newcastle by the Royalists, October 19th 1644 when the town won its proud motto 'Fortiter Defendit Triumphans'*
Above: *An artist's impression of the seige.*

The names of many of those dead 'foemen' are recorded in the Parish records. They included: *'Ather Herron … bured … which was kild with a grenad. George Fishbourne … bured … which was kild by ye Skotes at the Spittl. Edward Mylburne … bured … which was kild in Pilgrim Street by the Scotes at the skirmes'*

The fighting continued for two hours until the defenders finally capitulated in the Bigg Market - except for a group which included Mayor Marley who had retreated into the castle and held out there for a further two days until 21st of October when the siege was finally ended and the town was entirely in the hands of the enemy.

Newgate, 1644.

You might think that the occupants of Newcastle had put up a pretty impressive resistance and that they had been well led by their Mayor and I might think that you are right, but the Scots were scandalised by Marley's behaviour. Euen Lindsay, a soldier in the Earl of Loudoun's regiment wrote that Mayor Marley, *'having threatened to use Scots prisoners as human shields, promptly quit the defence and scuttled to the castle … it remains a mystery why this creature was not put to the sword as custom permitted following an unnecessary storming.'*

But he wasn't. Marley's subsequent history was quite interesting. He had quite clearly been a thorn in the Scottish flesh. Having been knighted for his resistance to them in the Bishop's War and having humiliated General Leslie at the beginning of 1644 *for 'refusing the fair proposition urged for the surrender of the town'*, he had gone on to lead Newcastle through a major siege but instead of being sentenced to death as Euen Lindsay thought he should have been, his possessions were all sold and he was exiled to the Netherlands. Sadly, when he was abroad, he seems to have behaved with rather less glory. He was penniless, and in desperation he offered to disclose his fellow Royalist exiles' plans to the authorities for £100. But when it was all over, when the Puritan Commonwealth had come to an end and the Restoration of the Monarchy had occurred, he returned to Newcastle, regained his seat as an Alderman and was elected an MP.

But that was a long way in the future. In the meantime the Scots stayed in Newcastle as occupiers for almost three years – until 30 January 1647. They seem to have been quite pleased with themselves and eager to publish their kindness and clemency, suggesting that there had never been a town captured in a siege where there had been less cruelty and plundering or more mercy involved. You might want to temper this rather self-satisfied view of things with the information that it was only the houses of the rich that were protected from plunder and the Scottish soldiers (poor old things) had to make do with what they could loot from the houses of the poor, which were given no protection at all.

It's not quite clear to me what the situation was like in the town when the siege was over because not a lot seems to have been written about it, but I suspect that the atmosphere was pretty volatile. The Scots were in charge – subsequent events were to demonstrate that forcefully – but they weren't the actual rulers of the town. The old Royalist members of the Corporation had gone, cast aside, exiled like Mayor Marley or brooding darkly in the background, and their places had been taken by a new group of men who were sympathetic to the parliamentary cause. These people must have been in the town all the time, unable to express their religious or political sympathies while the town as a whole had gone Royalist but now they emerged and took over. Most prominent among them was a man called John Blakiston who became the mayor in 1645

He was a local mercer, a coal merchant and a Hostman. He was also a puritan, a passionate puritan, totally opposed to the church reforms that the king and Archbishop Laud were introducing and in fact he was so vociferous in his criticisms of the changes that he was excommunicated by the Archbishop. (Incidentally, he was also an enthusiastic supporter of emigration to America and his son went on to become the Governor of Maryland.) In 1640 he had been elected as the town's MP. How odd for such a man to have been, nominally at least, representing a town that had chosen exactly the opposite position to his own, and how satisfying it must have felt to have watched things turn full circle and to find himself in power.

But there were others who would have felt no such satisfaction. William Grey, Newcastle's first historian, who published his *Chorographia* in 1649, took exactly the opposite side to Blakiston. He was passionately Royalist and prepared to be pretty forthright about the victors. About the Scots he wrote *'In former times, the Aldermen of the town had their scarlet gowns, but the proud Scot*

got them by conquest as they did other ornaments of the town, thinking no English in authority worthy to wear them but themselves; and so they continued lording over us for two years until they were hired out as they were bought in, being a mercenary nation, for any nation for money'

Elsewhere in his book he said that there are three things you can find anywhere in the world *'...a Scot, a rat and a Newcastle grindstone.'* Ouch!

But if he didn't like the Scots he disliked the Parliamentarians even more. He wrote, *'We live in an age where meckanicks will presume to step into Moses chair and become politicians'* and accused the new rulers of contradicting all the laws of God and man.

What an extraordinary situation – you can imagine that victorious Scots, triumphant Parliamentarians and disappointed Royalists were all mingled in a bitter whirl of conflicting emotions and into this maelstrom came another, entirely unexpected element. Suddenly, on 13 May 1646, the king became part of the mix.

In the Laing Art Gallery there is an early 20th century mural by James Tucker (1898-1972) that shows King Charles I entering Newcastle. The town has been painted so that it looks like somewhere in Renaissance Italy. The residents who are bowing down before the king are elegant Renaissance figures while Charles himself looks every inch a king – calm, controlled and dignified.

He was here because he had finally surrendered outside Newark, but rather than fall into the hands of the Parliamentary forces that he clearly feared, he had given himself up to the Scots who brought him to their Northern stronghold. The contemporary description of his arrival makes the event seem grand and powerful, not unlike its depiction in the Laing. He walked into the town, across the bridge from Gateshead along a lane of muskets and pikes. There were bonfires, bells, drums and trumpets and he was guarded by 300 horsemen, those closest to him bareheaded. If he did behave with the dignity of the picture it was a good performance because he is described as having been 'reduced to a condition in the last degree disastrous and melancholy'. And for all the show of respect, he was still a prisoner, still on foot and completely surrounded by enemy troops. He might have hoped to find friends in this loyal town but a proclamation was issued saying that '*no Papists or Delinquents*' were allowed to approach him. The town he entered was still clearly a war zone. There were sunken ships in the river below the bridge, the defensive walls were breached and broken, the mines beneath the town had been flooded. St Andrew's, one of the four parish churches in the town, was battered and broken. The suburbs beyond the walls had been burned and destroyed. It was a town without trade; for four years the coal business had virtually stopped. It was one of Newcastle's lowest moments.

The King was given a room in The Newe Place, the gigantic mansion of the Anderson family that I described in the previous chapter. That house has gone but a bronze plaque on the wall of Lloyds Bank on Grey Street marks the spot where he stayed. He had some freedom – he was allowed to leave the town and go to Shieldfield with his retinue in order to play golf (or 'goff' as it was called at the time) but essentially he was a prisoner in a hostile environment, strictly guarded and treated, as one contemporary put it, with '*distant ceremony and feigned respect*' . We get odd vivid glimpses of the way life was for him. He is said to have tried to escape, for example, by sneaking down the Lort Burn towards a waiting ship on the Tyne but he was caught, trapped behind a grille that protected the end of the sewer he was in; and there is a terrific story about what happened to him in St Nicholas' church. Inevitably the services were conducted by the victors and at one service the puritan minister after preaching a sermon which berated the King, announced that they would sing Psalm 52, which starts '*Why dost thou, tyrant, boast thyself/Thy wicked ways to praise?*' But the King stood up and called instead for Psalm 56 '*Have mercy, Lord, on me I pray/ For men would me devour.*'

Among the men who no doubt wanted to devour him was the Mayor. John Blakiston was to become one of the 'Regicides', the twelfth of the fifty-nine signatories to the execution of the King. But that was still in the future and before that happened Charles left Newcastle. In January 1647 the Scots handed him over to Parliament and a few months after that they themselves withdrew from the town. The next few years saw a second and even a third Civil War and though the fighting came close (Sir Arthur Haselrig, the puritan Governor of the town, had to fight off a Royalist force and recapture Tynemouth Castle in July 1648) Newcastle's extraordinary involvement in the Civil war was more or less over and the town began to get back to normal.

But, you know, 'normal' isn't quite the right word to describe 17th century Newcastle, because even ignoring the war in the middle, it was a time of extraordinary extremes – there were great things happened and there were terrible things.

Among the worst … one of the worst things that ever happened in Newcastle occurred in 1636; it was an outbreak of the plague. I mentioned it briefly at the end of the previous chapter but I've been reading two, extraordinary, meticulous and yet passionate accounts of it recently (by Keith Wrightson) and I find I can't dismiss it as a sort of footnote to an earlier century because it was an absolute catastrophe – one of the worst medical disasters to have ever struck this country. We have had mass infections and panics all over the world in recent years and we have been inevitably and rightly appalled by the misery and suffering they have caused; we have all read about the Great Plague that wracked London in 1665 and we know about the dreadful Flu epidemic that killed so many millions of people in the years after the first world war; but while events like these and others killed far more people than the Newcastle plague of 1636, it's likely that none ever killed a higher proportion of the population in a single community.

The figures are startling. It has been calculated that 5,631 people died of the plague in Newcastle between 6th May and the beginning of December, 1636.

That means forty-seven per cent of the population.

One in two.

Two lists of all the burials in the town over that period have survived and they not only provide an accurate figure for the total number of deaths but they also give a clear indication of the development of the epidemic. There were four churches with burial grounds and by working out how many burials took place in each one and on which dates it is possible to follow, eerily and inexorably the pace and the route of the plague as it moved through the town.

It started in Sandgate down by the river, where the seafarers lived so it is probable that one of them brought the disease into the town. It was also the poorest and most overcrowded part of the town and there were two vast middens in the area so it was an ideal breeding ground for the infection

From Sandgate it moved west along the river bank into the parish of St Nicholas and began to attack Sandhill where the municipal centre was and where the rich merchants had their homes. It took a while to reach its full, horrible effect in the upper reaches of the town and the St Andrew's area near Newgate in the north west corner was the last to feel the full impact, but by the end of July the whole town was in the grip of the epidemic.

And that grip was fearsome. Dr Jenison, a puritan preacher in the town described its progress in these terms *'it increaseth, it rageth, runs and spreads like wildfire'.*

Dr Jenison published an account of the plague almost immediately after it had receded and to it he added eighteen weekly totals of burials in the town between early May and 11th September, and one final list showing the funerals from September to the end of the year, by which time the Plague had come to an end. The lists make desperate reading.

In normal conditions there were about fifty funerals a month in Newcastle but during May that figure had become fifty a week and it soon got far worse. By the end of July each of the four parishes was burying at least five or six people a day and sometimes as many as fifteen or sixteen. The worst period of all was 11-13 August when four hundred people died. It is hard to imagine how awful and remorseless this roll call of death must have been. Keith Wrightson finds brilliant evidence for the psychological pain that people were suffering by describing the entries written by the Parish Clerk into the St Andrew's parish register. As the plague got worse the entries became odd, more personal and less detached; the Clerk draws pointing fingers to mark the names of people of rank; he adds extra little facts to show that these are not just names to him, but the names of people he knows, people who need to be remembered: *Robert Toddericke which had the honch back, Gorge the fiddler* and even the anonymous ones are given a touch of recognition, a moment of sympathy, a fragment of identity: *a powre one, a powre child.*

The last entries of all, the last recorded deaths in the outbreak are to be found in the St John's Parish Register and record the deaths of *'seven poore things out of the Warden Close'.* Warden Close was a group of ramshackle houses outside the walls near Westgate and the assumption is that this group died unnoticed and were found only after it was all over.

Such deaths fit the stereotypical view of the Plague – people abandoned and dying alone in an atmosphere of unrelieved horror, shunned by their neighbours and family – and left to die by the community as a whole. The quarantine regulations that were introduced by the authorities rather support this picture; they were draconian and frightening. The sick had to be isolated; houses were boarded up, *'shutt up for suspicion of the plague'* and nobody was allowed to enter or leave them. By the summer large numbers of the sick were being kept (until they died?) in lodges beyond the walls, safely out of harm's way on the town moor.

It seems as if these measures had the effect of creating pockets of death – that by shutting houses up whole households were being condemned to die. This meant that the deaths weren't spread evenly throughout the population but came disproportionately from the hardest hit families. In John Collingwood's house, for example, he himself died but so did *'his children and servants being seven in number'* and in the same house the three girls who had been entrusted to the care of John Collingwood by their dying father, were also among the dead. There are lots, and lots of stories like these

And yet, the books that I've been reading create a more complicated picture. As well as examining the awful records of death, Keith Wrightson has also examined the wills and the probate records of the time, particularly the records left by a young lawyer called Ralph Tailor who worked throughout the plague months doing his job –

> the job of making sure that people's dying wishes were recorded. He made the wills of ninety-one people, sometimes by standing on ladders and leaning in through their windows, sometimes by sitting on the town wall outside their houses and taking down their instructions by word of mouth, but sometimes he visited them and sat with them and listened to their final wishes. What he recorded was quite different from the stereotypical picture of plague. The wills reveal that people remained desperately keen to maintain their normal life, to record their love of their families and show their gratitude to the people who had helped them even in those desperate times. Unborn children are included in the wills and tokens are left to friends and neighbours. It's clear that some people at least were prepared to break the quarantine rules and risk their lives to help or sit with a dying friend or neighbour.
>
> And the wills show that it mattered to people where they were buried. They wanted to be near

Anderson Place (formerly the Newe Place) in 1795, long after the King's stay.

their husbands or '*soe neare unto my deare mother and sister as conveniently may be*'.

When it was all over, Ralph Tailor's next job was to write up inventories of what had been left behind for probate purposes and those lists are equally revealing because they suggest that there was no evidence of crime or disorder, there seems to have been no looting. There was food left on the shelves and cash untouched in the houses.

So the picture that is created of Newcastle in the 1636 Plague is of a town under desperate pressure and quite unbearable grief and suffering, but a town in which the normal ties of life, family and community were not broken. As far as possible life went on. There was still some trade on the river, not as much as normal, but ships still came and went, people did their jobs whenever possible and when it was over life went on. As Keith Wrightson puts it '*Life went on, Ralph Tailor kept working, apples were imported from Germany … and afterwards survivors cleaned houses, re-married and sued each other.*'

Robert Jenison, a local clergyman wrote an account of how the plague decimated the City in a book titled: Newcastle's call to her neighbours…to take warning by her sins and sorrows lest this overflowing scourge of pestilence reach unto them…

Good grief! So much harshness and so much sadness and yet the 17th century also brought really positive changes to the town and the broader region. Take industry for example.

The coal industry expanded from exports of 160,000 tons in 1603 to about 600,000 tons on the eve of the Civil War and to even greater volumes after the war was over. Pits got ever bigger and deeper and new inventions began to appear, which marked the start of huge changes in the technology of the industry. After 1605 the first horse-drawn waggonways were built; and shortly after that there were horse-powered engines to drain and ventilate the mines. After 1655 there were even early prototype steam engines, invented by the 1st Marquis of Worcester, which were capable of lifting water from the depths of the mines. These things were going to have a much greater effect in later centuries, but they are evidence that the coal industry was growing and becoming much more complex and the coal brought about the introduction of new industries …

A glass blower by Thomas Bewick.

Glass, for example. Before the 17th century glass had been made using wood-fired furnaces but wood was getting scarce and in 1615 the Government banned its use in glass production. But then, in 1617, a Royal Naval officer called Sir Robert Mansell, was granted a government monopoly to make window glass using coal and after much research he came to Newcastle to do it because, as those of us who live here know, you can't come to a better place. He built his first two furnaces on the banks of the river, near the mouth of the Ouseburn, just east of the Quayside. It was a brilliant place because everything that he needed in the production and trade was immediately to hand. First of all the site was beside the ballast hills. Collier ships returning from London after delivering their coal needed to take ballast on board to keep themselves stable so they filled up with rubble from the places they had delivered to. When the ships arrived back home again they were unloaded and, the ballast was carried along the river bank by women with baskets on their heads and dumped in a suitably vacant space. The ballast, which was rich in sand and limestone, provided the raw materials for making glass – and it cost nothing! And then there was coal, plentiful cheap coal to power the furnaces, and of course there was a navigable river right on the doorstep to export the finished glass. It was all so convenient and as a result, glass making became a huge industry, until eventually most of the window glass in England came from Newcastle – which was a big plus for the Toon.

Coal led to brickmaking too. The bands of clay that are almost always associated with the coal seams were perfect for making bricks and, as ever, vast quantities of cheap coal were available for firing the brick kilns. And it led to shipbuilding as well. The coal merchants of Newcastle were too bright to leave the export of coal to 'foreign bottoms' or to the ship owners of East Anglia who had dominated the trade so far and so in the 17th century they started to build their own ships to give themselves an even tighter grip on the whole process. Salt

production became massive too - inevitably powered by cheap coal . Limestone was burned to make lime, which was made into mortar for the building industry. The emerging metal industries in the Derwent Valley depended on cheap coal. The need for pit props encouraged trade with Scandinavia and the increased shipping led to the export of grindstones … I'm sure I could go on but you've probably got the picture by now – in the 17th century, Newcastle (and the Tyne as a whole, of course) was rapidly becoming a big, complicated, interrelated industrial giant.

So, what effect did all of that have on the town itself?

What you would hope is that such a place, with all the wealth that was being created and all the contacts with other cities and countries that trade entails would develop a nice looking face and keep up to date with modern styles, and I think it did. I think there's enough evidence that 17th century Newcastle was a pretty exciting place with its finger on the pulse of changing fashion.

Take the 1630s for example and imagine a group of lads coming up north for a stag weekend (always assuming they had them in those days) – what would they have thought of Newcastle? What might they have written on Trip Advisor. I'll just click on the old Jacobean laptop and find out. Ah! Here's one – an army lieutenant from Norwich on a trip with his mates in 1634. I wonder what he thought …'*We found the people and the streets much alike, neither rich nor clean.*'

Hm, that's not very positive; perhaps he got a better impression of the people at the top of the social scale. What about the mayor?

'*Fat and rich.*'

Is there nothing he liked? Thank goodness for that! Even old misery guts seems to have liked the Nag's Head. He enjoyed '*a cup of good wine*' there.

Well, there's always one moaning Minnie but fortunately, the following year, in 1635, one of Newcastle's best ever tourist notices was written. A

Baronet called Sir William Brereton from Cheshire described Newcastle as *'Beyond compare the fairest and the richest town in England, inferior for wealth and building to no city save London and Bristol.'* This is the sort of advertising we like. The tasteful Bart keeps going. He's impressed by the number of salmon in the river; he thinks the Quay is *'the fairest in the land.'* The Nag's Head is terrific, the bridge superb, the streets have *'the daintiest flagged channels'* to give horses footing, the markets are beyond compare. He had a lovely little trip out to Tynemouth and South Shields (the Metro must have been running that day) and he's not even fazed by the fact that the town is placed on the highest and steepest hills he has come across in any great town in the country.

He sounds like a man after my own heart – all you need is a bit of nice architecture (and Newcastle, as we know was rich in Medieval magnificence and all of those fine Tudor merchants' houses), an interesting townscape and a decent pint – what more could you want? And if Sir William happened to have a taste for modern design – well, he would have found that too in 1635.

For example, he might have seen one pure Jacobean room which is part of a complex of buildings that I haven't mentioned so far, though I should have done and I meant to. It is the chapel of Trinity House, which became the property of the Guild or Fraternity of the Blessed Trinity of Newcastle upon Tyne, whose purpose from the earliest times was the welfare of mariners and their families. They acquired their site down beside the river from Ralph

Top: *Trinity House in 1930.* Below right: *In 2016.* Below Left: *The Chapel, 2016.*

Hebburn in 1505. It cost them a single rose, to be paid yearly on Midsummer's Day. There were already buildings there when they got it and some early bits and pieces are still there. One complete medieval building survives pretty well intact; the 'rigging loft' is probably the oldest surviving domestic building in Newcastle and the lower floor beneath the chapel has a 14th century doorway and window and timbers that have been dated to the 1300s as well. But on these earlier foundations the Guild immediately started to build a new chapel and a hall and some almshouses. The present chapel is almost certainly part of that original 16th century building. These are the things that I should have already been telling you about in earlier chapters but the problem with Trinity house is that they never stopped building. They added stuff in the 17th century; most of the site was remodelled in the 18th and they kept on making changes in the 19th century as well. What they ended up with is a fantastically picturesque and atmospheric little warren of beautiful buildings created over 400 years and extraordinarily enriched inside with the things they've kept hold of over the whole of that time. So my problem was when to talk about it. I still don't know. I'll probably come back to it a bit later but in the meantime I have to mention the early 17th century chapel because church buildings of that date are really rare in England and this one is completely delightful. It was started in 1634 and the whole room seems to be made of wood. The furniture is entirely Jacobean; there's a splendidly elaborate pulpit and an equally elaborate screen at the west end. The seats are box pews, richly decorated with strapwork and cherubs' heads, the walls are panelled. The ceiling is so lovable. It has close-set beams all of them slightly arched like the hull of a ship; in fact the whole room seems like the 'tween decks of a ship. You can almost hear the creaking of the timbers – the most satisfying and appropriate atmosphere for the chapel of a Guild of Mariners that you could possible imagine.

Another 'modern' thing Sir William might well have seen is a monument in St Nicholas's church that commemorates the Maddison Family, in particular Henry and Elizabeth Maddison who are portrayed kneeling and facing each other on opposite sides of a prayer desk. Behind Henry are his parents and behind Elizabeth is a figure in armour which (it was suggested by the 18th century historian, the Rev. John Brand) might be her son, Sir Lionel Maddison, who was knighted by Charles I in 1633. Kneeling beneath these principal figures are all sixteen of the Maddison children – ten sons (including Lionel) and six daughters. It's quite a small but brilliantly entertaining monument, richly coloured, absolutely packed with incident and character and carved sometime after 1635 when Henry died …

… but why did it survive the Scottish iconoclasts when so many of St Nicholas's ancient monuments didn't? I have an idea, no more than a guess really but I'll tell you about it anyway. The eldest son, Sir Lionel, who was knighted by the king, changed sides as the war approached and became an ardent puritan. During the occupation, along with John Blakiston the puritan mayor, he was among the first to re-open coal mines and begin to supply the 'enemy'. I find myself wondering if the memorial was spared by the puritan invaders because he was on their side. Underneath his figure is a space for an inscription which was never carved – a suggestion perhaps that when he died, after the restoration of the monarchy in 1660, he remained an unpopular figure in the town (and possibly in the family).

Both of those designs from the 1630s are smashing examples of a very English style and I like to think that Sir William (who was clearly a man of taste and discrimination) would have enjoyed them; but he might have been even more impressed by a series of absolutely superlative carved fireplaces that were to be found in various buildings in the town. There were probably more of them at one time but as far as I know there are only three still in existence. One, which used to be in the Beehive Inn on the Quayside, has ended up in the Beamish Museum, where it looks fantastic in the Bank room; a second is at Chipchase Castle in the North Tyne valley, but the third is in the Merchant Adventurers Court, which is part of the Guildhall down by the river. All of these are brilliantly carved and rich in allegorical figures and scenes. They are thought to have been carved in Newcastle but inspired by styles and craftsmanship from elsewhere in northern Europe and they are evidence of two things – firstly of the amazing standard of craftsmanship and design that was available in Newcastle in the early 17th century and secondly of the town's close connections with the wider European world …

… which brings me to the Guildhall itself and to the group of remarkable buildings that face it from the opposite side of the road.

Sandhill had long been the posh bit of town. It was the centre of municipal government and where the *'opulent and knightly inhabitants lived'* according to William Grey. There were lots of *'shops and stately houses'* and the perfect place for all the *'merchant adventurers, merchants of coals and all those who have their living by shipping'*. Henry Bourne, writing a few years later, says that these houses were *'where the principal inhabitants lived. Sir William Blackett, Sir John Marley, Sir Mark Millbank and the houses of many other gentlemen…'* and they really are pretty splendid. Bourne goes on to say that inside they have *'magnificence and grandeur; the rooms being very large and stately and for the most part adorned with curious carving'*.

They are all four or five storeys high and they are all timber-framed (though some of them were given brick fronts in the 1700s). They nearly all contain timber which dates from the 1500s but they all seem to have been rebuilt or restored in the 1650s , in fact Bessie Surtees' House, the best known of the bunch, contains a fireplace dated 1657, which seems about right. The facades of all the ones that are still clearly timber framed have unbroken strips of glass on each of their floors. As Eneas Mackenzie put it *'Many of these houses were built before any window tax was contemplated. The entire front of the dwellings is occupied by windows.'* It seems to me that the amount of glass is probably a reflection of the fact that they are in Newcastle, the new window-glass capital of the country, on the grounds that if you've got it you should flaunt it; but all that glass also makes them look foreign, un-English, rather exotic as if they come from somewhere like Lubeck in the Baltic. Bruce Alsopp, who was a professor in the School of Architecture at Newcastle Uni and who wrote a book about the historic architecture of Newcastle back in the 60s, was very enthusiastic in his response, specificaly to Bessie Surtees' House. He said that it was 'perhaps the finest of its kind in Europe, because it is not only a superb example of a timber-framed town house, it is also a rare example of this kind of design refined by the Renaissance and it is so advanced as a form that it anticipates in most essentials the modern idiom of frame and curtain wall'.

You can't say fairer than that.

Opposite Bessie Surtees is the Guildhall, where the municipal government took place. That's where all the courts were held – the Sheriff's and the Mayor's Court and the Assizes. It's where the Freemen held their Guild meetings. The Mayor and the Corporation met in the Mayor's Chamber to conduct all the normal business of the town.

It's a building that was completly encased in new walls in the late 18th and early 19th centuries so now it looks entirely Georgian from the outside, but inside it's much older because there has been a Guildhall on this site for hundreds of years.

There have been guilds in Newcastle since the time of King John and they must have had a place to meet from the beginning but the first actual mention of a guildhall was made in 1400. In 1425 a chapel called the Maison

Dieu was added to it, paid for by that exceedingly wealthy medieval merchant, Roger Thornton. That original hall seems to have been rebuilt in 1509 and then rebuilt yet again at the same time as the houses across the road, between 1655 and 1658.

It was designed by an architect called Robert Trollope who came from York, lived in Gateshead and was to be a major influence on the buildings of Northumberland. His Guildhall was quite extraordinary. It was richly decorated and fanciful like nothing that had been seen in Newcastle before. It mingled classical details with Gothic ones in a strange and eclectic way. It must have reminded well-travelled Newcastle merchants of the public buildings in the main squares of towns like Ghent and Bruges. All of that has gone now (sadly) but inside the later walls quite a lot of Trollope's decorative scheme is still there. The hall itself is a fabulous room, now filled with the intensely picturesque and atmospheric fittings of an 18th century law court but its ceiling is by Trollope. It's a double hammerbeam roof such as you might find in Medieval great halls like St Stephen's Hall at Westminster – except that here, as he did outside, Trollope has mixed Classical details in with the Gothic ones. You might need to be a bit of an architectural nerd to get as excited as I do about this – but be nice, humour me, recognise that it is deeply unusual (and deeply original too) to find the Gothic and the Classical mingled together at this time in history.

And the Mayor's Parlour next door to the main hall, well, that's unusual too but in a different way – it is just a small but beautifully decorated room with a magnificent plaster ceiling, a splendid fireplace and fascinating panelling. If you saw it anywhere in the country and knew it had been decorated in the 1650s you would say that it was spot on the fashionable button.

I'll tell you something else about Robert Trollope's Guildhall; it's very difficult to think of another seat of local government, anywhere in England, from that period in the middle of the 1600s, which is anything like as ambitious as the one that Newcastle built, so the question is ....*Why?*

In 1655 the Civil War had only recently come to a close and Newcastle had been on the losing side. The Scots had left a few years previously and the town (if we are to believe William Grey) was still visibly damaged by the effects of a lengthy siege and a catastrophic final battle. The rulers (of the town as well as the country) were not sympathetic to the stance that Newcastle had taken and the Restoration that would bring back Royalty was still five years in the future. It seems an odd time and odd circumstances in which to start a rebuilding programme of such ambition right in the heart of the town so it seems reasonable to wonder why it happened.

It might have been necessary, of course. The area might well have been so badly damaged during the siege and the final battle that rebuilding was the only way forward. Or the inspiration may have been different. There may have just been a determination to start again. I'm sitting writing this in the middle of a time of profound austerity and economic depression and yet virtually every street and back lane I walk down is dotted with skips and scaffolding as people refuse to give up on their dreams and ambitions in the face of hardships. Well, a lot of Newcastle's ambitions and self image must have been thoroughly dented during the war and when I look at the Guildhall and the houses on Sandhill the message I get is 'You can't keep a good Geordie down'. It seems to me that they were absolutely determined to rise again and regain their rightful position as the lords of the Tyne. After the Restoration of the Monarchy in 1660 there don't seem to have been any real setbacks for the rest of the century. The industrial scene continued to flourish. The Corporation made a number of improvements to the town. They built the Holy Jesus Hospital, for example, to house thirty-nine poor Freemen or their widows, which shows a reasonable level of responsibility and they paved over the lower Lort Burn, which show an impressive awareness of town planning possibilities. The Lort Burn, which runs to the Tyne on the line now followed by Grey Street and Dean Street, was a major obstacle between the lower and the upper parts of the town. It was also effectively an open sewer and rubbish tip and turning it into a culvert and a street showed a level of imagination that other towns didn't show for many years after.

And the town continued to improve and modernise its face. New buildings were built of brick, which was a local product, less likely to burn down than timber-framing and more fashionable than stone. Alderman Fenwick's House on Pilgrim Street is the great example - a fine design from the end of the century with an elegant staircase and a magnificent panelled room with a beautiful plaster ceiling. There were other buildings like this at one time, especially the Mansion House, which the Corporation built in 1691 as a residence for the Mayor and a venue for civic events. It was on the river bank near the Guildhall. It was a very plain and rather austere design but extremely dignified and built in a perfect Classical style. Inside it seems to have been rather fabulous with painted panels (the ones that are now in the Mayor's chamber in The Guildhall), collections of rare books and displays of all the civic regalia including the massive silver gilt mace which was made for Mayor Cole in 1687 and remains the largest post-Reformation mace in the country. Both of these buildings (and there must have been many others once) are evidence that Newcastle was no longer remote and backward. It was becoming a metropolitan and sophisticated town influenced by all the places its merchants traded including, of course, London so when the great 17th century traveller, Celia Fiennes, visited the town in 1698 she was able to write 'it most resembles London of any place in England, its buildings Lofty and Large, of brick mostly or stone'.

Well said, Celia.

Showing four and five storeys of timber frames, buildings at Sandhill, 1879.

To Sir Matthew White Ridley Bar.ᵗ M.P. ALDERMAN and GOVERNOR of the Company of MERCHANT ADVENTURERS of NEWCASTLE upon TYNE, This View of the Exchange of that Town, engraved at his Expence, is most respectfully inscribed by his very obliged & most devoted faithful humble Servant. John Brand

E. Edwards delin   J. Fittler sculp.

MERCHANT ADVENTURERS.

BAKERS & BREWERS.

BARBER-SURGEONS & CHANDLERS.

Top: *Trollope's Guildhall in 1786.*
Left: *Various Arms of Newcastle incorporated companies or guilds.*
Far Left: *Inside the courtroom of the Guildhall 1950.*

(Dr Tom Yellowley)

(Dr Tom Yellowley)

Top: *The Mansion House, on The Close, this engraving is from around 1827.*
Top right and above: *Alderman Fenwicks House on Pilgrim Street and its interior.*
Right: *The Holy Jesus Hospital, 1910.*

The Eighteenth Century

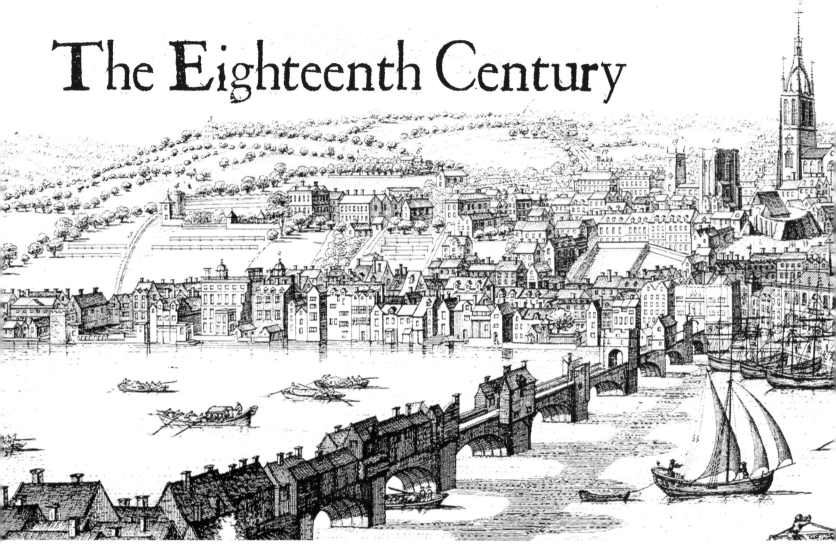

Newcastle's first building of the new century appeared in 1701. It was built of brick like everything else that was going up at that time but it wasn't as austere and formal as the mayor's Mansion House where we finished the last chapter; it was (well it still is) a classical building - but a nice, informal, rather jolly version of the style. It wasn't put up by the Corporation or anybody posh because it was the Keelmen's Hospital, which was intended to provide accommodation for elderly or sick keelmen or their widows. What makes it especially interesting, apart from its design, is that the money to pay for it didn't come from well-to-do sources but was raised by the keelmen themselves and they were thoroughly working class Geordies.

There hasn't been a lot of stuff about the working class so far in this book. They've been there, of course, hanging about in the background – being poor and getting the plague, their houses unprotected from the plundering Scottish soldiers, called upon to fight other

people's battles, sent down ever deeper pits and so on but all is about to change and the pitiless glare of the Grundy attention is going to shine on their lives for a bit.

Nowadays working class Geordies are presented in rather an odd way when they appear on the telly or in the papers. Lots of the blokes, of course, don't seem to possess any clothes except stripy black and white tops (unless they've got big bare bellies and they're trying to put the nut on police horses outside the football ground). They hardly ever get mentioned without drink entering into the equation. Geordie women are pretty well the same; the media only shows them when they're out on the town in their scanties whatever the weather. And falling down.

And of course the Geordie language is a constant source of fun and bemusement to the rest of the world. An American friend of mine once tried to buy something in Greggs.

'Could I have a starty?' he said to the woman behind the counter.

'Ugh?'
'Could I have a starty please?'
'Ugh?'
The person behind him on the queue leant over and said,
'The man wants a stottie, pet.'
'Way, why couldn't he say so?'

I made the mistake of trying to tell my American chum the joke about the woman who went to the hairdresser and asked for a perm. The hairdresser replied, 'I wandered lernly as a cloud.' It took him a fortnight to get it.

Stereotypes like these are nothing new. When the traveller and antiquarian, William Stukely, passed through Newcastle in 1724 gathering information for his *Itinerarium Curiosum* he recorded that, *'They speak very broad, so that as one walks the streets, one can scarce understand the common people but is apt to fancy oneself in a foreign country.'*

How one would have liked, if one had had the good fortune to be standing behind Mr Stukely, to kick him in his antiquarian pants. But the problem for outsiders was that they weren't used to places like Newcastle where the very air smelt of coal and the work was dirty, grim and seemed brutalising. Even John Wesley, the founder of Methodism, who loved Newcastle and thought there was *'no place in Britain comparable to it in pleasantness'*, even he talked about preaching in *'the poorest and most contemptible parts of the town'* by which he meant the working-class area of Sandgate down by the river where he found *'so much drunkenness, cursing and swearing, even from the mouths of little children'*. He described it as worse than he had ever encountered before. Lots of visitors were shocked in a similar way. They saw the locals' blackened faces and thought of them as less than human, as brutes and savages. One writer talks about the *'carbonated physiognomies'* of the miners as if they were actually made of coal.

And to be fair it wasn't just outsiders who gave us early examples of the modern Geordie stereotypes. There were snooty insiders as well. The well-to-do Judith Milbanke who lived in one of the big posh houses near the Guildhall moaned about the pong from the

Left: *An 1886 image of the Keelmen's Hospital.* Above: *Today, the hospital stands waiting for a new purpose.*

nearby tanning yards and mocked the tough market women carrying freshly butchered carcases 'dangling over their brawny arms.' Other observers were less snooty but equally critical. Edward Chicken was a teacher and the Parish Clerk of St Andrew's church in the early 1700s. He wrote an extraordinary poem called *The Colliers Wedding*, a bit of which I am going to quote to you, even though you are probably delicately nurtured and living as you do in our nice, well behaved, modern world, not used to stuff like this. So, here we are, in the church …

> *For some, perhaps there were three score*
> *Were never in a church before …*
> *… Our couple now kneel down to pray*
> *Much unacquainted with the way …*
> *… Whole troops of colliers swarm around*
> *And seize poor Jenny on the ground*
> *Put up their hands to loose her garters*
> *And work for pluck about her quarters*
> *Till ribbons from her legs are torn*
> *And round the church in triumph borne …*

But eventually the scene moves on to the reception. You might want to slip out for a cup of tea at this point if you are easily shocked because…*Dead drunk some tumble on the floor...*

> *And swim in what they'd drunk before.*
> *'Hiccup', cries one, 'Reach me your hand'.*
> *'The house turns round. I cannot stand'.*
> *So now the drunken senseless crew*
> *Break pipes, spill drink, piss, shit and spew.*

Gosh!

And then there was sex, of course. Lots of nice, respectable middle class chaps were shocked (or pretended to be) by the dangers and the prevalence of prostitution in 18th century Newcastle, but there seems to have been a lot of it about. The engraver Thomas Bewick, looking back on his early years as an apprentice in the 1770s, seemed more concerned about the effect that the trade had on his fellow apprentices whose health and lives were ruined by contact with it but he also felt sorry for the 'street walkers' as he called them, girls who had been seduced and abandoned. Sweetly, but rather embarrassingly he seems to have stopped them and given them little lectures on the dangers they were in and a few coins to help them on their way.

Remember the curous way Eneas Mackenzie had of describing the prostitutes who worked in the narrows chares off the Quayside in the late 18th century? He called them 'Cyprian Nymphs', I have no idea why, I saw no nymphs of any sort when I went on holiday to Cyprus, but he said that 'their blandishments were of the most coarse and vulgar description' and he went on to say that most of the dark lanes 'were inhabited by very dangerous, though not very tempting females'.

Gosh again!

So, back in the 18th century there were all sorts of stereotypical and prejudiced attitudes being expressed about the local working classes, very similar to the images that we still get today, and on top of all the other criticisms, they were accused of that other curse of the underclass so beloved of the modern mass media – ANTI-SOCIAL BEHAVIOUR – an attack that needs to be examined with a glance at the keelmen.

I'm sure you already know who the keelmen were but I'm going to tell you anyway, just in case. They were the people who took coal from the staithes down to the collier boats waiting near the mouth of the river. They were needed because the Tyne was twisting, shallow and tortuous and the bigger sea-going boats couldn't make it to the source of the coal. The keels, the boats that they used, were low and flat-bottomed (quite unlike myself) with a shallow draft which meant that they could get under the arches of the bridge at Newcastle and wouldn't get stuck on the shoals in the river. They used the current as their source of power (with a sail if the wind was helpful, and the incoming tide to get them back upstream) and an oar to steer with. Initially they were supposed to carry about sixteen tons of coal but grasping and unscrupulous owners sneakily added to that amount in order to transport more coal for the same cost until by the 1800s they were carrying about twenty-one tons. The work was incredibly arduous because the colliers were much higher in the water than the keels and all those tons of coal had to be manhandled up and over the sides of the sea-going boats.

The Keelmen were first mentioned in 1516, though they may well have existed earlier than that, and in 1565 they became an independent society. They always wanted to go one stage further and become an incorporated company or a guild like so many other trades in the town had done and there was no reason, really, why they shouldn't have done that. Lots of other trades which we might nowadays think of as being essentially working class jobs, trades like cobblers and glove makers for example, had become guilds, but the Keelmen never achieved their aim because of the opposition of the Hostmen who employed them. The Hostmen were convinced that the wage bill would go up if the Keelmen achieved the higher status of becoming a guild, so instead they were bound to the Hostmen by a yearly bond and it was a very fractious and unsettled relationship between the two groups.

The Keelmen's Hospital provides a good example of what the relationship was like because the institution which the workers had paid for with such unselfish pride turned into an ongoing source of contention. They were never allowed to run it themselves. How irritating must that have been? The management was handed over to the bosses and the Keelmen were allowed no role in their own creation. The below inscription is over the main door.

'White', 'Grey' and 'Carr' were among the most powerful names in the town and they are the ones in charge but the phrase, 'for the time being' tells another story. We built it, the words seem to say, and at the moment they're in charge, but …

It would have rankled with me, I would have been as sore as a gumboil and it clearly ranked with them. In 1707 they rioted over the issue. In 1710 they held a petition complaining that the money collected for the hospital was 'partly detained, partly wasted and misapplied.' None of this had any effect and the Hostmen kept tight control.

That was an issue to do with pride and status and you can't underestimate the importance of that for people who felt that they were being held down by those who employed them, but money was the usual source of conflict. It wasn't exactly that they were badly paid – in the 1700s they earned about seventeen shillings a week, which was a reasonable sum in the country as a whole and much more than an agricultural worker (for example) could get. They could even own their own keels and buy shares in ships; they owned property at times and did alright when things were going well. A handbill issued during a strike in 1793 says 'We can live comfortably, support our families decently, give our children an honest and a useful education.' But the problem was that there was no safety net, the work was entirely seasonal – virtually no sea-going collier boats risked the journeys they needed to make in the depths of winter so there was no work at that time. The job was also affected by the level of trade. If there was a war, or if London was in a recession, for example, the work dried up; and finally, like anybody else in the labouring classes, they were entirely at the mercy of the weather. In bad summers the price of corn (and everything else) went up and people like the Keelmen risked starvation.

And when the Keelmen were desperate the town soon got to know about it. There were about 1,600 of them at the beginning of the 18th century and they weren't shy about making their presence felt. They rioted in 1709, 1710, 1740 and 1750 but I think in all of these cases they were rioting because they were desperate for food and the disorder seems to me to have been pretty understandable - caused by treatment and inequalities that we would find entirely unacceptable nowadays.

The winter of 1739-40 was a classic example, though on that occasion the rioting keelmen were joined by the pitmen and all the other workers in the town. The weather had been absolutely awful and at the coldest times many of the poor would have died of the excessive cold if Alderman Ridley hadn't allowed them to take as much coal from his stockpiles as they needed. But as 1740 progressed, food shortage became the key issue. By June corn was in such short supply that the Corporation stepped in and gave £50 to the four different parishes for poor relief and promised that corn prices would be kept low. Sir Walter Blackett actually gave two-hundred guineas of his own money for the relief of the poor but sadly the corn dealers wouldn't play ball and shut up their shops rather than sell corn cheaply so the pitmen plundered their granaries and seized a cargo of rye from a ship in the harbour. On the 25th June, according to a frightened member of the middle class, 'the keelmen entered Newcastle in terrible numbers and with all sorts of weapons, swarmed into Sandhill.' There was an angry confrontation with town officials during which a demonstrator was killed. The crowd attacked the mayor and other members of the corporation. They broke into the Guildhall, carried off lots of the town's money, burnt lots of the town's records, ransacked the town court …

Can you imagine what the media would have to say about something like that in these days when a few sloshed binge drinkers falling down on a Saturday night or when a handful of arrests among over-enthusiastic supporters on derby day can generate weeks of soul searching; but mass class-based riots were relatively common events in the 18th century .

Left: *The inscription over the door of the Keelmen's Hospital.* Above: *The Tyne with keels (and the Mayor's Barge) in 1783.*

Later on for example, in 1795, at the heart of the war against France, there was another bad harvest which led to another round of violence. Because of the shortages food prices had risen to terrifically high levels and on the 10th November a crowd of workers took over the markets, seized all the butter, wheat and potatoes and promptly sold them cheaply to the poor. That's seems like quite a good crime to me? They seem like TTRHs (Tough Tyneside Robin Hoods) and it appears that the authorities thought so too because no action was taken against the culprits. It reminds me that there are other, less negative perspectives from which to look at Newcastle's working classes in the 18th century, indeed there were even some people who were prepared to say nice things about them.

Which brings me back to John Wesley. He was, as we have heard, a touch shocked by the rough edges of Newcastle society, but he was moved by it too.

His first visit to Newcastle was in May 1742 and he went down to Sandgate with his local supporter, John Taylor, and at noon the two of them began to sing Psalm 100. You may well have forgotten that one but it's the psalm that begins 'Make a joyful noise unto the Lord all ye lands'.

Recently I was persuaded to take part in a Nativity play, which was performed up and down Northumberland Street at five o'clock on a pre-Christmas evening. Now I have done some odd things in my filming life including running into the sea on a crowded Scarborough beach clad only in a flesh-coloured and deeply uncomfortable thong, but performing a Nativity play among crowds of festive shoppers and early evening revellers in the heart of the city was the hardest of all and so my heart goes out to Mr Wesley making his 'joyful noise' in the most 'contemptible part of town' among 'drunkenness, cursing and swearing' but his description of what happened next is remarkable. There was a slow response at first but then 'three or four curious people became four or five hundred' and by the time he finished

preaching there were about 1,500 in his alfresco congregation. At 5 o'clock he preached again from a hill that was crowded with people from top to bottom and when he was finished he said, 'The poor people were ready to tread me underfoot out of pure love and kindness.'

I'm not telling this story to suggest that one sermon, or even the rapid spread of Methodism (which undoubtedly occurred) dramatically changed the nature of working-class life, but it does show that people have always been more complicated than the stereotypes might suggest. Nowadays Newcastle people tend to boast that they might be a bit rough but they're friendly too and more open than people down south. That's a stereotype too, a story that we still like to tell about ourselves and it seems to me that it might have been born in the 18th century because at that time the lives (and the image) of working people began to change.

It's not that it got much easier. Half of the population were still living in poverty – indeed there was absolutely grinding poverty in some parts of the town - and the work was hard. At Walker Colliery in 1765 (and I am sure at lots of other places as well) children worked down the mines for between twelve and eighteen hours a day, much longer even than the adult miners; there were still strikes and pit disasters. Keelmen still suffered awful depredations at the hand of the press gang, and there was still no belief that you could really do anything about it. Society still believed that poverty was part of the natural order, but gradually, especially over the second half of the century, attitudes began to change and increasingly people began to look for ways to take a bit more control of their own destiny.

It was partly religion. All of the Nonconformist sects took root in the town. There were lots of Methodists as I've implied and there were even more Presbyterians because of the number of Scots who had settled here. Those were the main working-class groups but there were Unitarians, Congregationalists and Baptists, eventually, after early persecution there were Quakers. It even gradually became easier to admit to being a Catholic. In 1746 the first Catholic meeting house was burned down by a mob but by the end of the century there were at least two other places where they could worship. The point about this growth is that it was evidence that there was a more liberal attitude among those with power and that people had choice and freedom of conscience in a way that they never had in earlier centuries.

Another growth area was to be found in clubs and organisations set up by and for working-class people. There were loads of them; I've heard mention of there being thirty or forty societies for working men and possibly as many for women. They can sometimes sound a bit quaint and even naïve …The Flourishing Society of Women, Love and Unity, Peace and Unity, The Unanimous Society of Men, The Friendless Poor Society and The Good Intent… but they were evidence that life extended beyond the stereotypes, beyond poverty, roughness and drink, that people wanted to be involved in the community, that they had ideas about life which they needed to express. Middlebrook estimates that at least five-hundred working class men (out of a total Newcastle population of about 30,000) were members of clubs like these and the Reverend John Baillie, who wrote a history of the town in 1801, was convinced that the rules and the fines imposed by these clubs had the effect of softening the rough edges of life in the town. He said that the keelmen were 'losing that ferocity and savage roughness by which they were characterised not many years ago.'

Well perhaps … and perhaps education helped. As we know the Royal Grammar School had been in existence for a couple of hundred years but in the 18th century there was an amazing increase in the number of schools and many of them were intended for the education of poor girls and boys. Between 1705 and 1709 the four parish churches each got a school supported by public subscription or private charitable endowments. Two of them accepted girls as well. The pupils were taught to knit, sew and read – or perhaps that was just the girls? They got a free uniform and footwear. The uniforms were apparently grey, green or blue according to the school and – yes, I know that's only three colours for four schools, perhaps the others went in the buff –

Various seals and sigils of Newcastle including the town's (centre) and the hostmen (centre middle).

and when they left school they were given forty shillings to set themselves up for service or to buy their way into an apprenticeship and they were give four books – the bible, a prayer book, a catechism and *The Whole Duty of Man*, a pretty impressive haul, indeed a pretty impressive commitment to the education of the poor.

There was actually a municipal school at St Ann's Chapel which eventually had one-hundred children paying 8d a month for reading and 1s 2d for writing and arithmetic. Several other schools that get mentioned were maintained by private subscriptions but to make sure that the schools were 'appropriated entirely to the education of the poor' the subscriptions were topped up with 'liberal help from the corporation.' I really like that; it makes Newcastle seem unexpectedly forward thinking. This was especially true of the Royal Jubilee School that opened early in the next century which was, by the standards of the age, quite a liberal institution. It had entirely non-sectarian religious instruction which I think is amazing for the time and they clearly thought so too; among the many important visitors who were shown around it was the Czar of Russia. Mind you, it was a different world from the schools where I have taught, evidence that the past really is a foreign country. The older boys acted as monitors (I was a monitor once. I was a milk monitor at junior school; it is the only position of power I have ever held). Presumably the monitors kept control and presumably they were necessary because the writer claims that 'it is a pleasing spectacle to see above four-hundred boys in one room cheerfully engaged in acquiring the elements of education.'

Four-hundred boys! In one room! That deserves a 'gosh' as well.

The girls' school next door had two-hundred and four on the books but it was apparently a very cold building so they often didn't bother to turn up, and who can blame them. I bet it was nice and warm at the fifteen private academies where 'the softer sex' were taught cookery, address, deportment and accomplishments like dancing, music, drawing and perhaps just un petit peu de Francais.

And finally, there were lots and lots of other schools – some were set up by the various nonconformist chapels in the town, but many were small commercial ventures set up by … well … by whoever wanted to set one up. Sometimes they are called Dame Schools because they were owned and run by elderly ladies in their own homes, some were run in the local church by the vicar, or the parish clerk or it could be anybody else who felt there was a market and they had the talents. These schools obviously varied wildly in their quality but some were clearly capable of providing children with a proper education and some pupils took full advantage of what they offered.

Charles Hutton, for example, was the son of a pitman, born in 1737 in a thatched cottage on Percy Street (which was quite an agreeable but very poor part of the town). He started off at a dame school run by an elderly Scotswoman but over the years his father moved to different pits at Benton and High Heaton and Charles changed to new schools in whichever neighbourhood he was living. When he was eighteen he became a miner but he couldn't cope because he had a bad arm from a childhood accident so he gave up and went back into education – not as a pupil but as a teacher. He took over his former teacher's school in Jesmond. At the same time he spent his evenings back at school himself, learning maths from a Mr James. In 1760 he left Jesmond and opened a school in Newcastle that moved around the town a bit until it finally settled in a new building at the bottom of Westgate. He was clearly a very good teacher and the children of the great and the good were sent to him – the family of Robert Shaftoe of Benwell Hall, for example, and lots of boys from the Royal Grammar School including the future Lord Chancellor of England, John Scott, Bessie Surtees' future co-elopee (if such a word exists). In 1773 he was appointed professor of Mathematics at the Royal Academy at Woolwich and ended his years with a national reputation.

Not bad for a failed miner and a pitman's son.

Another working class boy who used the system well and went on to make a name for himself on the national stage was Mark Akenside.

Mark's father was a butcher who was often heard to say, 'Mark, just keep out of the way when I'm using this meat cleav ... oooh dear...' so Mark grew up with a lame leg. His family were Presbyterians. He went to the Royal Grammar School and then to a Presbyterian Academy in the town. He was clearly bright and the local Presbyterian community paid for him to go to Edinburgh University to train as a minister but he gave that ambition up when he became a 'deist', which is what you call someone who believes in the existence of God but not in organised religion. In fact he seems to have been quite a radical thinker as a young man because he was a republican as well. Anyway, having given up the church his new idea was to become a surgeon ... and a poet.

His poetry was successful. People spoke well of it at the time. One critic said it was 'of great beauty in its richness of description.' Samuel Pope praised it as well but J. Grundy (of this parish) finds it almost impossible to read. I start, but find myself immediately drawn to cups of tea and bickies and little walks and things. Still they liked it at the time.

It took him longer to become a doctor and he had several unsuccessful attempts to set himself up in practice in Newcastle and Northampton and various places in London but eventually he became the medical bees knees – a Fellow of the Royal College of Physicians, the Principal Physician at Christ's Hospital and even physician to Queen Charlotte, the wife of George III ...

... but he doesn't seem to have been well liked. It has been suggested that he was overly conscious of his humble origins and compensated for it by being exceedingly haughty and disagreeably rough with poor people and women. He is said to have done his ward rounds in full periwig with a sword by his side and an escort of attendants who kept his patients at a distance. And on top of all that he left Newcastle and never came back! How many successful Geordies down the years have done that?

Still, they were proud enough of him in his home town and he did get a street named after him. Butcher Bank where he was born was renamed Akenside Hill in his honour.

And finally I would like to include one other successful chap from a relatively humble background who did come back and stayed in the town for the rest of his life. His name was Charles Avison and he is my personal favourite of the lads-done-well group.

He was born in 1709 into a musical family. He was probably educated at the charity school attached to St John's church. His father, who might have been a member of the town waits, died when he was twelve having taught his son to play the violin, flute ~~bongos~~ and harpsichord. In his twenties he went to London (like vast numbers of ambitious Geordies have done before and since) and studied with a composer called Francesco Germiniano but in 1734 he came back home to Newcastle, I don't think anybody knows why. Perhaps he missed his mum or his girlfriend; perhaps he got sick of Londoners mocking his accent; nobody knows, but he got the job of organist at St John's Church. The following year he moved on to do the same job at St Nicholas' Church where he stayed until he died. The salary was £20 a year. In 1737 he married Catherine Reynolds and they had nine children of whom, sadly, only three survived past childhood. She died before him as well and when he died himself, having been caught in an unexpected blizzard in May 1770, his will made two specifications – he didn't want a fancy funeral and he wanted to be buried beside his beloved wife.

That's a life in itself, it seems to me, a life of gentle usefulness and niceness with the inevitable sprinkling of sadness over it - but it is only a fraction of Charles Avison's achievements. He was a teacher as well, and he was a composer, quite a major composer. He wrote fifty concertos, twenty-four sonatas and a handful of religious pieces. They were all in the Baroque style … I can't believe I'm telling you this; I have no qualifications for talking about the history of music except that I listened to a nice podcast about him on Radio 3 and really liked the music. It was like listening to Vivaldi or Scarlatti, both of whom I have heard before and I have to tell you that his music seemed just as good as theirs. It was jolly and very tuneful

and I was assured that he ranked alongside the best of his English contemporaries. It seems to me to be rather remarkable that it was written for performance, not in Rome or Leipzig or somewhere, but in Newcastle, beside the coaly Tyne. What happened was this. In July 1738 he became, on top of everything else, the Musical Director of the newly formed Newcastle Musical Society and in that role he started a series of fortnightly subscription concerts that continued season after season throughout his life and for decades afterwards. They were the first regular concert series in the country except for the ones in London and Edinburgh, a nice bit of evidence that Newcastle had its finger on the pulse of changing taste and culture. If you were a gent you could buy a season ticket for these concerts for half a guinea but for the same price you could get season tickets for two ladies. Does that seem fair? Well, it certainly is significant because these concerts were not just concerts in the sitty-downy-listeny sort of way, they were also Assemblies - elaborate social occasions, which included card games and food, listening to music, dancing, seeing and, of course, being seen and none of those activities would have been half so interesting if there had been no pretty ladies to see and be seen by. You had to get the ladies there, even if it meant giving them half-price tickets.

You have probably guessed that these Assemblies were not places to meet pitmen or keelmen or similar rough and ready people – these were the haunts of those at the opposite end of the social spectrum – they were where you went to find Newcastle's POLITE SOCIETY.

You have seen fashionable gatherings like this on a hundred BBC period dramas so you know what they looked like and the only surprise is that they were happening in Newcastle where you weren't necessarily expecting to find polite society; but that's where you would be wrong. My Radio 3 podcast made it clear that Newcastle, in the middle of the 18th century, had a musical life, indeed a cultural life as rich as anywhere else. The town had been made wealthy by coal but there was

sophistication here as well as money. It was a
fashionable town with international
connections. There were visiting merchants from
all over the country and beyond. A shipping list
from the middle of the century records that
ships arrived in the river from places as far
afield as London and Edinburgh, Riga,
Copenhagen, Hamburg and Bremen; there were
boats from Bordeaux, Cadiz and Oporto and
even ships from across the Atlantic, from
Boston, New York and Charleston. It wasn't
just about coal going out of the river, there were
luxury goods coming in - wine from southern
Europe, tea and coffee from the far east, sugar
from the West Indies and tobacco from America.
Every day, coaches from London and Edinburgh
brought wealthy visitors into the town just like
there are nowadays – for a few glasses of wine,
a bit of a laugh and a spot of shopping …

And just like today, it was good for shopping.
First of all there were terrific markets. Charles
Hutton, writing in 1770, said (with
appropriately mathematical precision) that the
population was 'supplied from the very plentiful
markets of the town … here being used
annually above 5000 beeves, 10,000 calves,
143,000 sheep and lambs with swine, fish,
poultry, eggs, butter etc in a prodigious
abundance.' All towns had markets of course
but not on that scale and Newcastle was even
better off for shops. Specialist shops were still a
rarity in most parts of the country, especially the
new sort of shops with attractive window
displays - but not here. Even as early as the
1690s Celia Fiennes (who we met in in the
previous chapter) was just the first of a very
long line indeed of visitors who were impressed
by the shopping possibilities of Newcastle and
by the middle of the 18th century the town was

Named after a Newcastle poet, Akenside Hill in 1925.

rich enough and there was enough of a middle class to create a genuine market for luxury goods. In 1736, Henry Bourne said that The Side was 'from one end to the other filled with shops of merchants, Goldsmiths, Milliners, upholsterers etc.' Now The Side is a long street; it stretches from Sandhill right up the hill as far as the castle and there were over a hundred shops on it. There was fantastically high quality glass on offer and superb silverware. If you go into the Laing Art Gallery you'll see examples of the sort of quality that was being made in Newcastle and sold in its shops. There were grocers and milliners and tobacconists and wine shops. There were specialists in musical instruments and a range of different drapers and dressmakers. There were goldsmiths, tea dealers, book shops (the town had eleven bookshops and it had publishers too, it published more children's books than any other town in the country outside London.) By 1790 buyers had a choice of four different china dealers to select from. Coffee shops became increasingly common; Katy's opposite the Guildhall always got a good review on Trip Advisor, I believe. And there were services and creative industries too. Around St Nicholas's Churchyard at the head of the street there were music teachers, and a dancing master; Thomas Bewick, the engraver, had his workshop there where he produced wood carvings of incomparable quality and the workshop of the Beilby family was there too. Ralph, to whom Bewick was apprenticed, was a silversmith and engraver; William, his brother produced engraved and enamelled glass of superlative beauty and skill. Across the lane there was a free lending library called The Tomlinson Library attached to the south side of St Nicks.

So the town centre seems to have been a pretty vibrant and exciting place to be and, a little further out, housing was getting better too, especially middle class housing. Some of the merchants and Hostmen (like Bessie Surtees' dad and the Milbanke family) were still clinging on to their old haunts down on Sandhill, but most middle class families began to move away from the river bank to new

housing developments on the outskirts of the town. Hanover Square and Clavering Place (which were behind where the station is now) and Charlotte Square (which still stands off Westgate Hill) were the first proper Georgian developments inside the walls and there were lots of other nice suburbs just outside. Northumberland Street was pleasantly middle class and there was an attractive area near St Andrew's Church. Pilgrim Street was considered the most desirable place to live in the town because there were no markets there, no shops or pubs, no rough people, just nice houses and pleasant walks in the surrounding countryside; it was the street of choice for the gentry and the clergy who could stroll out to take the air in Carliol Croft on a summer evening.

Only one full-blown gentry mansion remained within the walls. The Newe Place, built in the 16th Century by Robert Anderson, had become Blackett property and extended; it was surrounded by a superb garden or series of gardens in the formal 17th century style - but there were lots of other mansions outside the town (though often close enough to be within the city's modern boundaries). The Ridleys had Heaton Hall overlooking the Ouseburn Valley, the Brandlings built themselves a splendid mansion at Gosforth Park, there was a manor house in Jesmond and another in Fenham. Fenham had (and still has) a splendid country house as well and at Benwell the Shaftoes had a country house. They might have lived beyond the town, but all of the upper-crust families from these stately homes were part of Newcastle society as well.

We underestimate Georgian Newcastle you know. Nowadays when we look at Newcastle, our view is dominated by the vast and extraordinary changes that have taken place over the last two-hundred years and we tend to miss its Georgian legacy and yet there is plenty to see. There's Trinity House and St Anne's church, the Guildhall and the splendid early 18th century survivals like Alderman Fenwick's House and the Keelmen's Hospital. The surviving 18th century housing in Charlotte Square and Ridley place off the top of Northumberland Street, on

Dean Street and Saville Row, is mainly quiet, simple and plain and made of brick but really pretty; a few houses remain that give a sense of the posher end of the Georgian housing market. There is Clavering House behind the station and 35-37 Westgate Road (which has a fantastic mid-18th century interior) but the best Georgian building of all – this is my own little opinion – is All Saints church, one of the most elegant, beautiful and ambitious Georgian churches in the country. It was designed by David Stephenson, the first Newcastle architect to study at The Royal Academy. When it was finished, the steeplejack John Burdikin climbed to the top of the steeple to fix the weather cock. He did a handstand on the very top – the sort of flourish that Geordies love and it made him the stuff of legends. Twenty years later, when repairs were needed, his son repeated the whole thing. I myself have offered to re-enact these spectacles for the cheering multitudes but sadly my offer has been turned down.

Buildings are nice, of course but are they enough? Indeed they are not and as the century progressed the town increasingly developed not only a more elegant architectural face but also a richer cultural and intellectual life. Three newspapers were available from a remarkably early date. England's first daily newspaper, the *Daily Courant* appeared in 1702 and by 1711 Newcastle had a *Courant* of its own. It was followed by *The Newcastle Journal* in 1739 and *The Chronicle* in 1764. There were innumerable societies for gentle folk just as there were for the working classes. By 1793 they included the wonderful and extraordinary Literary and Philosophical Society, which was destined to become of immense significance and which we will undoubtedly be coming back to in subsequent chapters. There were new subscription libraries. There was a Theatre Royal opened in 1788, there were pleasure gardens (the New Ranelagh Gardens) which provided outdoor summer concerts and over the next few decades all of these were to be joined by the Society of Antiquities (another provincial first for Newcastle), a Mechanics' Institute and the Natural history society …

… and there were the Assembly Rooms which is where the soirees and elegant entertainments and subscription concerts organised by Charles Avison took place. In the Assembly Rooms patrons were entertained by his particular brand of Baroque music. I have already told you that it was very tuneful, rich and varied, popular music that was in great demand for dancing. The particular form that he chose (said my podcast) was the

All Saints.

(Dr Tom Yellowley)

concerto grosso, which was a slightly old-fashioned form by the time he was writing – a little outmoded perhaps but especially suitable for the Newcastle circumstances. In a full-blown concerto you have an orchestra alternating with a soloist but in a concerto grosso the music is passed between a small group of soloists and the full orchestra. That was appropriate to Newcastle because these concerts were largely performed by local amateur players beefed up with a few professionals and it was easier (and cheaper) to play a concerto grosso because you didn't need so many highly qualified professional soloists. This mingling of amateur and professional musicians didn't happen in other countries, it was a peculiarly British way of doing things and it is evidence that the music teachers and musical instrument makers of Newcastle (not to mention the 'academies for the softer sex') were doing their job among the town's polite society at that time.

Avison's concerts were performed in the Old Assembly Rooms on the Groat Market, but shortly after he died, Newcastle society decided to up its game and build a new and more splendid set of Assembly Rooms. In 1774 they raised money by public subscription. 128 subscribers gave of their bounty and they acquired land in what had been the garden of St John's Vicarage on the north side of Westgate Road. William Newton, who was the town's other principal architect of the time, provided the design in a very up-to-the minute Neo-Classical style. Inside there was … well, there still is because it is all still there … a richly-decorated saloon where dancing and concerts could take place and round it other equally elegant rooms - a coffee room, a library and a news room where it is said, though I am not clear how it was possible, that people could read the London newspapers on the day they were published. It was opened in 1776 and people were immensely pleased with it from the start. It was described as 'the most elegant and commodious edifice of its kind in the kingdom, except the house of Assembly in Bath' and it has a foundation stone that expresses the confident satisfaction of its founders to perfection:

In an age
When the Polite Arts
By general Encouragement and Emulation
Have advanced to a state of perfection
Unknown in any former Period
The first stone of this Edifice
Dedicated to the elegant Recreation
Was laid by William Lowes Esq.

So that's the two extremes of Newcastle society – the tough and rough labouring classes, constantly on the edge of hunger and insurrection, maybe doing a bit better than they had in former centuries – and polite society, inventing new sophisticated forms of entertainment and supremely confident that they were doing OK.

But there was another group, a very interesting section of Newcastle society which I haven't mentioned yet and they were the radicals, the dissatisfied, the reformers.

You would be surprised, given the state of world politics in the later 1700s, if there had been no radicals and revolutionary thinkers in England at that time. With the American Revolution in 1776 and the French Revolution in 1789 and the spirit of revolt clearly out of the bottle all over Europe, there were bound to be home-grown free thinkers and, as it happens, Newcastle was especially well endowed with them and was considered a bit of a hotbed of revolutionary thought, sufficient to provide sanctuary to a revolutionary as important as Jean-Paul Marat (who was so famously murdered in his bath by Charlotte Corday). He lived here for five years from 1770. He wrote and published *The Chains of Slavery* here, working in one of the town's libraries, living for three months (he said) on black coffee and practising as a vet (and a human doctor) to keep body and soul together. He was voted in as an honorary member of the Newcastle Patriotic Society (and, to be fair, of similar societies in Berwick and Carlisle as well). Other radicals didn't live in Newcastle but were popular here. James Wilkes, who was creating political mayhem demanding reform of Parliament in the 1760s, was warmly supported in Newcastle. The *Newcastle Chronicle* wrote enthusiastically about him. Thomas Paine, one of the great advocates of the American and French Revolutions was a firm favourite too. His *Rights of Man* which is a devastating critique of monarchies and of most other traditional social institutions, was hugely popular and sold almost a million copies when it came out in 1791. Newcastle was one of its best markets; people said satirically that every pitman had a copy of the book in his back pocket.

So the town was a great supporter of free thinking radicals but interestingly it also produced one of the men that the radicals most hated. John Scott, the man who eloped with Bessie Surtees, didn't only climb up the ladder to Bessie's window but up the political ladder as well. He became Solicitor General first, then Attorney General and Lord Chief Justice and eventually Lord Chancellor, in which position he was passionately despised by the radicals because he opposed almost any reform you could think of and his response to the French Revolution was to impose as many repressive policies as he possibly could. He was described as the most hated man in Britain. The poet Shelley described him as a 'foul, knotted, many-headed worm', which is a good line; you could use that on someone who was irritating you in the pub – if you were confident that you had enough speed to get away afterwards. He must have had supporters in the town though, people who shared his political beliefs, because, like Mark Akenside, his name features among the streets and shopping malls in our modern city – the title he was given later in his life was Lord ~~Square~~ Eldon.

So there were lots of radicals in Newcastle and prominent among them was the Rev James Murray, the minister of the High Bridge Congregational Meeting House whose feelings about the New Assembly Rooms (to whisk you back a couple of pages) were just the teeniest bit different from the people who built them. This is the version of the Foundation Stone inscription which he wrote and published in the *Freemen's Magazine:*

Left: *Guildhall, 1827*. Right: *Charlotte Square.*

18th Century buildings: Left: *The Assembly Rooms (etching from 1830).* Right: *The Theatre Royal on Mosley Street, image dated 1804.*

In an Age
When the tide of corruption
By Royal encouragement, deluged the land
When a stagnation
Of trade and the high price of provisions
Had reduced the poor to the greatest extremity
To their everlasting disgrace, the gentlemen of Newcastle
Continued to waste their time
And spend their substance
In celebrating the rites of Venus and the ceremonies of
Bacchus …

Wow!

There's not much that you can read about the beliefs and behaviour of the Reverend James Murray that doesn't make you say 'Wow!' Here's a description of him from *Myers' Literary Guide to the North East.* He was 'outspoken, egalitarian, democrat, frequently in trouble … a constant thorn in the flesh of the Newcastle establishment. Almost arrested for preaching on the text, 'He that hath not a sword, let him sell his garments and buy one'.

He was a Congregationalist minister who had arrived

from Scotland via Alnwick, where he'd been sacked for being too radical, but in Newcastle he found enough followers to allow him to build his own Meeting House on High Bridge. He was a reformer who wrote that no man could be a real Christian 'who was not a warm and zealous friend to civil and religious freedom' and he wasn't scared to attack anybody or anything he disapproved of. He preached sermons on the divine right of subjects to criticise their King and he was savagely opposed to heavy taxes, tithes, political corruption and poverty. His great underlying theme was the contrast between what the bible said and the harsh social reality of life in 18th century Newcastle. When the poor rioted against the high price of food he preached sermons in their support, claiming that there would be no need for food riots if the rich used their money to offer relief to the poor.

One of his followers was a man called Thomas Spence, another feisty little firebrand who came from a very strictly religious family. He was brought up on the Quayside with his mum and dad who had come down from Scotland and were members of a now extinct sect called the Glassites (don't ask, their beliefs seemed incomprehensible to me). His father ran a hardware stall on Sandhill and as he worked he made Thomas read constantly to him from the bible. Let this be a lesson to all pushy parents because unsurprisingly Thomas grew up to denounce religion as a delusion. He became a teacher and set up his own school on Broad Chare. He invented a system of teaching based on a phonetic alphabet for which he became quite famous – but he was (and remains) more famous for the extremity of the political beliefs that he developed under the influence of the Rev Murray. They were beliefs that would still set him on the fringes today.

He believed in the abolition of all private property. He believed that everybody should live in self-governing communes where everything was owned in common. Quite generously he accepted that some people might want to hold onto their personal possessions – their books and clothes and so on – but all bigger possessions like land and property – share them.

You can imagine that his ideas rather stirred people up at the time. He was a member of a club, a debating club called The Philosophical Society, which had been founded by James Murray and which seems to have been full of people with pretty radical opinions. On the eve of the American Revolution, for example, they were, along with lots of other people in Newcastle, passionately pro-American and debated the question, 'Is the resistance of the Americans to taxation without representation constitutional or unconstitutional?' A few years later one of his fellow members and friends, the engraver Thomas Bewick, looked back on those times and wrote this about America, a country he described as '… the wisest and greatest Republic the world ever saw … filled with an enlightened population … its government like a rock, founded on the liberties and the rights of man …' He imagined that in the future America 'will cast a compassionate eye on the rest of the world, grovelling under arbitrary power, banish it from the face of the earth, and kill despots with a frown.' Those were quite dangerous opinions at the time so, since those were the views of his fellow members, you can imagine that

Thomas Spence probably felt that he was in relatively safe territory on 11th November 1775 when he gave a speech expounding his beliefs on the common ownership of property.

They chucked him out, not an easy thing to do since the meeting was being held in Thomas's own schoolroom. Thomas Bewick went one stage further and had a fight with him. They liked each other. Bewick liked him. He described him as having a 'cheerful disposition, warm in his attachment to his friends and in his patriotism for his country' but he had gone too far and Bewick refused to support his proposition so Spence produced a pair of cudgels and they set about beating each other up. I'm not sure what cudgels were in a sporting context, I had always assumed that they were just the things used by baddies to biff goodies, but evidently Bewick was *proficient in cudgel playing* whereas Spence was no use at it. He was very small, only about five feet tall and Bewick 'blackened the inside of his thighs and arms' at which Spence began to be 'quite outrageous' and acted very unfairly so Bewick was forced 'to give him a severe beating.'

Such drama; and on our beloved Quayside too! It had no effect on Thomas Spence however. He continued to hold his beliefs for the rest of his life. Among many other pamphlets and poems and broadsides and other writings, he published the text of his Newcastle speech and included a sardonic note on the title page that it had got him banned from the club. He moved to London, got arrested and put in prison on numerous occasions and remained one of the poster figures of the radical movement of the late 18th century.

One of the endearing things about the Newcastle radicals is that while they were concerned to address the big social and moral issues of the day, they weren't above getting stuck into more down-to-earth local controversies. In the 1770s the corporation (believing implicitly in private ownership like many a government we have seen in more recent years) decided to privatise part of the Town Moor which, you may recall, had belonged to the townsfolk since time immemorial. They decided to lease part of it off (probably to their chums) and allow it to be enclosed and used for cultivation. There was uproar. This was obviously meat and drink to Spence with his passionate beliefs in common ownership and he and James Murray joined forces with the members of another set of stirrers in a society called The Constitution Club and devised a strategy to fight the proposal. They had leaflet campaigns, they brought in a top anti-establishment London lawyer called Sergeant Glynn to take the corporation to court and, being fiery hotheads, they engaged in some direct action too – they broke down the fence that the Corporation had put up, pulled down the new gates and they won. The plans were thrown out by the courts and the Moor remained the property of the Freemen and the people of Newcastle. Time for three democratic cheers.

But the big social and moral issues of the day weren't going away and needed tackling. We tend, I think, to see the 19th century as the great period of reform in England but all of the great issues, health and education, political reform, prison reform, working conditions, all of these and lots of others that were going to be of importance in the next century were already under examination, change and protest in the second half of the 18th too.

Some of these reforms happened in Newcastle but in just the same way as they happened in the rest of the country. Prison reform was like that. John Howard was the main man and he was remarkable, instantly and immensely effective, but nice with it. He was a vegetarian and ate nothing but fruit and veg, milk and tea. He died in Russia on his way to do a report for the Czar on the state of Russian prisons and was buried there. His grave has the inscription, 'Whoever thou art, thou standest at the grave of thy friend'. He was the Sheriff of Bedfordshire when he became obsessed with the dreadful state of prisons. His initial reports to Parliament in 1773 galvanised MPs and tremendous improvements were

made almost immediately. His continued research, which was published as *The State of Prisons* was inspired by visits to gaols all over the country and the rest of Europe, including Newcastle where there were two prisons: the County Gaol in the Castle basement and the Town Gaol in Newgate. Howard came here in 1787 and was disgusted by the filthy conditions in the castle where prisoners awaiting trial were chained to the wall and exhibited to visitors by the gaoler at '2d a piece'. He was much more encouraged at Newgate where he commented on the cleanliness, the adequate bedding, the good fires and the humanity of the gaoler.

In a similar vein, lunatic asylums, which had been places of disgusting horror, began to see a new approach in the later years of the century. Newcastle's asylum had been built in 1767 and was a forbidding, overcrowded place with no ventilation, no light, no segregation of the sexes and no cleanliness. Eneas Mackenzie looking back on it a few years later said that the cells were 'less comfortable than cow houses.'

Improvements to public institutions like these all started in the 18th century. Health improvements were a similar area of concern that I'm going to come back to shortly, but the big issue, the biggest of all issues in the late 18th century, and one in which Newcastle played a very active role, was the abolition of the slave trade.

Because it faces east and not west, Newcastle isn't normally seen as being involved in the slave trade but to be honest, the whole country was made rich by the trade and Newcastle was no different. Lots of local firms and families benefitted …

Crowleys, the great iron masters from the Derwent Valley, were an extraordinary, socially responsible and forward thinking company, but they exported a bewildering array of iron goods, including restraints for captured Africans and there were lots of families who owned plantations or sold goods or imported sugar, or ran sugar refineries. The richest were the Graham Clarke family who were major shareholders in North East banking. They had five ships engaged in the African trade, owned three plantations in the West Indies and several sugar factories in Newcastle and Gateshead. They made a huge fortune out of it and lots of other well-known North Eastern families were in the same trade.

But interestingly, at the same time as this was happening, Newcastle was also in the forefront of the movement to bring about the abolition of slavery. It hadn't started in Newcastle, Thomas Clarkson had started the campaign in London but Newcastle was the first provincial town to respond to it. In 1787 Thomas Clarkson's London Committee wrote to all of the mayors in England, urging them to petition Parliament to bring about an end to the Slave Trade. Newcastle was the first corporation to do so. It passed a resolution from 'the Mayor, Aldermen, Sheriff and the rest of the common council, to the Honourable, the House of Commons, praying the said house to taken into serious consideration the hardships which many of the natives of Africa suffer by means of the trade carried and the purchase of slaves.' John Erasmus Blackett, who served as mayor of Newcastle on four occasions, personally took the petition to London and handed it to Parliament.

Almost immediately the campaign became widespread in Newcastle. There was a second, extraordinary nonconformist minister in the town. The Reverend William Turner, minister of the Unitarian church on Hanover Square, wasn't as politically radical as James Murray but he was a pretty impressive individual. He became the minister when he was twenty-one and stayed in post for another fifty-nine years and there wasn't much going on in Newcastle that he didn't have a hand in. He was the main mover in the foundation of The Lit and Phil in 1791 and of the Natural History Society a bit later. He founded The Bible Society and, in 1791 he started the Newcastle Anti-Slavery Society, the first such organisation outside London. Its members decided that the best way forward was to print a pamphlet calling on people to sign a petition in support of Abolition. Thomas Bewick engraved a wonderfully powerful medallion of a kneeling and manacled slave pleading for mercy (inset). It was printed on the pamphlet and subsequently used as the symbol of the movement throughout the country. 2,000 copies were printed and over 3,000 people voted; only Manchester and Edinburgh had larger numbers. 3,000 was roughly the number of Newcastle people eligible to vote in general elections, which suggests that virtually the whole voting population of the town was prepared to declare itself anti-slavery. It suggests that there were a lot of Geordies with radical and humanitarian leanings. I find that so comforting.

In *Hidden Chains* by John Charlton there's a story about a letter written to the *Newcastle Courant* in 1792. It was signed by a man who called himself Humanus. He writes that he had been away from home and came back to find that the women in his family had been reading an article urging the people of Great Britain to give up using West Indian sugar and rum, not because it was too expensive but because it was created by slaves. 'I was surprised,' he wrote, 'to find that they had entirely left off the use of sugar and banished it from the tea table.'

So there you are – ethical consumerism in 18th century Newcastle. I raise my (Beilby) glass to the splendidly radical ladies in Humanus's family.

Town Improvements (in the 18th century)

Eighteenth century Newcastle was ruled by pretty much the same Corporation as had been in charge for hundreds of years. The names had changed – but not very much and not very often. To take just one example, the list of Newcastle's mayors for the 100 years from 1700 to 1800 contains just seven different surnames. If I'm being fair (which isn't like me at all; too often it spoils a good story) there are a few gaps in the record on the internet so the range might be a bit greater – but not much. There were Andersons and Carrs, Claverings and Ridleys, names that had appeared in the 17th century list as well. Various Claytons held the post on eight occasions, while another, Nathaniel Clayton, bought the job of Town Clerk for £2,100 (about £2,000,000 in modern prices) and kept it for thirty-two years before passing it on to his son. Members of the Blackett family, who were mayors on innumerable occasions, included Sir Walter Blackett who was mayor five times (and an MP in seven different parliaments as well). There are a number of examples of fathers being followed by their sons in the role. They were all posh and most of them were Hostmen or at least members of the most important guilds in the town. All of them (as far as I can tell) had their principal homes in the countryside beyond the town and all but one of them also held the position of MP. I have never seen a list of the full members of the corporation but I would be really surprised if there had been much difference. I suspect that Newcastle's rulers were drawn from the same narrow elite that had run the town for ever. Often they didn't even get elected, they were just co-opted onto the council by their chums and once they were there they tended to stay for life.

As a corporation they didn't have much money either – no English corporation did. They got their income from market stall rents and tolls and any property the town owned. That never amounted to much; because of all the tolls from the river Newcastle was one of the richest corporations in the country but even they only had an income of about £25,000 a year, which wasn't enough to do all of the things that a town really needed to do.

None of the above is to say that they were inevitably a bad bunch but it does make you wonder how they got on. How much impact did they have on the town they ruled?

There were things they didn't handle well – we've seen some of them in the previous chapter. They didn't handle the poor well – providing meagre support in times of need and leaving the bigger moves to be made by private charity. They could be oppressive and (as we saw with regard to the Town Moor) show scant respect for the traditions of the town. They were slow to act. After the Guildhall was ransacked by food rioters in the 1750s it took them nearly forty years to put the damage right.

There were bigger problems too – well there was at least one bigger problem and that was their failure to do anything about the state of the river. Newcastle depended

Governors of the Hostmen's Company,

Chosen annually January 4th.

1600. Mr. William Jenison
1601. Mr. George Selbie
1602. Mr. Francis Anderson
1603. Mr. Robert Dudley
1604. Mr. Thomas Riddell
1605. Mr. William Jenison
1606. The fame
1607. Mr. George Selbie
1608. Mr. James Clavering
1609. Mr. Henry Chapman
1610. Mr. Thomas Liddell
1611. Mr. Francis Anderson
1612. Mr. George Selbie
1613. Mr. Francis Anderson
1614. Mr. Thomas Riddell
1615. The fame
1616. Mr. George Selbie
1617. Mr. James Clavering
No entry in the old book of any governor till
1627. Mr. Peter Riddell
None afterwards till
1636. Mr. Thomas Liddell
1637. The fame
1638. Mr. John Marley
1639. Sir Lyonel Maddifon
1640. Mr. Robert Anderson
1641. Mr. Nicholas Cole
1642. Mr. Leonard Carr
1643. The fame
1644. Sir John Marley, mayor
1645. Sir Lyonel Maddifon
1646. Mr. Ralph Grey
1647. The fame
1648. The fame
1649, 1650, 1651, 1652. The fame
1653. Mr. Leonard Carr
1654. The fame
1655. Mr. Robert Shafto
1656, 1657, 1658, 1659. The fame
1660. Mr. John Emmerfon
1661. The fame

1662. Mr. William Blackett
1663. The fame
1664. Sir James Clavering, bart.
1665. Sir Francis Liddell, efq.
1666. Mr. Henry Maddifon
1667, 1668. William Blackett, efq.
1669. Ra. Jenifon, efq.
1670, 1671, 1672, 1673, 1674. The fame
1675. Thomas Jennifon, efq.
1676. Sir Francis Anderfon, knt.
1677. Sir Ralph Carr, knt.
1678, 1679, 1680, 1681, 1682, 1683. The fame
1684. Sir William Blackett
1685. William Aubone, efq. mayor
1686. Sir Henry Brabant, knt.
1687. Nicholas Cole, efq. mayor
1688. Sir William Creah, knt.
1689. Mr. Thomas Bewick
1690. William Carr, efq. mayor
1691. Sir William Blackett
1692. The fame
1693. Mr. George Harrifon
1694. Nicholas Fenwick, efq.
1695. William Aubone, efq.
1696, 1697, 1698, 1699, 1700. The fame
1701. Matthew White, efq.
1702, 1703, 1704. The fame
1705. Sir Ralph Carr, knt.
1706, 1707. The fame
1708. Mr. Henry Liddell
1709. Robert Fenwick, efq. mayor
1710, 1711. The fame
1712. Matthew White, efq.
1713, &c. The fame
1716. Richard Ridley, efq.
1725. Sir William Blackett
1728. Geo. Liddell, efq.
1740. John Ord, efq.
1745. John Simpfon, efq.

4

APPEN.

on the Tyne. It owned the rights to all of it as far as the mouth and upstream as far as Wylam. It had defended those rights savagely for hundreds of years but increasingly it wasn't an easy river to manage. Downstream there were twelve shallow, twisty, tidal miles of it; shifting shoals of sand obstructed the channel and there were dangerous reefs in a number of places. The shallowness was made worse by what we would call 'fly-tipping' nowadays – the illegal dumping of ballast by ships trying to avoid the charges they should have paid. Even the legal ballast was just dumped on the river banks from where it could easily be washed back into the river whenever it rained (Joyce Ellis, in *The Black Indies*, says that 100,000 tons of ballast were washed off the banks at St Anthony's in Walker on a single night). The bar at the mouth of the river between North and South Shields was so pronounced that at low tides it is said that market traders could walk across the river with their goods on their heads and if the winds and the tides were wrong, ships could be trapped in the river for days or even weeks at a time. By the 18th century the main pits were upstream, beyond the town and the sea-going colliers were getting bigger and bigger – all factors that massively increased the difficulty of exporting the ever increasing volumes of coal.

One independent organisation had taken some responsibility for all of this. Trinity House maintained buoys to mark the channel. In 1727 they built new leading lights at North Shields to mark a safe entry into the river, they provided pilots and charged boat owners according to their tonnage in order to pay for the ongoing work that needed to be done (and to provide exquisite extensions to the Guild's own headquarters on Broad Chare, it should be said) but the corporation did nothing and were much criticised for it. Captain Phipps, a nautical chap and Parliamentary candidate in 1774 wrote that the Tyne could be a great river but that '*avarice, inattention and ignorance*' had made it '*a cursed horse pond.*'

The situation was dangerous for Newcastle. The town was still a major industrial centre with lines of glass works and lead works, iron, steel, shipbuilding and dozens of other industries stretched along the river frontage within the town boundaries but by the second half of the 18th century most of the coal in the North East and most of the other valuable industries were situated outside the town. They might be managed by Newcastle industrialists and merchants and they might be organised from company HQs in Newcastle but the work was increasingly being done in other places up and down the river and those places were very keen to get a bit of the action or at least a reduction to the charges demanded by Newcastle. Landowners in the Tyne Valley went so far as to build a whole road from Hexham to Alnmouth to avoid the charges, and mine owners south of the river offered the Government £8,000 a year to help them fight against the '*ill-bred, ill- minded and insolent inferiors*' of Newcastle; but the only thing the corporation did was cling on to their rights and privileges, squash the opposition and collect all the taxes they could … and there were quite a lot of them to collect. Middlebrook tells a tale about one ten-year period when their income from the river was £217,833. Of that they spent a measly £1265 on improving the river and gave £30,526 to their pals on the council for the '*conveyance of ballast*'. My very inadequate maths suggests that about one per cent of the river income was spent on the river and about twelve percent was spent on themselves.

At best it sounds lazy and misguided; at worst it sounds … a lot worse. People certainly thought the worst at the time and there was much tutting over newspapers and moaning in the pubs. The Reverend Murray expressed the widespread disapproval when he wrote '*To their everlasting shame the gentlemen of Newcastle, continued to waste their time and spend their substance in celebrating the rites of Venus and the ceremonies of Bacchus*'.

Top: *The bridge over the Tyne 1771 damaged by the flood.*
Above: *A new bridge was opened in 1781.*

And on another occasions the Freemen of Newcastle wrote to the king complaining that the mayor and aldermen were '*entirely self-elected and irresponsible*' and that they were guilty of '*gross partiality to each other.*'

So … were they just inefficient, or were they inefficient and corrupt? Or was there more to it than that? I love the old radical Rev Murray and I do love a good corruption story but it seems to me that the 18th century wasn't all that different from today. Just like us, Georgian Geordies were inclined to think the worst of their politicians and assume that nothing was being done at all and that corruption was rife, and also just like today, it probably wasn't quite as black and white as that. It never is and, in fact some things *were* getting done. If the tolls weren't being spent on the river some of them were at least being spent on the town, which changed dramatically in the second half of the 1700s, often for the better; at least some of those changes were brought about by the Corporation.

What did they do?

First of all they built a new bridge – they had to of course since the medieval one had been washed away in the '*dreadful inundation*' of November 1771 along with seven of the shops that lined it and, sadly, the bodies of six people who lived on it. The loss of the bridge was an enormous blow and a terrible tragedy for those who suffered the worst losses. It was also a major inconvenience. The Reverend James Murray (my radical chum) gave a flavour of the difficulties that people experienced when he described the ferry that temporarily replaced the broken bridge. In particular he wasn't impressed with the little jobsworth who was in charge and who would do nothing to make life easier for his passengers '*You wait the pleasure of the little arbitrary bashaw who will not move one foot beyond the rules of his own authority or mitigate the sentences passed upon those who are condemned to travel in a stage-coach within a ferry boat.*' (I think I've met him; or possibly it was one of his descendants.)

For ten years the ferry was the only way across to Gateshead (or London) until Robert Mylne's new bridge was opened in 1781 and in fact the corporation took a lot of stick that the rebuilding took so long. But it opened eventually so that's one significant task that the corporation achieved with their limited revenue.

Another was the gradual demolition of those parts of the town wall that were causing difficulties - particularly the gateways, which were often so low and narrow that wagons got stuck in them. At the Pilgrim Street gate goods had to be unloaded, carried through the arch and then reloaded on the other side. The same was true of the Close Gate and Sandgate down by the river. All of these gates had been removed by the beginning of the next century but the first part of the walls to go was the stretch along the Quayside, which was knocked down in 1763. You are allowed to feel sorry about this and dream wistfully of those places like Carcassonne, romantically surrounded by the complete ring of their medieval walls, but the reality is that the wall along the river had become a major barrier to trade. The Quay itself was long but very narrow and overcrowded and the lane behind the wall … well, a long time ago (in chapter four) I mentioned the lane between Stowell Street and the town wall and commented on its medieval atmosphere (i.e. smelly and dirty). That's what the Quayside was like. So the removal of the wall was brilliant for trade and gave us what has become one of the most exciting parts of the town ever since.

In the rest of the town the corporation funded quite a lot of improvements – they got permission to make changes in a private Act of Parliament in 1763 so they were able to install the first street lights. This was relatively early by English town standards and they were quite basic. At first they were oil lamps and all inside the walled town. The service was extended to the suburbs only in 1812. Gas appeared in 1818. In 1827, Eneas Mackenzie records (with admirable precision) that the walled town was lit by 269 gas lamps and the suburbs by 280 oil and 122 gas lamps. There were some steps to introduce street cleaning as well. For a measly £1,620 a year a force of twenty 'scavengers' with ten carts collected the oojah and took it away. Sadly they didn't take it away very often and they didn't take it very far. The poshest streets were cleared daily, the less posh once or twice a week and the slums not at all. The loathsome droppings were taken to a series of vast middens at various points around the town where they were left to stew for months and only cleared once or twice a year.

In 1763 the corporation also got the permission of Parliament to raise money to pay for 'The Watch', a sort of rudimentary police force that employed twenty-six watchmen under the control of a constable, or Captain of the Watch, and his two assistants. They only worked in the winter months when the town was at its darkest and patrolled the streets calling out the time every half an hour from ten at night until six o'clock in the morning. They were rather oddly supplied. They each had a greatcoat (very necessary in Newcastle in the winter) a lantern (useful), a rattle (hm!) and a stick with an iron hook on the end (No, I have no idea either). They were paid half a guinea a week with an additional guinea at the end of the season. My correspondent (E. Mackenzie again) says that the whole business was 'wretchedly conducted', possibly because the watchmen also got a shilling every time they made an arrest. Call me a fool but that seems to be an open invitation to boost the arrest rate.

Yet another improvement occurred in 1783 when street names were put up. What a difference that must have made. There are places (Japan springs to mind) where there are still no street names so strangers (let's call them my son and daughter-in-law) can find themselves surrounded by crowds of helpful policemen, local butchers and elderly ladies all trying to get them to their restaurant of choice. It was no longer like that in Newcastle after 1783.

None of these efforts were enough of course and it was going to be the job of councils in the next century to take up the town improvement struggle – but they were a start and they were accompanied by the sort of support they gave to the education of the poor that I was writing about before and finally there was a whole new movement towards public health in which the corporation combined with private and charitable forces to make important changes.

In April 1751, Newcastle got its first proper hospital. A group of medical men, including a young surgeon called Richard Lambert, opened a subscription for the building of a General Infirmary. By May they were already fitting out a temporary hospital in a house on Gallowgate. The corporation was involved to the extent that it gave the group a site for the new hospital on Forth Banks and in September of the same year it was already under construction. It had ninety beds and was completed in time for opening on 8 October 1752 – start to finish in

less than eighteen months! That is substantially less time than it takes me to choose a new rug for the front room.

Hospitals, in the sense of almshouses had existed for centuries and there were a few ancient institutions like St Barts in London that had been rebuilt by rich philanthropists but the movement that led to the Newcastle Hospital was a mid-18th century nationwide phenomenon – a product of the Age of Reason. The first ones had been built in the 1740s, almost always, like at Newcastle, by public subscription under the inspiration of a small committee. Newcastle's infirmary of 1751 is among the earliest examples in the country and it was just the start of the health provision that was still to come.

In 1760 a Lying-in Hospital for poor married women was opened. Patients were looked after by a physician, two surgeons, a man-midwife (I suspect that means a midwife who was male rather than a midwife for males) and a matron. The following year a charity was set up that allowed poor women to have their babies at home

Left: *the Newcastle Infirmary, 1789*. Above: *Lying-in Hospital, 1820*.

with the support of a midwife and a doctor if one was needed. By 1777 there was a dispensary as well. These were remarkable developments. The rich had always had some sort of health care – they could rely on their servants or they could pay for professional advice, but it was an extraordinary change when the poor began to be included - and it had at least some effect. Deaths in childbirth decreased and life expectancy among the poor increased and as a result, after 1750 the population of Newcastle began to increase quite quickly.

So there you are – a whole heap of improvements carried out at least partly by the corporation, but the biggy, the really big and most significant alteration that the 18th century corporation was involved in was the plan to create a new route from the bridge to the upper town.

In an earlier chapter I mentioned that my little rounded form has long been aware of how steep the route used to be from the river bank to the rest of the town. Until Dean Street was created the ways up from the Quayside were formidably steep and a confusing maze of narrow dark alleys. One of them teetered up past All Saints church and the other followed the difficult route up The Side towards the castle and St Nicholas's. Between them was the Lort Burn, which had presumably once been a nice Jesmond Dene-ish sort of stream but by the 1780s was described as *'a vast nauseous hollow … a place of filth and dirt'*. The idea of filling it in to create a new route had been on the agenda for decades but inertia and the need to build new bridges had got in the way so it wasn't until the 1780s that anything was done about it. Even then the corporation didn't actual get going themselves; it was a couple of members of the committee who got the ball rolling. Nathaniel Clayton, the Town Clerk and Alderman Mosley were the prime movers and Mr Mosley even put his money where his mouth was and advanced the cost of the whole scheme. The plan was drawn up by David Stephenson. The work was started in 1784 and completed five years later.

The main thing they did was fill in the valley, with the Lort Burn flowing through a culvert underneath. They built Dean Street on top of it and then they laid out a new road (Mosley Street) which went west along as far as St Nicholas's where they created a new square in front of the church, and east to join up with Pilgrim Street. It wasn't a vast scheme, just two streets and a little square. Nowadays most of its buildings have been replaced by Victorian and Edwardian ones and there are only a few of David Stephenson's quiet brick houses still to be seen on Mosley Street and down the east side of Dean Street. It seems like quite a modest precursor to the vast changes that were to revolutionise the town in the 1830s but it was clever; it was an intelligent way of dealing with the town's difficult topography and it created a new area that rapidly became fashionable with its fine broad streets, neatly paved and lit. As it opened, the new Theatre Royal was being built in Drury Lane just off Mosley Street; the Post Office moved there almost straight away and within no time at all the town's two principal banks had shifted there as well.

So, did it matter that the corporation did virtually nothing about the river and focussed almost all of their attention on making the town a bit nicer? Were they being selfish … or were they being clever?

The answer is probably both but, you know, I find myself sneakily applauding their choices despite the fact that they were an unreconstructed, possibly corrupt, mainly reactionary bunch of old rich chaps whereas I am … well, I'm only some of those things. I can't help feeling that if Newcastle was going to hold back the ambitions of its neighbours and stay top dog in the area (and that's what it was always aiming to do) it was probably more important to make the town attractive, to make sure that the shopping was good and you could have a decent night out at the Assembly Rooms than to faff around with the river.

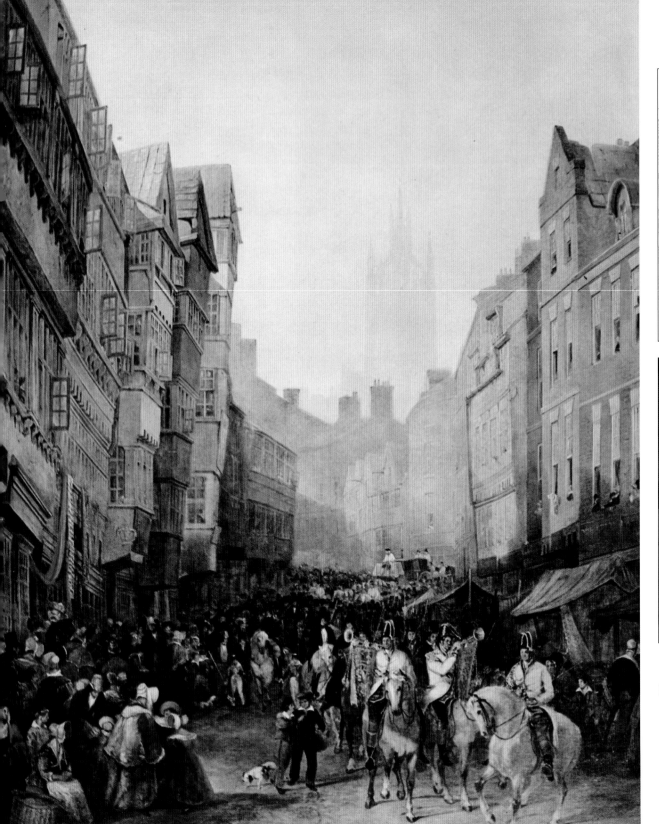

Side (T
Left: *Procession of the High Sh*
of Northumberland going to r
the Judges, 1835 (Mansion H
Collection). Top: *A small br*
across the Lort Burn . Abov
painting of Side and the
Burn in the Mayor's Chamb
the Guild

The Nineteenth Century

Well, who would have thought it! Here we are already on the cusp of the 19th century. Where have all the years gone to? I bet you all have very firm ideas about Newcastle in the 19th century. Some of you will be agog with girlish (and boyish) enthusiasm, eager to finally explore our great city's finest hour, its triumphant industrial success. You may even have heard that story about the moment in the 1870s when the Swing Bridge opened for the first time to allow a ship through on its way to pick up a gun that was being exported to Bari in Italy – an incident when the largest moving bridge in the world opened to let the largest ship in the world get to the largest factory in the world where the world's largest sheer legs loaded the largest gun that had ever been made. Inevitably, when it arrived in Italy, the gun had to be unloaded using the largest hydraulic crane in the world – and not only did all of these things come from here but they were all the work of one man, of Lord Armstrong, the great Newcastle inventor, industrialist and entrepreneur. Others, of course, gloomier and more pessimistic souls, will be muttering darkly, 'Ah but what about the workers? Tell us about the century's suffering, the overcrowding and poverty, the dreadful health and appalling housing.' Some will be keeping a watchful eye on the narrator lest he should forget to explore the extraordinary changes that the century wrought in the physical appearance and shape of the city, its wonderful classical renaissance in the 1830s, its Late Victorian splendours and the vast expansion beyond the walls that had constricted it for so many centuries. Yet others will have their mind on the city at play, at the growth of leisure time, of parks and sport, art galleries and …erm … what are they called? Oh yes, the pubs.

I am hoping to be able to cover all of those things, the highs and the lows of this remarkable century but I do have to warn you that whatever glories emerge later in the story, it didn't start well.

By the time Napoleon was defeated at the Battle of Waterloo in 1815, Britain had been at war with France for twenty-two years. That's an awfully long time and you might have hoped that when it was finally all over everybody would have been pleased, things would have settled down and life would get better again.

But we know better than that, don't we boys and girls. We know about the Cold War that followed WWII. We've watched the misery left behind after all the other nasty little wars that have happened in recent years, we know that wars don't end tidily and the five or six years after Waterloo were no different. It was a horrible time all over Britain and it was a horrible time in Newcastle.

There was a dreadful post-war slump. Industry was in the doldrums because there was no war to provide for any more; there was massive unemployment because of all the discharged soldiers and sailors. A series of terrible harvests meant there was an agricultural recession as well, and the situation of the poor was made worse because the price of bread was being kept awfully and artificially high by the Corn Law which prevented the importing of foreign wheat. Taxation was high; inflation was high and almost inevitably there was a real tension in the air. Protest movements sprung up all over the place. In some places factory workers revolted against the new machinery that they thought was threatening their jobs. In Newcastle the keelmen attacked the new coal 'spouts', which had been invented to speed up the loading of colliers (and rightly so, from their point of view since the spouts were a new technology that were going to put them out of work and bring their way of life to an end). Unemployed Newcastle sailors blockaded the Tyne and there was growing protest demanding the repeal of the Corn Law. In November 1816 the *Newcastle Chronicle* waded into the debate, claiming that in some parts of the region half the families were living on less than two shillings a head, a week (at a time when a small loaf cost a shilling). The middle-class radicals and the working class set up three Anti-Corn Law petitions. Each of them was said to have been sixty yards long and to have contained about 25,000 signatures. Lots of reform societies were set up. The Newcastle one had the catchy little title of the 'Political Protestants of Newcastle and Neighbourhood' and there were others in places like Benwell and Fawdon. Almost inevitably the keelmen rioted …

All of this terrified the ruling classes in case there was a full-scale armed revolt like there had been in America and in France. They seemed too thick to realise that it was all to do with food and instead of trying to find ways to feed people, the only solution they could come up with was repression. It was a deeply repressive Government led by Lord Liverpool and the toughest of its members was the Lord Chancellor, the old Geordie eloper, Lord ~~Square~~ Eldon. He encouraged local magistrates to enrol special constables and set up local yeomanry. Civil liberties were restricted. Habeas Corpus was suspended in 1817 but the situation certainly didn't get any better, in fact it came to a head in August 1819, not in Newcastle or the North East, but in Manchester, where a peaceful crowd of about 80,000 gathered on St Peter's Fields for a protest meeting. The cavalry were sent in to arrest the ringleaders and in the chaos fifteen were killed and hundreds injured. In a bitterly ironic reference to the brilliant British triumph at the Battle of Waterloo, it became known as the Peterloo Massacre.

The country was shocked and horrified but the only response that the Government could make was to pass even more restrictive laws. In the weeks after the massacre they passed the Six Acts whose big aim was to restrict individual liberties and the right to hold public meetings. Really, really draconian punishments were introduced for breaking these laws (fourteen years' transportation, for example, for writing nasty things about the Government) but in fact their only impact was to stir people up even more and on 11 October the Newcastle protesters organised a massive protest meeting on the Town Moor.

They met in the town at the Haymarket (it was called the Parade Ground in those days) and then marched up to the Moor. There were about 100,000 of them - I think I might write that again, actually, because it was such an extraordinary number – there were about *100,000* of them - all of the societies, of course, each bearing lots of placards and led by a banner, lots of them with bands. The speakers' stage was on a wagon pulled by three horses festooned with red ribbons. There was a huge banner which read 'Truth! Order! Justice.'

The man who presided over this vast event was one of my Newcastle heroes, a man who has already appeared several times in this book. Eneas Mackenzie had started off as a teacher (so many of the best people do) before becoming one of the finest of all local historians, but he was a radical all the time and on this occasion he and the other speakers demanded all sorts of reforms including, most boldly, universal suffrage, the vote for everybody (all chaps, I think they meant; let's not get carried away here).

The magistrates were in a frenzy. They had heard rumours that the iron workers at Crowley's iron works in Winlaton had been secretly making pikes and other weapons and they were convinced there were going to be outrages so they had sworn-in a large body of special constables, they had formed a Volunteer Cavalry from 'loyal inhabitants' who were prepared to fight in support of the Corporation. The Mayor himself had raised and commanded a troop of Dismounted Yeomanry.

It amazes and depresses me that there were so many people living in the town who were prepared to fight against the reformers. I had always assumed that the local Yeomanries had been set up as a defence against a possible French invasion and it saddens me that that in fact lots of them started life as volunteer right-wing militias supporting the authorities against the protesters. Maybe it's just the wisdom of hindsight but it seems obvious that so much needed doing, so much change needed to happen; there was so much suffering and unhappiness and yet all of those people thought that the best way to deal with it was to join a militia and prepare to attack their neighbours.

Well, in the event they weren't needed. No outrages occurred on either side and over the next few years the situation began to get better. There was a new, more moderate government. Lord Square had his protest-biffing tendencies curbed by gentler colleagues. The Corn Laws weren't repealed but they were toned down a bit and there was a general move towards some less aggressive policies and then …

And then … in 1830 the Tories were thrown out and a new Whig Government under Earl Grey came into power.

I have been worrying about this moment. The Earl Grey is an interesting man and a very important local hero – but he wasn't from Newcastle. His family home was at Howick up the Northumberland Coast and as far as I know he never lived in Newcastle. Can I talk about him? Can I artificially confer Geordie status on outsiders merely because I want to include their story in my history of Newcastle? It's a problem. I've been very firm about such matters so far in this book. I've risked the wrath of Gateshead for not being Newcastle and ignored important things happening at all sorts of places outside the town. It's a worry, but I have resolved that I am going to include Mr Grey (and by extension other local heroes like George Stephenson) because they stand in the city every day (even if they only do it on statues).

So in 1830 the Whigs came into power and suddenly the only topic of conversation in the pubs was parliamentary reform and the question of who should get to vote. As it stood, in Newcastle about 3,000 people out of a total population of about 50,000 were eligible to vote. I believe that's six percent or, to put it another way, not very many at all. As we've heard, the radicals who had been stamping their feet on the Town Moor, and the working class who had never had a look-in wanted everybody to have the vote but the new Government, even though they were a bit more cuddly than the Tories

didn't want to go further than the middle class so that led to another round of marches and speeches. Some of Newcastle's radicals marched off to Durham to support the reformers there who were rumoured to be threatened by Lord Londonderry and his 'lambs' (the Durham Yeomanry).

It was all very tense. The radicals did this, the king refused to do that, the Duke of Wellington and his right-wing chums threatened to do the other. Lord Square snorted. Three different versions of the Reform Bill passed through the House of Commons and were either thrown out or savagely mutilated by the Lords. In Newcastle and the North East there were threats of violence against all of the Bishops and the members of the local aristocracy who had voted against the Bill. Earl Grey resigned. Everything looked doomed to end in failure …

… and then it didn't. It all came together. The Great Reform Bill of 1832 was passed and yea, there was much rejoicing in those bits of the land that wanted it.

Strictly speaking, in terms of the number of new voters, it didn't achieve very much; in Newcastle the numbers went up from 3,000 to 5,000, which isn't a vast changes (and still none of them were women) (or working class), but in fact the bill was the beginning of a brand new world because the newly reformed parliament was a much perkier institution than the one it had replaced and it began to fire out new laws like a boy with a peashooter and one of the first new laws was the Municipal Corporations Act, which arrived in 1835.

The corporations that ruled English towns hadn't changed in centuries. If you were listening at the time you will recall that I went on about this at some length in the previous chapter and it was the Municipal Corporations Act which finally brought about the change that everybody (except maybe those on the old council) felt was necessary. From then on there were proper local elections. Councillors had to stand for re-election every three years, a new mayor had to be chosen by the council every year and aldermen could only retain their title for six years. The council had a new regular source of income from the rates as well as all its former dues and with the new money came new responsibilities – it had to pay for street lighting and the police out of the rates – and pretty soon the newly reformed parliament started firing new possibilities at councils all the time – to do with health and education cleanliness and town planning. What a difference it was going to make … eventually.

The other thing that the 1835 Act did was extend the size of the town – all the villages just beyond the old boundaries suddenly became part of Newcastle. The people of Westgate, Elswick, Fenham, Jesmond, Heaton and Byker no longer went into town of a Saturday, suddenly they *were* the town.

It was quite a different world after The Municipal Corporations Act was passed and we'll come back to how Newcastle handled it a little bit later, but meanwhile …

… back to the beginning of the century to explore what other changes had been happening in the toon.

A new style of architecture began to emerge in the North East in the early years of the century. It was still a classical style such as had been introduced by David Stephenson and William Newton at the end of the 1700s but a new, rather grander and more monumental version of it. It was the Greek Revival style and as far as the North East was concerned it first peeped its rather impressive little head above the parapet at Belsay Hall, a few miles outside the town. Sir Charles Monck, who owned and designed Belsay, went on his honeymoon, not for two nights in Bamburgh like Sir John Grundy, but for eighteen months. He set off, heading down to the Med like all the other Grand Tourists but he didn't go through France because we were at war with them, instead he went via Berlin and Dresden to study new German architecture which was dominated by the Greek Doric style (think of the Brandenburg Gate) and then, once he got to Italy, he went a bit further than most. He went on to Athens, which was still part of the Ottoman Empire and still a rare and dangerous place to visit and there he spent his time doing what all newly married honeymooners do – he made detailed drawings of the ruins of ancient Greece that he turned into a design for his new home when he got back.

It was a hugely influential design. North Easterners took to the new style with great enthusiasm and within a decade a whole heap of newly wealthy mine owners and industrialists had hired John Dobson, the head honcho of north east country house architecture at the time, to build them mansions in the Greek style. They are all over the place but it was Newcastle that provided the first example of the new Belsay style. The Moot Hall, the new County Court and prison, was designed by an elusive local architect called William Stokoe. It was begun on the site of the old Moot Hall in the grounds of the Castle in 1810, opened in 1812 and it was the first use of a full-blown Greek Doric style for a public building in the whole country. Within a few years they were going to be everywhere. The British Museum, the Ashmolean in Cambridge, Birmingham Town Hall, St George's Hall in Liverpool to name but a few – scores of the most impressive early 19th century public buildings in the country were to be built in the Greek Revival style – but Newcastle's Moot Hall was the first and weren't the local chuffed. Eneas Mackenzie wrote this about it *'This building is certainly one of the grandest public structures that have been erected in the North of England and is amongst the finest and purest specimens of ancient architecture ever attempted in this kingdom … the classic sublimity of the design accords with the dignity and importance of a hall of Justice … In short it is one of the proudest ornaments of this metropolis of the north.'*

He loves the fact that it is visible from all over the town but especially that it is seen to best advantage from the Tyne Bridge where it can't avoid impressing visitors from the south as they arrive in the town.

Bizarrely, and rather touchingly though, the prime mover of the new building wasn't a desire for grandeur but a sense of shame – a shame that arose directly out of the humanitarian passions of the 18th century radicals. In 1808 the gentlemen of the grand jury seem to have been so stung by the savage criticism that the old County Gaol in the castle had received from John Howard and others in the 1780s that they were determined to build something which would reflect better upon their *'liberality and humanity.'* They were determined to remove *'the reproach … which arose from the dismal and horrid prison in the castle'* and they were tickled pink with what they got. The cells were *'dry, well-lighted and ventilated and furnished with fireplaces'.* It sounds positively cosy but the prisoners might not have felt quite so pleased with their new home because *'the cells are arched over by massive stones, nicely jointed and as they support the superincumbent buildings, prisoners are as safe within these walls as if they were confined in the centre of the earth.'*

I've gone on a bit about the Moot Hall because it was a game changer. Suddenly the town seems to have been keen to see itself as a metropolis, to be stressing its credentials as a regional capital and even to be thinking of itself in the same breath as London. I

warned you way back at the beginning of this story that Geordies were going to turn out to be wildly sure of themselves – this was one of those moments when the self-confidence started to show.

And it continued.

The second Greek building was a new headquarters for the Newcastle Literary and Philosophical Society, which had been founded by the Reverend William Turner in 1793. In its early years it had drifted around a number of places in the town but was already a pretty formidable organisation. Religion and the politics of the day were forbidden topics but it was open season on anything else. They were responsible for setting up the Newcastle Anti-Slavery Society and in 1799 a lady called Miss Deer was among the first women to be admitted to a learned society anywhere in the country. They were sent a

(Frank Manders)

The south elevation of the Moot Hall, 1984.

wombat and a duck-billed platypus from New South Wales. They picked up a major museum-load of stuffed birds from the Wycliffe Museum in Teesdale and drawfulls of beautifully preserved insects from Nova Scotia. There were birds from Russia and 1500 geological specimens. They didn't know where to put them all. In 1821 they were all but overwhelmed by the public's interest in a mummy they had acquired ~~and you should have seen what happened shortly after when the daddy arri~~… In 1815 George Stephenson demonstrated the miner's safety lamp he had designed in response to the dreadful disaster at the Felling colliery in 1812. All of that and so much more happened before they even moved into their new, splendid, hugely fashionable, Greek Doric premises in July 1822. There was a dinner of epic proportions to celebrate the event; it defeated the reporter from the local papers – he gave up (or passed out) after fifty-three speeches and thirty-five toasts.

The building was designed by the father and son partnership of John and Benjamin Green who are a bit like Ant and Dec to me. I can never remember which was which but it doesn't seem to matter. They were a team and very, very good. Among other things, they seem to have pioneered the use of laminated timber in Britain (the roof of Cambo church near Wallington is probably the oldest surviving example in the country) and they will get a number of other rave reviews in the next few pages but the Lit and Phil is a perfect introduction to their ability – restrained, elegant, learned and dignified – words which might not leap instinctively to the lips of southerners when they're talking about Newcastle but which can be applied to lots of other buildings that were soon sprouting up all over the town.

Actually, that's not strictly true, the next set of Grecian buildings were all concentrated in the northern part of the town, they were all houses and they were all built by the same man.

He was called Richard Grainger and he was born in 1797, the son of a Quayside porter. His father died when he was quite young but his mother, Amelia, showed remarkable strength to keep her five children housed, fed and educated. They lived in a poor tenement just off Blackett St and she made gloves and took in sewing and laundry. Richard went to the Charity School at St Andrew's church but left when he was twelve to become an apprentice builder. His elder brother, Robert, was in the same trade and in 1816 the two of them went into business together as jobbing builders but sadly Robert died the following year so Richard was left to carry on by himself.

Only one little group of his early houses survive; they're in Higham Place next to the Laing Art Gallery. They were put up in 1819 when he was only twenty-one and they're really nice, brick Regency houses with pretty classical doorways. Above all they are a very impressive testament to his ability. Could I have run a business and built a row of houses to this standard when I was twenty-one? I could not. But for Richard this was the merest beginning. He went on to build a substantial group of houses on Blackett Street which have since been demolished and then, in 1821, he made a really, really smart move, a move that you might want to consider yourself and that many of us might have made had the opportunity arisen. He married somebody with money. Rachel Arundale was the daughter of a wealthy businessman and she brought £5,000 with her as a marriage settlement. That was a lot of money in those days, probably equivalent to about £500,000 nowadays (I sigh wistfully) and it clearly made a substantial difference to the business. I'm not saying it was the be all and end all of their relationship. They were a close and affectionate couple with lots (and lots) of children (thirteen in fact) and a quiet domestic life. She worked as a sort of in-house company secretary with him for many years and he was entirely devastated when she died in childbirth in 1842 but at the beginning the £5,000 launched the company into a new level of ambition that allowed him to build Eldon Square.

Next page, clockwise from top left: 1) *Early 19th Century Lit & Phil.* 2) *Higham Place* 3) *The Theatre Royal on Grey Street, 1841.*

Eldon Square through the ages.
Top: *Looking north, 18*
Middle: *Looking west, 1*
Left: *Today's view.*

Unless you're older than you want to be with a good memory, you won't recall Eldon Square in its complete form because two sides of it were pulled down in the early 1970s to make space for the shopping mall of the same name. Only one rather isolated side remains to remind you of the grandeur it once had – because this was a square on a London pattern and metropolitan scale, made up of seriously posh houses, quite unlike anything Newcastle had seen before.

The architect was another local man of terrific ability. His name was Thomas Oliver and you need to file him away in your memory alongside John Dobson and Ant and Dec. They are all going to remain part of the Grainger story for some time. John Dobson designed St Mary's Place for him in 1827 and the Greens were to play a major part later on but in 1829 it was back to Thomas Oliver again for a block of houses even more stupendous than his Eldon Square.

Leazes Terrace now lies between Leazes Park and St James's Park, neither of which existed when it was built; then it was on open territory right on the edge of the Town Moor – a wonderful situation for a building of real splendour. It's big, it's Grecian and it's built of beautiful stone. There wasn't a terrace to match it in the North when it was built – there probably still isn't.

And then there was just time for Grainger to have one last push to get the town into top fashionable gear. The Pilgrim Street roundabout now sits on the site of the Royal Arcade and houses a rather tragic replica of the Arcade's interior within the 1960s walls, but when it was built in 1832 it was another sophisticated moment of excitement and the town was bubbling with enthusiasm for the achievements of Richard Grainger. The following year, in 1833, the Mayor and council gave a Grand Public Dinner in his honour, to celebrate his extraordinary contributions to the town of his birth. He was just thirty-six years old and had risen from a tenement and charity school background to a position of civic honour. He must have thought it couldn't get better …but he had hardly started.

At this time there was an appetite for town improvements in Newcastle. The new streets built at the end of the 18th century had suggested what was possible but there was clearly room for more. You sense it was in the air, waiting to get started. As early as 1827 Eneas Mackenzie, my favourite radical, school-teaching historian, complained that nobody was taking such matters seriously. He obviously wanted something to happen. *'No master mind,'* he wrote, *'conceives and directs the public works.'* But by the 1830s several people were busy conceiving (if you will excuse the metaphor) though nobody had yet got round to actually directing. Grainger's architects, Thomas Oliver and John Dobson, had both come up with big bold plans for remodelling the middle of the town but it was Grainger himself whose plan was accepted and built.

You know it well. I have no doubt you have marvelled many a time at the splendour of Grey Street. You have probably stood at the foot of Grey's magnificent Monument and enjoyed both of the main streets together – the slope and gentle curve of Grey Street, the more restrained dignity of Grainger Street. I bet you have been impressed by the triangular block that forms the junction between them– the Central Exchange Building with its elegant curves, its beautifully carved Corinthian columns and big green domes dominating the corners. You might well have been a little less impressed by the third main street because Clayton Street seems a bit out of the way and forgotten these days but even there you will have been aware of the grandeur of the buildings, row after row, tall and beautifully built in finely cut, buff-coloured sandstone. And I bet you have been amazed that despite there being so much consistency in the overall look of this massive scheme there is still room for variety and personality in the individual buildings as well – Lloyds Bank at the top of Grey Street is like a magnificent Italian palazzo, the Theatre Royal is a transplanted Pantheon from ancient Rome. In places (down the west side of Grey Street, for example) there are great temple fronts and throughout the scheme big, blocky, powerful pavilions give wonderful emphasis to most of the corners. It is fabulous architecture on a titanic scale.

Grainger presented his plan to the council on 22 May 1834 and it was accepted almost right away. He already had a reputation as somebody who could deliver big schemes and good schemes and on this occasion he also had the support of the extremely influential (and extremely rich) Town Clerk, John Clayton, which might have helped, but nevertheless the council, the old unreformed council remember, showed quite a lot of courage to be so decisive because an awful lot of things had to come together before the whole thing would work.

First of all it depended on Grainger being able to buy the enormous Anderson Place. This was the huge Tudor house which I've written about before that had stood in the north-east quarter of the town for the last 250 years and which had recently come on the market along with its enormous gardens and the adjacent Nun's Fields, twelve acres of open ground that had never been built on since the Benedictine nuns left at the dissolution of the Monasteries.

If he could get all of that it would provide a solid basis for his plan – it would need clearing and grading of course but it was available land and hardly anybody would have to be displaced in order to build on it; but outside the area of open ground the whole thing got quite a bit more problematic. The route of Clayton Street, for example, was through entirely built-up streets and little courts that would have to be demolished; and south of the Nun's Fields, following the line that Grey Street would eventually take, the Lort Burn had already been covered over and extensively built on. For example there was a large and almost new Flesh Market and beside it, David Stephenson's very popular Theatre Royal of 1788 was in the way as well. If Grainger's plan was going to work, both of these would have to be pulled down. Around them, as you can see from Thomas Oliver's map of 1830, the route of Grainger's principal street had become a densely-packed mass of houses and little lanes. All of this would have to go.

All of it did go. At astonishing speed. The moment he had the council's approval on 16th June Grainger completed the purchase of Anderson Place for a measly £50,000 (perhaps £5,000,000 modern equivalent) and within two weeks he had started to demolish it. The rubble of the house became the new contours for the valley of the Lort Burn. He bought the Flesh Market too; he gave the council £15,000 pounds for it and promised to sell them a brand new one, twice as good, for about £36,000. He bought the Theatre as well with a similar promise and his workmen started to demolish it within three hours of him signing the deal.

I imagine people must have been intensely unsettled about what was going on. Inevitably there was huge disruption. There were carts and dirt and mud. Streets were blocked by scaffolding. I bet people complained bitterly just like we do nowadays:

'You can't keep your shoes clean anymore.'
'it's costing me a fortune in laundry…'
'… and the parking! I had to leave me carriage three streets away this morning.'

Vast holes in the ground allowed for foundations more than fifty feet deep. There was a brickworks built in the middle of the site. The English Heritage book on Grainger Town tells about a dreadful accident when three partly-built houses on Market Street collapsed, killing seven men and injuring eight others. A lightning strike was blamed at the time and perhaps that *was* the cause. And people must have been desolate at the loss of their theatre and worried sick about when they were going to be able to get their their market stall going again. Parliamentary Commissioners who had come from London to work out the new boundaries of the town in the light of The Municipal Corporations Act were aware of a sense of nervous but hopeful unease *'The Corporation are at present erecting a large and handsome*

Market-house and individuals are at the same time building on speculation entire streets of shops and houses of a superior description. There are various opinions as to the result of this speculation but it is hoped … that it will attract inhabitants'.

Two things might have offered some comfort to the worriers. The extraordinary speed with which things were happening must have amazed them and so must the quality that was appearing before their eyes.

Take the market for example. Grainger had bought the Flesh Market in the summer of 1834; by October John Dobson's design for a replacement was ready and the foundations of the new indoor market were already in place. A year later it was done, finished, and the town had a beautiful building with splendid classical facades. Inside there were 234 shops and stalls. It was the largest indoor market in Europe and a source of intense pride. On 22 October 1835, they held a giant civic dinner to celebrate its opening with thousands of men (and the inevitable sloshed reporter) getting totally trolleyed on pints of wine. One local writer (I have pinched this quote – and much else – from Yvonne Young's book on the Grainger Market) wrote:

'It was a glorious vista … irradiated by gas light'

Collard and Ross, in their *Architectural and picturesque views of Newcastle* said in 1841 *'nothing can exceed the bustle and animation displayed here on a market day.'* They called the building a *'cathedral-like temple of trade'* and seemed particularly impressed by the ducks awaiting sale being allowed to swim in the fountain with its large stone basin.

The new Theatre Royal took a little longer to complete – but not much. It was up and running by the beginning of 1837 which seems astonishing when you look at the complexity and magnificence of its design. It makes me wonder how it was done. How did John and Benjamin Green get to be so good? And how did Grainger find enough masons capable of work at this level? John Dobson wrote that Sir Charles Monck at Belsay was so

finicketty about the quality of the stonework of his new house that afterwards the workmen he used were so skilled that Northumbrian masons were in huge demand around the country. And you can believe it when you look at the quality of the Theatre Royal and the crisp splendour of its Corinthian capitals.

J (father) and B (son) were the designers of Grey's Monument as well, with the statue of the noble Earl done by a London sculptor called Edward Hodge Baily. The Earl's head fell off once, struck by lightning; it was replaced with a new one but the right hand must have fallen off at some point as well because if you look at it through binoculars (I can't believe you haven't!) it's huge and uncarved, almost like a club, but then he was a politician who always packed a punch…

There was no monument in Grainger's original plan and the idea only emerged in 1837 and was paid for by public subscription. The beautifully carved inscription on it reveals that it had been erected in gratitude for the passing of the Great Reform Bill of 1832. It looks absolutely magnificent and seems like a perfect focus at the centre of the scheme and for the centre of Newcastle as well, but in fact it was extremely contentious at the time. The Earl himself wasn't at all keen on the idea and refused to come for the opening and you can't really blame him, it would have made him feel as if he was already dead, having memorials put up in his memory. But worse than that, 1838 wasn't a good time to be recalling the Reform Bill because the People's Charter had just been issued and all over the country the Chartists were rising to demand that the working-class, which had been left out of the original bill, should be given the vote. It was a very scary and dangerous time. There were massive protests in Newcastle, just like there had been earlier in the century, and as the monument was nearing completion, there were two dangerous riots. At one of them the rioters armed themselves with 'stones and brickbats'. I was interested to find that a 'brickbat' is just a bit of a brick, and bits of bricks were indeed

Britain's Best Street
The Commission for Architecture and the Built Environment found Grey Street to be 'Britain's Best Street' - '...a street on a human scale with a grand vision.' Clockwise from below: 1) Grey Sreet from Grey's Monument, 1957. 2) A water colour of Grey Street, 1835. 3) A modern view down Grey Street and Grainger Street. 4) Artwork outside the Theatre Royal, 2007. 5) A beggar boy on Grey Street, 1898.

heaved through the windows of banks and one of the local newspapers, which is bad enough but the mayor was stoned as well. The Riot Act was read four times but the crowds wouldn't disperse. Troops were brought down from Fenham Barracks and the cavalry broke up the crowds and patrolled the streets until after midnight. Lots of people were arrested and banners were seized. It's no surprise that the Council was (once again) convinced that it was the beginning of an armed uprising and there were lots of people in the poorer districts who would have been in favour of that happening. Robert Colls reports that pamphlets on 'Street Warfare' were being sold for a penny each down by the riverside. Because the situation was so volatile the monument got no official opening.

What an extraordinary juxtaposition that two equally significant but massively different things were happening in the same place at the same time. I'm reminded of a diary I was once shown, a sort of house diary which had been written in 1933 by the great Northumbrian historian, G.M. Trevelyan. It comprised of a list of things that had been happening where he lived and included the number of new roses that had been planted in his garden, the number of pheasants and grouse and blackcock which had been shot on the estate, the redecoration of a bedroom, all completely ordinary country housey sorts of things – but right in the middle of this long list was an extra item which read, 'That bounder Hitler burnt down the Reichstag'. In 1838, Newcastle was a bit like that. One group of people, mainly the posher sort, were keen to celebrate their local pride in the political revolution that had recently occurred, another, the poorer sort, wanted the opposite; they wanted a new revolution to improve on the one that had gone before.

As for the wealthier group of people, there was probably another, unspoken reason why they wanted a huge public monument. 1837 was the date of the first meeting of Londoners pushing for a memorial to Lord Nelson to be erected in Trafalgar Square and it seems likely that Newcastle didn't want to be left behind. In 1838, pretty much the same group of leading Newcastle citizens who had been responsible for the Grey Monument started meeting again to discuss another monument, this time in memory of another local hero, Admiral Collingwood. Their deliberations, as quoted in the local papers, were absolutely oozing local patriotism and a real pride in the achievements of the town. Captain Blackett, one of those present, said he hoped they would erect a monument which would be *worthy of this magnificent county and this now splendid town* and another notable bigwig (C. W. Bigge Esq) made the motivation even clearer. He was quoted as saying '... *they only now saw the metropolis preparing to do the same justice to the memory of Lord Nelson and he was glad that they were not behind-hand with the great city of London, but were as ready to express their admiration ... as London was ...*' So in the monument stakes Newcastle was in a race against the capital and in fact Newcastle won. Both places got a tall Corinthian column with a hero on top; both heroes were carved by E.H. Baily ... but Newcastle's got there first – by five years! Haway the Geordies.

Around these splendid set-pieces, Grainger's team was creating houses and shops – shops on the ground floor and two or three storey houses above them. It seems an odd way of living now. Only students, young people and the poor tend to live above the shops today (above the chip shops in my experience) but it was what middle-class Newcastle had been used to for centuries. Since medieval times Newcastle's well-to-do merchants had lived above their shops and warehouses so Grainger's plan was following an established pattern. In other places – in Edinburgh, for example, which was experiencing similar levels of rebuilding, people lived in apartments above the shops but the English weren't ready for flats yet, so they got houses.

Top: *A detail from* The Royal Arcade *by Dobson and Carmichael.*
Top right: *The Central Exchange Building seen from Grainger Street*
Right: *Grey's Monument surrounded by tram tracks in 1900, the Central Exchange Building in the background.*

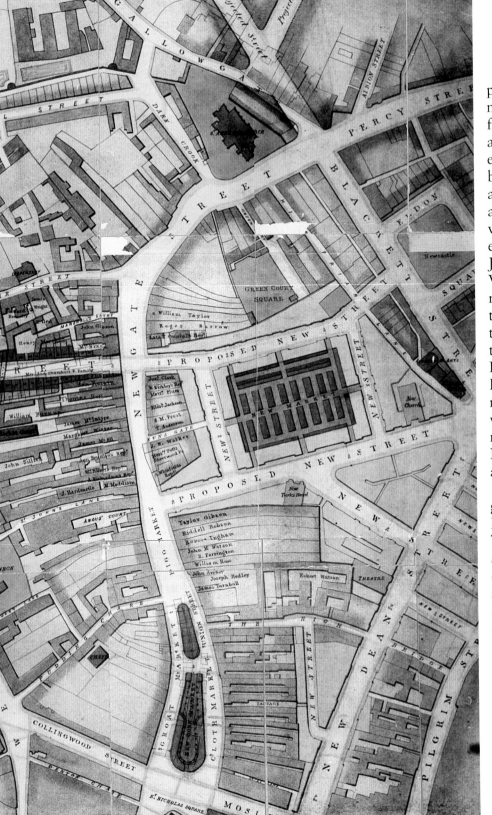

The houses and shops were as grand as the public buildings and the rich variety that Grainger managed to bring to this vast unified scheme came from a piece of brilliance – he didn't have a single architect – he had a whole pile of them who were each able to bring different interpretations to the brief. I've already mentioned Dobson and Oliver and the Greens, all of whom were independent architects with practices of their own, and there were two others who seem to have been directly employed in the Grainger office. They were called John and George by their chums, that's John Wardle and George Walker to you and me. They remain much less well known than the others but they created some of the most beautiful parts of the plan – the whole west side of Grey Street is theirs and the magnificent Central Exchange Building. These were all local chaps. Except for Baily, the sculptor, everybody involved was local, not necessarily from Newcastle itself but born very close and all based here. It was a stroke of massive luck for Grainger (and even more, for Newcastle) that such richness of talent should be available at one time and in one place.

So as the scheme developed the town must have gained in confidence. In 1837 the Parliamentary Boundary Commissioners expressed the mood. They wrote '*The great improvement in the buildings of the town is taking place in the Parish of St Andrew … the project seems to indicate the increasing prosperity of the town. When these buildings are completed, the whole Northern part of the Town will present an appearance of comfort and beauty exceeded by few commercial towns in the country*'.

A map showing the 'Building Ground with Proposed and Projected Improvements', 1834. Although not all of the proposals came to fruition, the map can be recognised as the 'Graingertown' we know today.

That confidence was borne out. By 1842 the whole thing was finished and Grainger had delivered:

- Ten inns and twelve pubs
- A market and a theatre
- A Central Exchange
- A dispensary, a music hall and two chapels
- Grey Street had ten posher houses for posher people (a good advertising slogan for developers nowadays, possibly?)
- 325 combined houses and shops

They weren't perfect, some of them need later remedial work to put right weaknesses in their construction, but they were pretty, damn impressive. All of the houses had water closets, which was almost entirely unheard of in those days and they looked superb as they still do. People were massively impressed. The English Heritage book quotes the novelist, William Howitt, who visited the town in 1842, as saying:

'You walk into what has long been termed the coal hole of the north and find yourself at once in a city of palaces, a fairyland of newness, brightness and elegance. And who has wrought this change? It is Mr Grainger.'

For Mr. Grainger himself, 1842 was a very sad year. His wife Rachel died and he had fled Newcastle to escape his creditors. The whole scheme had been funded in risky ways. It was done on loans and what you might call rolling mortgages where each completed and sold property was used to fund the next one down the line and in 1839 the system imploded and he fled. In 1842 he returned, persuaded and supported by John Clayton, to confront his problems. When he died in 1861 he was still massively in debt and it wasn't for another forty years that his estate was clear … but when he died in 1861 the town was in his debt. When the news of his death was announced, the bells in all the churches were rung and the shopkeepers in all of his shops put up the shutters for the day in honour of his memory. It's not a bad record, but …

But what about the workers? Not one of Grainger's houses was meant to house the poor or the working classes. The simpler buildings on Clayton Street are said to have included some for artisans and tradesmen but the rest were all for the middle class. Even those from Grainger's own background, families that were hard-working, respectable, religious but unfortunate, were given no consideration at all so, as the great spate of town improvements drew to an end and as the new municipal council completed its first few years, how were the poor doing?

Not well.

One of the relatively early things that the new, reformed national government did was to start to look at public health and in 1843 they set up a Commission on the Health of Towns to find out what was going on. Commissioners were sent to all the major towns to report on the situation; the man who came to Newcastle was called Dr Reid and his report was published in 1845. It made grim reading.

The poorer parts of the town had long been called 'the fever districts' and there was appalling overcrowding. Mackenzie, writing in 1827 and looking back at the Quayside chares of a few years previously, had described them as 'the most crowded part of his majesty's dominions' and by 1845 there hadn't been any improvement. The poor lived in old houses that had been split up into multiple apartments. Often a family would just have a single room, sometimes with no more than a single bed. Lodgers were often given three beds to a room and three people in each bed. Because of the window tax and the meanness of the street there was dreadful ventilation and there was often no sanitation at all.

According to Dr Reid, the worst places of all were the lodging houses down by the river where he found *'the most deplorable exhibitions of the want of sanitary regulations to be found in this country.'* He said that they were crowded in the extreme and dirty, ill-managed, occupied promiscuously by both sexes.'

Even among the main streets (The Close, Newgate Street and Groat Market were examples) there were thirty-three that still weren't paved and had no drains or sewers and in '*the narrow, dark, stinking alleys*', which formed the oldest parts of the town, the conditions were far worse. In 1854, Sandgate had a population of about 5,000 living in 350 houses. Alan Morgan records that between them they had one public privy, three private privies and four private WCs – eight toilets in total for 5,000 people! Imagine what it was like there late on a Saturday night. So in the absence of privies, the stuff was just piled up in corners or thrown out onto the streets and only cleaned away occasionally. The public middens held about 2,000 tons of '*putrefying manure.*' There were still no regulations or bye-laws that required builders to include privies or drains or sewers in new developments and as a result even new streets in places like Westgate outside the boundary of the historic town were in a 'neglected and filthy condition.' Any streams that still existed (Pandon Dene for example) had become no better than open sewers.

All of this was nasty, of course, but it was dangerous too. Since the 18th century doctors had been getting clearer and clearer about the connection between hygiene and health but nobody had yet thought to do anything about it, so outbreaks of diseases like typhus and smallpox were common and in 1831 there had been the first of three visitations by cholera.

Cholera had existed as a pandemic for centuries in the Far East but it was a 'new and terrifying' disease when it first appeared in Newcastle in 1831 and the corporation's response to it was quite vigorous by the standards of the day. Emergency hospitals were opened and the theatres and other places of entertainment were closed. Ships were held in quarantine and soldiers confined to their barracks. The riverside chares were washed in hot lime; funerals couldn't take place inside churches and the dead were buried deep and in quick lime to make sure the bodies provided no risk.

Good measures then – but futile because they missed the point. It was still assumed that disease was carried by dirty air and nobody had yet realised that cholera was carried in dirty water and human faeces. It was going to take some time (and another far more serious outbreak in 1853) before that connection was made, but interestingly, the man who finally made the connection had worked as a colliery surgeon in Newcastle right through the 1831 outbreak.

His name was John Snow, born in York in 1813 and apprenticed to William Hardcastle in Newcastle at the age of fourteen. He was working as a surgeon in Soho in 1853 when the next great epidemic took place and he was able to identify that in his area the epicentre was a drinking fountain with water taken from a sewage rich section of the Thames. He has the reputation of being the father of British epidemiology.

Though the disease had been brought to England from the Far East by a sick sailor, dirty water was undoubtedly a factor in the Newcastle outbreak because the town's water supply was almost entirely inadequate. Only a few of the poshest houses had their own water supply, most people had to make do with about twenty public fountains or 'pants', which only ran for three days a week, and the situation in 1831 was even worse than normal because that winter had been unusually dry and the pants stopped working. Water had to be delivered by carts.

The town was supplied by a private water company that pumped water from the river at Elswick and from a small reservoir on the Town Moor as well – but it wasn't sufficient and Dr Reid's report was damning about it. He found the water inadequately filtered. Only one house in twelve had a supply and the poorer classes weren't provided for at all.

This is one of those rather low points for a man like me, writing an account of the development of a place of which I am very proud, because Dr Reid, the first objective, analytical, statistically literate person to look at Newcastle from the outside was clearly pretty disgusted by what he found. He makes no mention of the nice new developments that have happened so recently at the top of the hill but instead calls for things to be done in the poorest districts. His report formed part of a nationwide Health Inspectors' Report and that in turn led to the 1848 Public Health Act. The Public Health Act laid down the law that any town with a death rate that was over 23 per 1,000 could be forced to take action. Newcastle's death rate for seven consecutive years was 29.6 per 1000. Only Manchester and Liverpool were worse in England so you would think that the council should have been forced to take action - but the report contains a pretty damning assessment. It says '*Any report I might write on Newcastle so far as the local authorities are concerned would be a dead letter.*' Oh dear, what an odd chapter. There have been encouraging things in it; the splendid new town centre provided by Richard Grainger was a source of pride and optimism but round about that there have been so many worse things: civil and social upheavals, riots and repression, grinding poverty, bad housing and public health disasters and inadequacies. It has criticised the local authorities on a number of occasions and even drawn attention to the fact that the mayor was, at times, stoned by the populace. I do hope I find a few more optimistic things to say in the next chapter. Perhaps it's time I dipped my writer's toe into the inky waters of industrial innovation and invention.

'Graingertown' from Grey's Monument.

Newcastle's Inventive Genius?

I live in Gosforth and at the end of my street there's a very busy road that goes down the hill towards South Gosforth. It is busy with cars nowadays but originally it was busy with wagons taking coal from the Kenton and Coxlodge Colliery to the staithes on the River Tyne at Wallsend. For many years they used a horse-drawn waggonway with wooden rails but in 1808 the management had made an adventurous technological investment to replace the wooden rails with cast iron ones on stone sleepers and then, in 1813, they took an even more impressive leap into the relatively unknown and replaced the horses with three steam locomotives.

The thinking was pretty sound for at least two reasons. Firstly, the war with France had created a shortage of hay and other fodder and the cost of keeping a horse had increased massively. Secondly, evidence from Coalbrookdale in Shropshire and Merthyr Tydfil in South Wales had already demonstrated that steam locomotives, first invented by the Cornishman Richard Trevithick in the earliest years of the century, were capable of hauling more weight than a horse.

What happened next in the steam locomotive story had a strong Geordie connection and an even stronger connection with Gosforth. There was a pit at Middleton, just outside Leeds, which was owned by the Brandling family who were members of the old Newcastle ruling elite. In the 16th century alone, Brandlings had been mayors on at least 1,000 occasions (approximately); they were Hostmen inevitably, they had sunk pits in many parts of the country and their spankingly impressive 18th century mansion at Gosforth Park now forms the grandstand of Newcastle Race Course. John Blenkinsop, who was the chap in charge of their Middleton pit, was almost a Newcastle man too; he came from Walker and he'd been impressed by the Trevithick engines so he designed one of his own. He didn't believe that it would be possible to haul heavy loads using smooth iron wheels on smooth iron tracks; he thought there would be too much slippage, so his locomotive worked on the rack and pinion system; it had a cogged wheel that engaged with an extra toothed rail alongside the smooth rails. He patented it in 1811, had it made by another Geordie engineer called Matthew Watson, and in 1812 it started to work in earnest on the four-mile long waggonway into Leeds. It went well and, according to Stafford Linsley, was able to pull as much coal each journey as sixteen horses working for twelve hours … and it didn't need as much hay.

The Brandlings also owned the pits near my house and the viewer they employed to run them was yet another local man, a chum of John Blenkinsop's called John Watson, and so together they decided to bring the Middleton system to Gosforth. It opened on 2 September 1813 and if I had been alive at the time and my house had been built and there hadn't been a church in the way I would have been able to watch it from my bedroom window. The soon-to-be-very-famous George Stephenson was there and I might have been able to wave at him if I'd known who he was.

For many years after this, Gosforth stubbornly resisted being changed from a landscape of coal into the elegant abode of the sophisticated Grundy family that it has become. The Bishop of Newcastle's official residence on the edge of the Town Moor is on the site of another pit and from it there was a second waggonway where now there are houses of substantial poshness. In the Parish Church grounds there is a stone called the Main Dyke stone, which marks the occasion, in 1825, when the miners of the Gosforth Pit broke through formidable barriers to reach a rich new seam of coal far deeper than the one that had begun to run out. They held a banquet ninety fathoms underground to celebrate the achievement. Ladies and gentlemen, along with pitmen and their families were all lowered down the new shaft in baskets to feast on goodies and wine (for the gents) and beer (for the chaps).

All signs of these things are long gone of course but I have included them because what was happening in Gosforth was typical of Newcastle's involvement in those earliest days of the growth of the railways. In villages and at collieries all over the North East experiments were being carried out and improvements made which led to astonishing developments in the effectiveness and reliability of steam locomotives, not to mention the safety and efficiency of mines. At first, all of the great and memorable things were happening beyond the boundaries of Newcastle in places as far-flung as Wylam, Gosforth and Killingworth and even (whisper it quietly) as far south as Teesside. Newcastle was involved in so far as there were significant players who had been born and educated in the town and many of the mine owners were part of the Newcastle mafia; it's almost certain that the financial deals that made the developments possible were brokered in Newcastle but in the earliest years the actual inventions were made where the coal was and that was no longer in Newcastle.

The first sign that Newcastle was going to become even more closely involved in the changes that were taking place in the coalfield occurred in 1815.

In 1812 there had been a terrible explosion with massive loss of life at Felling, another pit belonging to the Brandling family. It led to the setting up of The Society for the Prevention of Accidents in Mines which offered a reward for anyone who came up with a practical miners' safety lamp. Two viable alternatives were produced. Humphrey Davy, exceedingly famous scientist and eminent member of the Royal Society in London, produced one, while George Stephenson, ordinary chap, born in a cottage near Wylam and working as an engineer in a colliery at Killingworth, produced the other. Both of the lamps worked – more or less.

Guess who was awarded the prize.

Humph got a gold medal and £1,000 from the Royal Society and a further £2,000 from the country's colliery owners. George was given a consolation one-hundred guineas – better than a kick on the shin but still a slap on the face.

An etching of Gosforth Colliery, 1844.

That was the sort of snub he had to get used to. Years later when he was summoned to appear before a Parliamentary sub-committee to answer question about one of his schemes, the MPs had to pause proceedings to send out for a translator. When he was being quizzed by a barrage of barristers representing those who were opposing the Manchester and Liverpool Railway he had to listen to constant abuse. He suffered days of virulent questioning and insults until he was on the verge of collapse. One barrister said he had '*an ignorance almost inconceivable*' and talked about the '*trash and confusion of his evidence*'. A fellow engineer called Francis Giles wondered whether he was in his right senses. Mr Alderman KC called him '*stupid and incredulous*'. That's what happened to ordinary people in an upper-class world. Humphry Davy might have been the first to insult him, but he certainly wasn't the last.

The problem with Davy, just like all the rest of them, was that he couldn't accept that an uneducated working man could possibly have the ability to come up with his design on his own so he was scathing in his rejection - but it was George who demonstrated his design first and inevitably he did so in Newcastle. On 5 December 1815 he came to the Newcastle Literary and Philosophical Society to show what he'd made and whatever the rest of the country thought, the North East was convinced. North East miners chose to use the 'Geordie' lamp instead of the Davy lamp and the members of the Newcastle branch of The Society for the Prevention of Accidents in Mines redressed the snub that had been delivered to Stephenson by awarding him a £1,000 prize of their own. The connection between Newcastle and George Stephenson was forged; it was going to get stronger, last throughout his life and beyond, and it was going to be underlined by many other extraordinary moments of technical brilliance as the century progressed.

George Stephenson's next big connection with Newcastle occurred a few years later in 1823. By that date he had already acquired a formidable reputation as a builder and repairer of engines, but he'd moved into new territory as well. He had turned himself into a civil engineer. He had built the Killingworth waggonway and in 1820 he'd designed the Hetton Railway, which was the longest and most complicated waggonway to have been built so far; it led eight complicated miles over hills and down dales from Hetton le Hole to the River Wear at Sunderland and it was the first railway in the world to be designed entirely for mechanical power (with not a horse in sight). It was so successful that on the back of it, in 1821, he was appointed as the engineer in charge of the proposed Stockton and Darlington Railway which was to be twenty-five miles long and the biggest railway scheme ever attempted.

His job was to survey and build the line but it was also his responsibility to provide the locomotives that would run on it and to do that he opened a factory called Robert Stephenson and Co. It was on Forth Street just behind the present Central Station in Newcastle. Its managing director was George's nineteen-year old son Robert, and it was the first locomotive works in the world! It firmly planted Newcastle's feet at the centre of the new railway age. The famous *Locomotion No.1*, which hauled 450 people and a load of coal at an average twelve miles per hour on the Stockton and Darlington's first day was built on Forth Street and the factory attracted a steady stream of visitors and potential customers from all over the world. The first two locomotives to run in America came from Newcastle and a Stephenson locomotive called *John Bull*, which is now in the Smithsonian Museum in Washington DC, is supposed to be the oldest working self-propelled vehicle in the world. *Rocket*, built on Forth Street in 1829, was the most famous locomotive in the world and very rapidly George Stephenson became the most famous engineer in the world. He surveyed and created the Manchester to Liverpool Railway and went on to provide railways all over the country. He had started his railway career building coal locomotives that struggled to travel at four mph on colliery waggonways, but by 1844, a year or two before he died, he made the journey from London to Newcastle in eight hours at an average speed of thirty-seven miles per hour - that's about the same speed as a Friday evening trip along the M1 and it's about three times faster than driving a car across Newcastle in rush hour! And no! I'm not exaggerating.

Some of the things that people used to say about him, he didn't do. He certainly didn't invent the steam locomotive and he probably wasn't the best locomotive engineer even in the north east. But what he did do was bring it all together. He invented, or at least developed cuttings and embankments; he became a master at building bridges so that trains could flow with ease over flattened landscapes. He realised that the technology wasn't just made for moving coal but for moving people too. He had the vision to work out what railways were for and as a result he was the first person to liberate us from the places where we were born. Whatever problems he had, he was a good egg.

And Newcastle loved him for it. He might have been born in far-off Wylam (seven whole miles away!) and he didn't live in the town very much (his house was on Eldon Place – a short street beside the Playhouse and opposite the Civic Centre) but Newcastle considered him its favourite son and eventually, though it took a while, they erected a statue to him. It's an odd object if I'm being

honest. He stands like a Greek orator wrapped in a blanket; four seated figures of 'workmen' sit at the foot of his plinth though none of them look as if they would recognise hard labour if they had it for breakfast. He's near the station, which wouldn't have even been there if he hadn't done so much to bring the Railway Age into existence, but he's looking the wrong way; he's got his back to it, which seems very odd. It's not a great statue and I think there were lots of people at the time who wanted a better memorial to his achievements but never mind, there were still 100,000 people who turned up to see it unveiled and to acclaim yet another local chap who put Newcastle firmly on the world map.

'Draped in a blanket, with his back to the station.' A monument to Stephenson, 1862.

From 1845-49 George's son Robert, along with the engineer T. E. Harrison, built the High Level Bridge.

Actually I had thought of starting this chapter by writing about the High Level Bridge because I can't think of a single structure that represents Tyneside and Newcastle, the Railway Age or even the whole 19th century better than this superb object.

It had to be built, or at least something like it had to be built because by that time, by the mid 1840s, trains from York and points south had to stop in Gateshead while the line north towards Berwick (and shortly Edinburgh as well) was up and running from the Newcastle side of the river so passengers wanting to do the whole journey had to get off, try to pick up a horse and carriage, or walk, or cadge a piggy back down the cliff, cross the river (among all the lewd and disorderly people) and climb the mountain on the other side along with all of their luggage. It was a complete contradiction of the whole railway system whose essence was speed and convenience. There

just had to be a high level connection across the river and (according to Pevsner) nineteen different proposals had already been considered before Robert Stephenson's design was chosen.

It was superb. It is superb, so superb in fact that I am going to describe it for you twice or at least copy down two other people's descriptions. This is what my chum, Grace McCombie, wrote about it in Pevsner's Northumberland. First of all she points out that it is a combined road and rail bridge with a clearance of 120 feet above low water. It is 1,400 feet long. 'Masonry piers on massive timber piles (first use of Nasmyth's Steam Hammer for piling) support the main spans, each of which consists of four cast-iron ribs … tied with wrought-iron chains; the rail deck above is supported by cast-iron columns rising from the main ribs, while the road deck is slung from the ribs by wrought-iron hangers encased in cast-iron box sections to match the columns above …'. There's quite a bit more of this technical stuff but she

A detail from J.W. Carmichael's painting of the High Level Bridge, c.1849.

ends up by pointing out that the only change needed in the 170 years since it was built was a little strengthening of the roadway to take the weight of tramcars in 1922.

I am but an innocent boggler and my mind definitely boggles when I consider the level of complexity, ingenuity, scale and sheer effort required to come up with a design like that. It is still an absolute thrill to walk across it. It delights and awes just as it did when the first visitors saw it. In 1852 F.S. Williams wrote about it in Our Iron Roads, his early book about the railways. He wrote '*It is scarcely possible to imagine a more interesting and beautiful sight than it presents, with the huge span of arches diminishing in perspective and the opening at the furthest end showing only like a bright spot in the distance. The pillars, which carry the bridge, add greatly to the picturesque effect ... such a combination of beautiful lines is seldom seen*'.

The bridge was opened, or at least inaugurated by Queen Victoria when she rode across it in a Royal Train on her way to Balmoral on 29 September 1849. People waved flags and things and there was a band. A year later, or at least eleven months later, on 29 August 1850 she was back again to open the Newcastle Central Station.

Now ... since the 1820s when George and Robert Stephenson had opened their pioneering factory on Forth Street, Newcastle had become a hotbed of railway activity and invention. By 1835-8, for example, the Newcastle and Carlisle Railway was by far the longest line in the country and the first to cross it from east to west. Lineside stations were invented for it. The earlier Manchester and Liverpool Railway had stations at each end of the line but initially there were no stations in between. The idea for intermediate stations happened here, in Newcastle; station hotels began to spring up alongside the Newcastle and Carlisle too, the first of hundreds of thousands around the world. In 1839 the Newcastle and North Shields Railway included the two remarkable laminated timber viaducts designed by John Green that I mentioned in the previous chapter. And as for the main line, the route from the south

was in the process of getting its astonishing High Level Bridge. Each of the railways that converged on Newcastle showed evidence of inventive genius – and they each had a separate station. The Central station brought them all together – gloriously.

Top: *The High Level Bridge in 1863*. Right: *The High Level bridge, 1864. The older stone bridge can be seen in the background.*

Call me biased (J. 'biased' Grundy; it's got a ring to it) but I don't think there is a finer station in the country than Newcastle Central Station. York Station's alright I suppose; if you like that sort of thing, but it was built ages later by a man (Mr Prosser) who had already cut his station-builder's teeth at Newcastle. I'm told there are some quite nice stations in London as well, but who cares; I bite my thumb at them. Newcastle Central is the station for me; it's big and classical and splendid from outside, and inside it is … I cast around for a word and find that my chum Grace McCombie has already given me one … inside, she says, the train shed is astonishing, and she is right, it is astonishing. It is wide and spacious and curved with a high, arched glass and iron roof of the type that became almost ubiquitous in later stations but was invented here, on Tyneside. John Dobson, the architect, recorded how he had come up with a way to make the curved wrought-iron beams for the roof by using bevelled rollers. They were made for him in Gateshead. The reinforced plate glass in the roof was invented a few years earlier by James Hartley in Sunderland. The sweeping curve of the whole building was introduced to allow the trains to turn smoothly alongside the platforms as they came across the river over the High Level, but it has the added effect of being both elegant and beautiful, a sinuous, animated building of iron, glass and steam.

You can call me boring as well, if you like (though it has less of a ring to it) but I was a train spotter in my callow 'youthy' days and used to come across to Newcastle from Carlisle so that I could stand with my little train-spotter's book of numbers at the end of Platforms 2 or 3 and smell the steam and listen to it and I can tell you it was pretty exciting. At the west end, the most complex series of crossings and intersections in the whole national railway system satisfied my railway soul while at the east end the line divided in two and swooped imperiously on both sides of the Castle Keep and excited my sense of history, and it still does. There's

The best station in Britain?
Top: *c.1850*. Middle: *1863* Left: *2015*.

a lot of swooping going on. One line swoops round to the south and crosses the High Level; the other passes within three or four feet of the north-west corner of the keep and swoops along a viaduct in the direction of Edinburgh. The first few arches of the viaduct are low and quite normal but just beyond the Castle the line is carried over Dean Street on a stupendous arch. It was the highest and widest stone arch in the world when it was built in 1845 and it is still extraordinarily impressive.

You can imagine that this whole network of lines and structures, the High Level, the station and the viaducts had a major effect on the town. With astonishing self confidence, or even arrogance, the builders were willing to slice right through the middle of the castle, for example; the line cuts right between the castle gatehouse and its keep. But the other effects might seem even more extreme. At a stroke the lower town, the quayside, the birthplace of the town, the source of all its earlier history and wealth was abandoned and isolated, cut off by a whole new system in the sky like the bypasses and motorway systems threatened to do in the 1960s. There must have been people moaning at the time (though I must admit I haven't heard about them) who were desperately worried about the level of change. There must have been poor people in Sandgate and the crowded alleys by the river, people who would have no chance to use the new trains, who must have felt even more left behind by history than they had before. And yet …

And yet without these things Newcastle wouldn't have become the place it has. In the event, the quayside has been made more unusual and much more thrilling than it could ever have been without the vast bridges towering above it. Without its viaduct, Dean Street would just have been a steep hill. Without the High Level (and the later Tyne Bridge, of course) the Quayside buildings would still be nice but without the drama they possess today. I stood once looking over the edge of one of these bridges at the roof of a building just a few yards beneath me and watched a man climb out of an attic window. He edged along the parapet and opened another window while I wondered what to do. Was I watching a crime, or a potential tragedy? Very carefully he reached inside the second window and brought out a watering can and began to water the geraniums on the window sill. Where else could I have been a witness to such a scene?

The arches of the viaduct show where the Castle and Black Gate have been divided by the railway.

At exactly this time, the years just before 1850, the Industrial Revolution was really beginning to rip off its mask and show the world who was boss and Newcastle was one of the places where the mask ripping happened in the most startling ways. I'm just going to make a list of things that were invented here and of the people who made them happen. Not all of the key players were born here and some of the big achievements happened a few miles up and down the river but Newcastle was the common denominator. As you will see.

In the 1840s: William Armstrong created the first hydraulic crane. I hear you gasp. You are amazed, and so you should be. He was a solicitor, born in Shieldfield and fond of fishing. One day (boys and girls) while he was fishing in the Pennines he looked properly at a water wheel and realised that even though it was working brilliantly it was only using a fraction of its available power; water was being lost and wasted, splashing over the sides. He realised that if you could control the flow of the water and use it more efficiently you could work miracles with it. So he did. In his spare time he started to experiment with hydraulics, had a couple of false starts, invented a hydraulic crane and Bob became his uncle. He had two of his cranes made for Newcastle's Quayside where they were a resounding success so he gave up soliciting (I hope that's the right word), bought five acres of land in Elswick and started a factory, which was vastly successful. Vastly. He sold cranes all over the country and the rest of the world.

Now, many a hugely successful entrepreneur would have felt satisfied and put his feet up following such a level of success but not William Armstrong because …

In 1855: William Armstrong produced the world's first breech-loading gun. There had been massive condemnation of the failure of the British Army's artillery in the Crimean War so William (as you do) invented a better gun – breech loading instead of muzzle loading; with a rifled barrel to increase range and accuracy; brilliant technical construction to make it stronger and

less likely to explode. It was a revolution and a revelation. Thousands were sold to the Army and to the Union Armies in America and once the war was over he had a cunning wheeze. He gave the patents for the gun to the government who rewarded him (a) with a knighthood and (b) with lots and lots of orders that he was able to fulfil by building a second factory in Elswick

The story became a lot more complicated after that. Competitors complained about the gun and about the special relationship he had with the Government. He defended himself against both sets of accusations but British Army orders dried up so, in 1863, he severed his connections with the Government, combined his two factories into one and became a major armaments producer. He made a fortune; Tyneside made a fortune. In 1868 he started building warships to put his guns onto and made an even greater fortune. His first warship was built at the Low Walker Yard in the east end of Newcastle, a shipyard that belonged to Charles Mitchell, another of the great industrialists, and eventually (in 1882) the two men combined their shipbuilding activities into one firm called WG Armstrong Mitchell and Co. The Low Walker Yard was used mainly (but not exclusively) to build merchant ships so Armstrong built yet another factory at Elswick to build his warships, by which time his works covered 230 acres and employed over 20,000 men – as I said in an earlier chapter – the biggest factory in the world.

On the 28th and 29th June 1859: Newcastle Town Hall hosted the world's first dog show. I thought you might like a break from engines).

From 1868-76: William Armstrong built the Swing Bridge. When Armstrong started his factory in the late 1840s it was largely cut off from the sea by the appalling, shallow, twisting and unreliable channel that Newcastle Corporation, the useless managers of the river, had done absolutely nothing about for centuries. Something had to be done.

Something was done which must have seemed like a disaster to the people of Newcastle. The town lost control of the river and its revenues! All the other settlements downstream from Newcastle, the ports near the mouth of the river and the towns like Jarrow and Wallsend, which were increasingly where the work was actually happening, the exporters and the ship owners, all of those people who needed the river to be usable, they were just fed up with all of the years of mismanagement; they were fed up that Newcastle got all the money and spent it all in the town instead of using it to improve the river; they were fed up with the corruption so they got together and in 1850 they persuaded the Government to change the rules. After about seven hundred years of Geordie control, the river passed into the hands of the Tyne Improvement Commission, which turned out to be a very different beast from the old Newcastle Corporation. Things got done for a change. Dredging started and channels were properly marked, the river was made navigable, which should have been great for Lord Armstrong but unfortunately there was still another problem - a low stone bridge blocking the way between his factory and the sea.

That was obviously no use to a manufacturer of very large things so he got permission to demolish it and build the Swing Bridge in its place to let his giant ships emerge downstream from his giant factory with their cargoes of giant cranes and guns. He designed it himself complete with his hydraulic engines and it was the biggest moving bridge in the world when it opened. It rarely opens now

Some Newcastle highlights, 1889. From left to right: *High Level Bridge, Castle, Cathedral, Swing Bridge, Moot Hall, Guildhall.*

but in its day it did so constantly to allow Armstrong's own boats through and colliers from the upstream mines. Its peak year, if I remember correctly, was 1924 when it opened and shut on 6,007 occasions. That shows you how busy the river was – even upstream from central Newcastle. Imagine what it was like further down towards the sea.

In 1879: Joseph Swan invented the incandescent filament lamp. Joseph Swan, Sir Joseph as he became later, was born in 1828. Later in life he started his autobiography with the words, 'The days of my youth extend backwards to the dark ages, for I was born when the rushlight, the tallow dip or the solitary blaze of the hearth were the common means of indoor lighting.' Poor people, he said, normally went to bed as soon as the sun had set, but he had set himself the task of changing all that.

He was a remarkable man in a number of ways. He had a remarkable beard, for example, one of those beards which make even strong men quake. It's not remarkable that he was born in Sunderland, lived in Gateshead and had his business in Newcastle, though he did all of those things, which was nice of him because it means that we can all claim him as our own – but it is remarkable that he achieved astonishing feats of inventive brilliance without the benefit of much education. He left school at thirteen but went on, as everybody knows, to invent the electric light bulb.

He had become fascinated by the idea of electricity at a lecture in Sunderland when he was just seventeen but it was over thirty years before he overcame the enormous practical and scientific problems that made the light bulb possible. Physics and chemistry have never been my strong points, so you're not going to get a brainy breakdown of the science involved but the main problems were making a good enough vacuum inside the glass jar and making a filament fine enough to heat up quickly but strong enough so it didn't burn out too quickly. He finally achieved his breakthrough in 1879. On 3 February of that year he demonstrated his lamp to an audience of 700 people in the Newcastle Literary and Philosophical Society. The audience included Lord Armstrong, who was so impressed by Swan's new light bulbs that he decided to use them to light his great country house at Cragside in the Northumbrian hills.

In the 1870s the inventive Lord had bought Cragside, a small country house near Rothbury and had set about transforming it. He planted seven million trees, for example – not on his own, of course, I expect he got the lads to help him; and he extended the house in stages and with extraordinary brilliance using the skills of the great architect, Richard Norman Shaw. He filled his house with the technical products of his own inventive genius. There were hydraulic lifts and spits for the kitchen, for example, and he started to dabble in the possibilities of electric light.

Early attempts at creating electric lighting had depended on battery power which, as we torch owners know, is notoriously short lived, but in the 1870s, 1878 I think, the German-British engineer, William Siemens, invented the electrical generator, one of the very first of which was bought in 1878 by our chum Lord Armstrong, driven by water from one of the many lakes in his grounds and used to power electrical arc-lights in the house, making Cragside the first building in the world to be lit by hydroelectric power. That was a remarkable achievement but the arc lights of 1878 no longer exist because in December 1880 they were replaced by Joseph Swan's incandescent light bulbs – a much brighter and more reliable source of light. At the time they were described as being 'perfectly steady and noiseless, free from harsh glare and shadows, casting no ghastly hue on the countenance;' Lady Brownlow disagreed; she thought there was 'nothing more unbecoming than the pitiless glare of electricity.'

I don't think that we would find it all that pitiless nowadays. There were forty-five of Swan's light bulbs in Cragside, each producing sixty candle power or forty watts – by today's standards not a lot of light for a large

Sideburns: *Armstrong*, Beard: *Swan*, Tash: *Parsons*.

country house, but people used to the dark ages could not get over the brilliance.

The bulbs weren't cheap either. Each one cost twenty-five shillings, or about £125 in today's money, so it cost Lord Armstrong the equivalent of about £5,625 for his light bulbs alone.

So now there were two houses in the world lit by electric light - Cragside and 'Underhill', Swan's own house in Low Fell, and from those beginnings things began to move with incredible speed. In 1880 Swan took out a patent on his invention. On 10 August 1881, at a public meeting in the Lit and Phil, seventy gas lights were switched off and replaced by the light from Swan's lamp, making it the first public room in the world to be lit by electric light. Swan's offices were on Mosely Street just along the road from the Lit and Phil and in 1881 he lit the street outside his shop so that it became the first street in the world to be electrically lit. In the same year he was awarded the Legion d'Honneur, France's highest honour, and he set up a factory in Benwell called the Swan Electric

Light Company, the first electrical lighting company in the world!

In 1884: John Henry Holmes took the invention of electric light one step further - he learnt to switch the lights off. J. H. Holmes was present among the seven-hundred people who attended Swan's historic demonstration at the Lit and Phil and he was clearly impressed, he is said to have pestered the great man with a view to becoming his apprentice; that never happened but he did become one of the great electrical pioneers in his own right. By 1883 he had already set up an electrical engineering business on Portland Road in Shieldfield. In 1884 he installed electric lights into his father's house in Jesmond, the first house in Newcastle to have them and in the same year he invented and patented what I have learnt to call 'the quick break switch with snap-off action'. I have been using them all of my life and never knew what they were called. After that, orders came flooding in from all over the town and increasingly from round the world. He invented other stuff too. In 1884 the Tyne Steam

Shipping Company's *Royal Dane* became the first boat to be fitted with electric lights ('no smells of oil in the saloon or the cabins') and there were electric lights for trains. An early dynamo called 'The Castle' followed in 1885 and there was even a portable lighting set for night navigation on the Suez Canal. You'll not be surprised to hear that he was hugely successful. His order books were never empty and the firm continued until it became part of Reyrolles in 1928.

And I had never heard of him. Fortunately other people had, and there is a replica of his shop, all of his tools and examples of his inventions in the Discovery Museum which is where I pinched this information.

Meanwhile, also in 1884, Charles Parsons invented the first steam turbine. Charles Parsons is a classic example of the 'Newcastle effect'. He wasn't from here; he was the son of an Earl (the 3rd Earl of Rosse), brought up in the family castle in Ireland, privately educated, got a first class honours at Cambridge. His main inventions didn't happen in Newcastle either. They happened in far off places like Gateshead and Wallsend and he didn't even live in Newcastle; his family home was Holeyn Hall in Wylam (listed by J. Grundy of this parish in 1984!). But none of these things would have happened if it hadn't been for the magnetic draw of Newcastle. In 1877 with his aristocratic background and his shiny new First Class Honours Degree he came to Newcastle to sign on as an apprentice at Armstrong's works in Elswick so that he could learn about water and power, about shipbuilding and armaments at the feet of a master. He only stayed a few years before going down to Leeds for a while (to research rocket-propelled torpedoes of all things) and it was to Clarke Chapman's in Gateshead that he returned in 1884 to invent the steam turbine – but it was Newcastle that set him going.

In case you happen to be as ill-informed as me about the nature of things I'll tell you that I had to look up 'steam turbine' to find out what it was and my dictionary said that it is a device that uses pressurised steam to drive motors. You are on your own, I'm afraid, in working out what makes a steam turbine different from a steam locomotive but whatever the difference is, everybody agrees that it was a development and an invention that revolutionised ship's engines, naval warfare and the generation of electrical power. He invented it while he was working for Clarke Chapman in Gateshead and to go with it he designed and built an electrical generator. His other most famous invention, the steam-turbine driven ship, *Turbinia*, is usually said to been have taken cheekily and uninvited to the Navy's Spithead Review in 1897 though a letter in *The Times* the following day claims it was officially invited by the admiral of the fleet to demonstrate its speed. Whichever is true, *Turbinia* ran rings round all the more conventional boats that were present/trying to catch it (delete as appropriate). It was built in 1894 at Wallsend and I have driven it – is that the right word for a ship? I have been at its helm. South Tyneside College, where I used to work, had acquired all of the technical specification of Parsons' ship and created a virtual version of it that could be sailed, virtually of course, through any waterway in the world using the college's 270 degree marine simulator. I chose to sail it into the Tyne, too fast as it turned out, and while rounding the steepish bend at Whitehill Point opposite Tyne Dock, I turned it upside down but fortunately, being a virtual ship, I didn't drown or even get wet and it continued to chug along merrily under water.

The point about this accident is that the ship was fast. It went at thirty-four knots which is about forty-three mph, no mean speed, far faster than the twenty-seven knots available to the next fastest boats in the world at the time. Some of this speed was derived from the revolutionary brilliance of its engines but some of it came from the sleekness and slenderness of the design, which tipped over quite easily as I discovered. But it was fast and Parsons' cheeky demonstration of the speed under the noses of the Admiralty at the Spithead Review changed the face of ship design from that moment onwards.

By the time *Turbinia* was built, Parsons had moved into Newcastle in a big way, as you will see in a moment but first …

In 1885/6: at the Low Walker Yard, Armstrong and Mitchell built the world's first oil tanker. It was called *Gluckhauf*. It was built for a German company to carry oil from New York to Europe. It was a bit of a revolution like all the other objects in this list and it almost caused a revolution. Literally. New York dockers were wild with fury about it; convinced (rightly) that it was likely to take away their jobs, they threatened all sorts of outrages against it. There were threats that it would be bombed as it passed under the Brooklyn Bridge and it had to be given police protection all the time it was in harbour. It survived though, briefly. It ran aground and was abandoned in 1893 but by that time Armstrong and Mitchell were churning out lots of other tankers in its wake, not to mention masses of other specialist ships like ice breakers and train ferries. Refrigeration ships and cable-laying vessels were developed in Newcastle. By the end of this period, in the years just before the First World War, Newcastle itself, not just the Tyne, was still a major shipbuilding centre. There were three huge yards in the east end at Walker and another upstream at Elswick. Huge battleships like the *George V* (which was to play a massive role in hunting the *Bismarck* in the Second World War) were still being built in Newcastle and so were the first submarines but there were splendid liners too. The *Mauretania*, for example, was so vast that it had to be towed stern-first until it reached Tyne Dock where the river was wide enough to allow it to be turned with only fifty feet of clearance at each end.

In 1887: All sorts of things happened.

Queen Victoria had her Jubilee which was celebrated in Newcastle with a grand exhibition on the Town Moor. Lord Armstrong and Charles Mitchell both played a big part.

Lord Armstrong made friends with the government again. He started selling ships and masses of guns to them and made even more of a fortune.

Top: Turbinia *at speed in the North Sea.* Above: *A very early photograph of the Mitchell yard at Low Walker, 1857. Mitchell's firm was to merge with Armstrong's in 1882.*

The first of these new ships was called the *Victoria*. It was very sleek and fast and possessed two mighty 110 pounder Armstrong guns. It was probably the finest warship in the world when it was built.

Lord Armstrong was made a Peer. His title was 1st Baron Armstrong of Cragside. I wonder if there might be a connection between this event and the previous two points.

… and in 1889: Charles Parsons moved into Newcastle in a big way. He did two key things that year. He opened a factory in Heaton for the manufacture of turbines, which employed 7,000 people and he built the world's first modern power station, coal powered and driven by his own steam turbines as virtually all power stations were going to be for the next century. It was on Forth Banks behind the train station and it provided the power for a private electricity company called The Newcastle and District Electric Lighting Company ('DisCo' for short, so I suppose you could say that Discos were invented in Newcastle too – but you would be wrong). DisCo lit homes and streets and provided the power for a tramway in the western half of the city. Meanwhile …

Also in 1889 John Theodore Merz started a rival electrical company called The Newcastle Electric Supply Company (NesCo), which had its power station in Pandon Dene and supplied electricity to the eastern half of the city. This company was run by John Theodore's son, Charles Hesterman Merz who was its Chief Consultant Engineer. NesCo was also a world beater in ways that even my *Ladybird Book of Electrical Inventions* left me incapable of explaining, but prepare to be amazed. It was the first company in the world to use 3-phase electrical power. How about that. It revolutionised the world of power supply and it started here, even if I don't know what it means.

In 1898 Merz was joined by William McClellan and their Newcastle firm, which was called Merz and McClellan, became the absolute world leaders in power-station design and construction for almost a century. They also lived together or at least shared a house together in a very nice house on Gosforth High Street, next to the County pub. There is a plaque on its gatepost recording their presence.

I have sort of run-out of steam in my list of Newcastle 'firsts' in the years before WWI though I am sure I could have extended it if I had tried a bit harder. Even as I speak I think of Charles Palmer, whose integrated industrial empire was based in far-off Jarrow and who was born in South Shields but who, from the age of two, lived and was educated in Newcastle. I realise that I have forgotten to mention Charles Parsons' 'Auxetophone' the world's first sound amplifier, which he designed (in Newcastle) in 1903 without a volume switch. When it was first used at Blackpool Tower people had to move away to avoid the pain; we would probably be turning it up higher nowadays – and listening to it on headphones on the bus. I have kept quiet about the world's first beauty contest, the invention of windscreen wipers and, of course, the introduction of Andrew's Liver Salts (so important after a neet on the toon) but around this stellar group of innovators there was a host of others, inventors, suppliers, makers, who made Newcastle, in those years, an astonishing hotbed of creative change and activity. The speed was bewildering. Just think – in 1878 there was no electricity anywhere except in the laboratories of experimental scientists but by 1890 there were house lights and street lights, industrial power and electric tramways. In 1896 the first movie was shown in Newcastle. By 1904 there was an electric railway that looped out from Newcastle to Tynemouth and back again.

The rate of change was extraordinary and the level of inventive genius astonishing. More happened in those two or three decades that you would think possible in one place and it is reasonable to ask how it happened. Some people say that Newcastle didn't have all that much to do with it. I've heard it said that if the Tyne Improvement Commission hadn't taken control of the river it couldn't have happened anyway because the transport links would have been too poor; even lord Armstrong's great factories at Elswick could never have succeeded without the improved channel and if he hadn't been there, what else might never have happened? It is also pointed out that a lot of the key players were outsiders, immigrants from all over the country and beyond, so it wasn't native Geordie skill that made it happen. Even Joseph Swan came from Sunderland, they say, so we can't lay claim to him.

There's some truth in all of that. There is no doubt that the Tyne Improvement Commission made a difference or that the river needed to be dragged away from the dead hand of the Newcastle Council; and there's no doubt that immigrants and outsiders played a massive role in invention and change. There's no doubt either that the other communities on the river played huge parts in what happened or that the people from those other communities were driven wild by the arrogant assumption of leadership that came out of Newcastle.

But there's another truth. There's equally no doubt that over the centuries, by accident and by design, Newcastle had created its sense of leadership. In far-off, rough,

earlier times it might have sometimes imposed it with force and bribery but later, in the 18th and early 19th centuries Newcastle had adopted softer methods and consciously created a sophisticated face to attract the key people and services to it. It might have neglected the river, but it made sure that the shopping was good; inventors might have been born elsewhere, but they came to Newcastle to demonstrate their discoveries. Joseph Swan came to demonstrate his light bulb and W. H. Holmes was part of the audience. There was continuity too – one thing led to another. If the difficult terrain of the coalfield hadn't encouraged the development of steam power, William Armstrong might have been less aware of the power of water and Charles Palmer might never have taken that power to another level.

And there were lucky accidents. Armstrong was a lucky accident. If he hadn't been born in the town and possessed such an extraordinary mixture of scientific and entrepreneurial skill, much of what happened later might not have happened; Charles Parsons wouldn't have come here, Charles Mitchell wouldn't have achieved the level of success that he did. Armstrong was a fantastic catalyst for success. He became one of the richest and most powerful people in the country and he had a dramatic effect on his city. He gave it two parks, for a start – Armstrong Park in 1878 and the utterly extraordinary Jesmond Dene in the 1880s. It had been his garden; he had acquired the land

Armstrong's memorial near the Great North Museum

in bits over the previous two decades and developed it into a perfect, picturesque pleasure ground of waterfalls and decorative bridges, exotic planting and wonderful native woodland. It included his Banqueting House, which had a hydraulic organ, powered by water from the pond at Paddy Freeman's on the east side of the valley. He dynamited the bed of the Ouseburn to create variety and littered it with boulders made of artificial stone, or 'pulminite'. Other towns have great parks, but no other town has a park like this one and Armstrong did lots more. He put huge amounts of money into the Hancock Museum (now the Great North Museum) and paid for the buildings of Armstrong College, which became the basis of the present university. He funded the School for the Deaf and Blind and provided massive support for the town's hospital. He designed and built the unique Armstrong Bridge over Jesmond Dene at the behest of his wife who felt sorry for the horses that had to struggle down the precipitous steepness of Benton bank and back up the other side.

In return he got a statue – the nicest of the statues of famous men in the town (though not of famous women: the statue of Queen Victoria outside the cathedral is a masterpiece of realism and personality – no monarch can ever have been celebrated with greater, but still affectionate realism). Lord Armstrong is outside the Great North Museum. He's not clad in a blanket like George Stephenson, but dressed in his ordinary clothes and on the screen walls beneath him are relief images of his greatest achievements, the Swing Bridge and a hydraulic crane loading his great gun onto the deck of a ship.

So … there we are. By the end of the 19th century and the first years of the 20th, Newcastle was doing extraordinarily well. The coal industry was still vibrant - there were at least fifteen pits still working within the boundaries of the present town. All aspects of the shipping industry were on a high. By 1903, on top of everything else, Armstrong's had become a car manufacturer and in 1913 they established an aircraft factory on the edge of the Town Moor. There was still a huge glass industry and an equally vibrant ceramic industry making everything from tea caddies to sanitary ware. The place was still leading the world in the technologies of electric power. Pevsner writes that because of Swan's incandescent lamp, Parsons' steam turbine and Merz's design for central power stations with integrated control, Newcastle can be described as 'the one true source of the electrical industry'. It was still a railway centre of international significance. Vast fortunes were being made and the economic power can be clearly seen in the commercial buildings that were put up in those years. Collingwood Street, Mosley Street, lower Westgate Road, Neville Street and the lower end of Grainger Street were all almost entirely rebuilt on a stupendous scale and with tremendous panache, creating a business district of a type that is rare in English towns. Middlebrook quotes the writer of a local guide in 1903, 'At no time in its history has the spirit of change been so active in Newcastle as it is at present' and that's saying something when you think back to the enormous activity that had taken place half a century earlier.

These buildings were all designed by local chaps; Newcastle was far too self assured to bring big London names up to do the work for them and the town was fantastically lucky in the quality of local firms that were available. Milburn House on Dean Street is one of the best examples of this. It is certainly one of my favourites. It is a magnificent and enormous building of 1903 put up by the local architects Oliver, Leeson and Wood and it is best seen from below, framed by the vastness of the railway arch of 1845. It wears its size lightly, brilliantly using the hillside and the curves of the road to create variety. Its construction reflects the new industrial world into which it was born. According to the papers at the time it was built round a steel frame (an unusually early steel frame). It was heated by steam and lit by electricity. There were electric lifts to service the six floors and its public spaces are decorated with exquisite taste. It was built to provide offices for the Milburn family, which owned a huge shipping company, supposedly the fifth largest Merchant Fleet in the world. They were also directors of the Ashington Coal Company, one of the largest mining companies in the world with an annual production of over 2,500,000 tons of coal so that company's office was in Milburn House as well. Coal was still hugely important in late 19th century Newcastle and of the 185 other companies that rented space in the new building, forty-three were to do with coal. There were coal owners and coal shippers, coal fitters, coke manufacturers and at least three gas companies whose output depended on coal.

But if coal was important, it was shipping that lead the way. At least forty-six of the offices were let to shipping concerns and once again all aspects of the industry were represented. You really get the sense that the whole business could be organised from one single building and that there was no expertise that wasn't available on the premises. There were shipbuilders and shipowners, ship brokers, steamship companies, professional and indemnity clubs (for marine insurance). There was a Petroleum

Tanker Steamship Co. And in the end, if everything went wrong, there was even The Society for the Relief of Widows and Orphans of Shipwrecked Sailors.

A glance at the brass plaques outside office buildings or the index boards inside the entrance of many Newcastle office buildings would have produced the same picture as emerges from a look at Milburn House – the picture of a town still dominated by industrial concerns; of a town that was acting as the HQ of businesses from way beyond its boundaries; of a town with international connections; of a regional capital.

Except, of course, that it wasn't a town anymore. In 1882 it had won promotion. St Nicholas's church had become a cathedral and the centre of a new diocese. The toon had become a city.

Milburn House.

(Dr Tom Yellowley)

1850-1914 – Life in the Town

Without realising it you may well have heard my toilet flush. You might have become aware of the distant rush of mighty waters because the sound is quite noticeable and I believe it can be heard in far-flung corners of the earth. There are wives, my own springs to mind, who feel that this toilet should have been replaced many years ago with one that has no high-level cistern, but I counter that it has been doing its job, noisily but efficiently, since 1906; so why change it now. There are wives, and once again my own springs to mind, who do not recognise the validity of such an argument and eyes have been known to be rolled when it is put forward but it seems to me that this toilet is an object of historical interest. The miracle about it is that it is there at all, indoors, in a little room of its own, properly plumbed in and fully connected to a comprehensive sewerage system. The bathroom next door and the kitchen downstairs receive the company's own water at the turn of a tap and that system connects to a separate but equally efficient drainage system.

My house is a terraced house and it was built with other amenities as well. It might even have had electric lighting from the start but I'm not quite sure about that. It has a tiny little front garden, not exactly an estate but enough private ground to separate me from the street. It has a backyard which used to have outside toilets and coal sheds and things, all of which have gone and been replaced by a seemly modern shed and patio furniture. This yard may be small ... but it is MINE, mine, all mine - a little bit of privacy that I cherish still but that must have seemed like a miracle to the tradesmen and their families, the policemen (No. 21), the nurses and the newly-qualified schoolteachers (such as I was when I moved here), the lower middle class residents for whom the houses on my street were built at the end of the Victorian period.

I've never seen the deeds to my house so I'm not sure about the restrictions placed upon me, but one of my neighbours told me that his deeds revealed that he was absolutely hogtied by byelaws that limited his freedom of action in his own backyard. You'll be shocked by the draconian harshness of these laws, but apparently he was denied the right to brew beer in his back yard, nor could he keep pigs and worst of all he was not allowed to have any erection over thirty feet in height.

There are hundreds, probably thousands of streets like mine in a ring around Newcastle just as there are round pretty well all English towns and they were all built in a few decades towards the end of the 19th century and early in the next and they were and they are one of the great revolutions to occur in English life. Suddenly, after centuries of failing to do so, society found a way of building decent houses for ordinary people.

It needed to happen for two reasons.

The first reason was the expansion of the town and the growth of the population attracted to it because of the relatively high wages available. There was massive growth: in 1841 the population was 76,000, by 1911 there were 267,000, almost four times as many. They had to go somewhere.

The second reason, at least as important, was to do with health.

I'd like you to cast your minds back to Dr Reid whose report on the health and sanitary conditions of Newcastle was published in 1845. At that time, you will recall, the housing situation was entirely awful and it didn't begin to improve for some time. In 1853 cholera returned worse than ever before and that was despite the existence

A busy Grainger Street, 1897.

of a new and improving water supply. In 1845 a private company with many prominent local shareholders had founded the Newcastle and Gateshead Water company and begun the process of building reservoirs at Whittle Dene, west of Newcastle on the Military Road. At the beginning, Whittle Dene was able to provide 700,000 gallons a day but by 1849 the amount had already increased to 1,500,000 gallons a day. Sounds a lot; wasn't enough. In 1853 there was a long, hot, dry spell and the supply was stretched so, just as in 1831, water was pumped directly from the river at Elswick, immediately downstream from a sewage outfall and the result was an epidemic that cost the lives of 1,527 people. Nothing like enough was done to prevent the catastrophe. The council didn't even discuss the situation for the first two weeks. Richard Grainger called for privies to be provided and proper deep cleaning of the filthy streets and courts to take place but everybody was slow to respond.

It wasn't just cholera either. The riverside areas were still known as 'the fever districts'. In 1853 it was recorded that 'Typhus is still endemic in the filthy courts of the Quayside' and all the other infectious diseases were still lurking there too, things like smallpox and scarlet fever. The dirt hadn't improved at all; it was still virtually unheard of for ordinary people to have a WC and even privies were rare. As late as 1885 only a third of Newcastle houses had an inside toilet and at least forty per cent of the population felt lucky if they had an outside ash closet. Hundreds of streets were still without drains or sewers and even well-to-do houses had to make do with cess pits that leaked into water supplies and allowed noxious vapours to seep up into the houses. Overcrowding was still as bad as ever and was going to stay a problem for most of the rest of the century. Mike Barke tells the story of the Moore family who lived on Pitt Street close to Westgate Hill in the 1890s. They weren't particularly poor and had several wages coming into the family but there were still eleven of them living in two rooms in a house they shared with two other families – a total of twenty-seven people at one address.

So it was awful … but moving gradually in the right direction as it was throughout the country. In some places the speed of change was much faster than in Newcastle. London's response to the cholera outbreak, for example, was astonishing. In 1855 only ten per cent of London houses were connected to a sewer; by 1870 the system was complete. Newcastle wasn't as sharp as that. The reluctance to act that Dr Reid had recorded in his 1845 Report was apparently a feature of the town council for quite a number of years. The members of the reformed council seemed to have needed to be pushed, kicking and screaming, into action in the first three or four decades of their existence but eventually they got there.

They didn't build houses themselves, of course. My goodness no; that would have been a step too far for the Victorian official mind. It was occasionally suggested that they might do so but there was always a horrified response. It would be like communism, they thought; it would make the working class lazy and destroy their self respect – and anyway they would be too scruffy … or too luxurious … or they would be too expensive and a liability. So council houses were still something for the future but the council did eventually begin to provide the infrastructure that made decent housing possible.

They started thinking about it properly in the 1860s and 1870s prompted by a series of Acts emerging from Parliament. There had been a Public Health Act in 1848 and a new Housing Act in 1858. A second Public Health Act followed in 1872 and all of these placed responsibilities and provided opportunities for even the most reluctant of councils to take action. This last Act, for example, the one in 1872, made it a requirement to employ a Medical Officer of Health. Newcastle Council was profoundly reluctant to do that. One Alderman, Alderman Plummer (how ironic it would have been, given the close connection between clean water, toilets and health, if he had spelt his name Plumber) said that 'the appointment was no more use to the town than an umbrella to a duck'; but of course he was wrong. Dr Henry Armstrong, who was appointed to the role, had a profound effect on the health of the town. He hammered home the message about 'sanitary imperfections' and in a few years was able to cut the general and the infant mortality rate by a dramatic amount. The message was definitely getting round that decent plumbing saved lives. In 1870 the Prince of Wales had almost died of infection and when he recovered he said, 'If I wasn't a Prince, I would be a plumber' (though not a short-sighted grumpy old Plummer).

So the council didn't build the houses but they did lay the drains and install the sewers. Under the power of the 1858 Housing Act they also laid down byelaws that still make my life better today. Back lanes in Newcastle, for example, had to be a minimum eighteen feet in width with a narrow footpath on both sides. The Act required that all houses should have an outside privy, a coalhouse and at least another 150 square feet of space at the back, but the Newcastle byelaws took that further and stipulated that the yards should be surrounded by walls eight feet high. Lots of yards in other towns provide much less privacy than that and the Newcastle byelaws also provided for individual privacy inside the house in a way that was not exactly rare but at least evidence of best practice. They insisted that every room should be reached by a corridor so that nobody's bedroom was a route to another room.

Looking up Penn Street, 1957.

Another thing that the Newcastle byelaws did was to provide houses that are bigger than those in many other towns. I'll give you an example. My daughter lives in Chichester, which is a beautiful city but I have been amazed by how small its 19th century terraces and cottages are. They are often very pretty but by comparison to Newcastle houses they seem tiny. Newcastle houses had to be a minimum eighteen feet wide (I think mine is twenty feet) and there were firm regulations laid down for the size and height of rooms.

I'll give you another example. Many towns built back-to-back houses where houses in neighbouring streets joined directly onto the back of each other leaving no space for a back lane or a back yard or even, of course, a back door or any light and ventilation at the rear of the house. There are no back-to-backs in Newcastle; the byelaws didn't allow them … and a jolly good thing too.

I suspect that Newcastle's precise obsession with space, light and privacy came from the past. Dr Reid and others had been damning in their comments on overcrowding and the 'promiscuous' mingling of the sexes in the local lodging houses in the 1840s and as late as 1861 it was recorded that Newcastle had the most overcrowded housing in the country. The byelaws were confronting that situation head on. There was equal concern about cleanliness too and for the same reason – as if the town was stung by the historic criticism. The back yard, with its outside loo and its coal shed was seen as a way of keeping the house clean and the byelaws contained minute details about it– about its construction, storage, refuse collection, lack of pigs, height of erections and so on.

Another thing that the council did (eventually) was to improve the related, back-up stuff of emptying the privies and ash closets and employing bin men to take away general rubbish – stuff that we absolutely take for granted nowadays but which was revolutionary at the time. As you might recall the council had employed scavengers since the 18th century to remove at least some of the stuff but what is noticeable is how the scale of operations grew. So, in 1833 they had spent £250 a year employing fourteen men with three horses and a cart to dump the poo in a public midden; by 1907 they had an inspector, two foremen, 530 men, ten women, ninety-three horses, a sewage works and assorted rubbish dumps and it was costing £50,000 a year.

So the council set the standards and provided the backup but the houses were actually built by private and speculative builders who would sell them or rent them out. My own street, I am delighted to be able to tell you, was built for a developer by a well-known firm of architects. When not providing my home comforts they were busy designing Tyne Bridges, Laing Art Galleries, Northern Goldsmiths and things. For reasons I am not prepared to explain they had my favourite name among all the architects in the North East. They were called 'Cackett and Burns Dick'.

Of course, everything I have said so far could have been written, more or less, about most other industrial towns and cities in the country but there is one other thing about this late 19th century construction boom that only happened in Newcastle.

I am talking about Tyneside flats.

At the beginning of the 20th century 3.7 per cent of the population of the United Kingdom lived in flats; in Newcastle 44.7 per cent did. That's a remarkable local difference, is it not? There are still thousands and thousands of Tyneside Flats in streets that at first glance look identical to the normal terraces of houses – but these are quite different. They are two-storey terraces of flats with one family occupying upstairs and another downstairs. They are characterised by pairs of front doors because each flat has its own entrance. Each has its own backyard as well with the yards cunningly divided to provide the level of privacy that the byelaws required. Occasionally, on the corners between two streets, there were even three or possibly four flats occupying one structure so the arrangements of front doors and backyards become even more complicated, but the standards applied by the byelaws never changed. Each flat, just like the full houses, had to be at least eighteen feet wide with rooms at least nine feet high. All habitable rooms had to be more than seventy square feet and must be reached by a corridor. The byelaws changed over time but only to make the accommodation better. Kitchens got bigger and after 1900 many new flats managed to squeeze a bathroom into the extension at the back.

They are not quite unique. There are similar groups of 'half-house flats' in South London where they first appeared a bit later than on Tyneside. The London ones look superficially a bit posher but they haven't got the private back yards of the Tyneside flats so don't be seduced by their sneaky London ways. The Newcastle ones are better; they are bigger, arrived earlier, have more facilities, more refinements and they were invented here.

And what a clever invention it was. It cost about £250 to build a house like mine in those days, a price that would have been well beyond the pocket of a working class family; but half of £250 provided more space and amenities than anybody had ever attempted to give Newcastle's working class before - and you can't say fairer than that.

I don't think that anybody has yet offered a decent explanation why Newcastle should have taken to flats when so few other towns did. Some writers have talked about the proximity of Scotland where living in flats is a normal thing; others have suggested that the steep banks of the Tyne had made people used to the idea of living on top of each other. There are all sorts of other explanations but none of them seem very convincing to

These photos taken in 1967 following their compulsory purchase, show Meldon Street and (rear) Maple Street, some of the first Tyneside flats built in the North East.

me. I think it is more likely that somebody just had a cunning wheeze, a clever notion of how to house lots of people relatively cheaply but with all of the advantages of modern hygiene and privacy.

Ah! But who was that somebody and when did the invention take place? That's the question … or, to be more precise, that's the two questions.

Well, the first Tyneside flats I have ever read about seem to have been built on Maple Street, which is in Elswick. They have been replaced now with 20th century housing but apparently their plans revealed that they were a full version of the Tyneside Flat style and they were dated 1854. Nowadays Maple Street is beside Newcastle College but in 1854 it was just a tiny little bit up the hill from William Armstrong's brand new factory on the Elswick shore, so it seems possible, even likely, that they were invented by Armstrong or his architects to house his brand new workers. That has never been proved but it seems quite likely to me given that virtually everything else was being invented by that company at that time and if it is true, it's yet another extraordinary accolade to add to the noble entrepreneur's role of honour.

Whatever their origins, by the 1870s they were being built in large numbers

In Heaton and Jesmond, Fenham, Byker, Elswick and Scotswood (and for the sake of fairness and with gritted teeth I need to acknowledge that some of the earliest and best examples are to be found in Gateshead and all over the rest of Tyneside) there are thousands of them. There is some evidence that families with children tended to get the downstairs flats to keep the level of noise and disruption down a bit and in some parts of the town they were built in close proximity to rather more upmarket houses which caused a certain amount of friction. In West Jesmond, for example, on either side of the railway line, there are many terraces of flats that were built after 1895 by a firm of developers called Forsyth Brothers. They had bought the land from the Duke of Portland who had made a stipulation in the sale that no intoxicating liquor should be sold in the area. These flats intermingled with full houses, sometimes substantial full houses at the end of the terraces and the posher residents were disturbed to find that 'there is now a perfect rush of Working Men to the flats'. This was bad enough but worse, there were complaints that the new neighbours were carrying jugs of beer back home from the pubs half a mile away in Brandling Village. There were letters to the paper about it. Little did they know that it was merely training for the arrival of students who were going to invade the same streets a century later.

I do but jest.

I have gone on about Tyneside flats a bit because they were a uniquely Newcastle response to housing the working class. Most towns and cities built no flats at all in those days. Sunderland built its unique (and splendid) terraced, single storey cottages. Teesside built normal (and frequently quite decorative) terraces of small houses. Points south built back-to-backs or even smaller terraces of small houses; but Newcastle built the Tyneside flat.

You will have noticed that in the first half of this chapter I have reported the occasional criticism of Newcastle's Victorian Council. Lots of historians have pointed out, often quite forcefully, that the councillors had to be forced into action. I'll quote you an example:

'Provision of even the most basic of public services –

police, utilities, public health, municipal housing, libraries, recreational facilities – was usually only won after prolonged public agitation and in the teeth of municipal apathy … apathy in election … blah, blah, blah … reluctant activity in all major fields … blah, blah, blah … limited range of municipal activity in comparison to other Victorian cities …'

That's a bit harsh isn't it but there's truth in it. There was a period, quite a long period after the 1835 Act brought the new council into being, when Newcastle Council seemed reluctant to get fully involved, or to grasp the possibilities that were available to them. In the early days I think that was partly because there wasn't all that much change in the sort of people who got elected. You won't be that surprised to hear that they were still mainly the same well-to-do older men, industrialists, coal owners, ship-owners and such like who had been used to getting their way for the previous six or seven centuries. There were businessmen and quite a lot of lawyers; there were newspaper magnates; families like the Brandlings, who had been bigwigs for centuries, were bigwigs still. There were no women, of course, how could you think it? – Women weren't eligible to be elected until 1907 and none were until after the First World War. There were a couple of prominent doctors. Maureen Calcott tells a great story about one of them who was called Dr John Fife. He had been a fiery radical, 'an idol of the mob' but he 'cast his former friends off like an old slipper' after he was elected. He was later knighted and went to London for the ceremony and immediately had his luggage relabelled, 'Sir John Fife, Newcastle upon Tyne'.

They were the sort of people, not to put too fine a point on it, who didn't take all that kindly to being told what to do.

Try to hide your astonishment when I tell you that there were no working class members either – partly because there weren't enough working-class people on the electoral roll to vote for them and partly because the council meetings were always held in the afternoon and no workers could get time off to attend. According to Maureen Calcott the first working man to be elected was a tailor called James Cuthbert Laird who wasn't chosen as the councillor for Elswick until 1883.

Despite that explanation, I don't really understand why the council should have been so reluctant to get things done. The tradition, the stereotypical image of Victorian councils throughout the country is that they were go-getters, empire builders, spreading useful ornaments of civic improvement around their towns like confetti – a waterworks here, a new cemetery there, a fine new Town Hall with which to display their civic pride, wash houses and public baths, museums, libraries and parks, but in Newcastle such things were slow to arrive. Even their duty to set up a police force was resisted ('a Frenchified thing ... unfit to parade before the free and well-behaved citizens of Newcastle', said one Alderman). Another good example of their reluctance was that the town was one of the last in the country to establish public parks. Despite the fact that in 1833 a government committee had called for towns to provide walks and places of exercise; despite the fact that Dr Reid had called for them for health reasons in 1845; despite a petition of 1857 signed by 3,000 working men and despite the 1859 Recreation Ground Act, which allowed councils to levy a rate for to pay for them, the first park wasn't laid out until the middle of the 1870s (Moment of Geordie shame alert! Sunderland's Mowbray Park had been started in 1854 and was already open by 1857!). The council was extraordinarily reluctant to do anything about it. Libraries were another facility that caused years of contention. The Government had passed the Public Libraries Act in 1850 but Newcastle's wasn't opened until 1878, twenty-eight years later. In most towns utilities like gas and water were publicly owned – but not in Newcastle. By 1900 more than two thirds of English towns had their own water company but Newcastle's water continued to be provided by the privately owned Newcastle and Gateshead Water Company. These things have irritated many writers and even the new Town Hall they built themselves in 1855 opposite the Cathedral tends to get criticised. Writers compare its ambition

Top: *Brandling Park, 1897*. Above: *The Stephenson Library and Wesleyan Church from Elswich Park, c.1900*.

and architecture unfavourably with the great Civic buildings in Manchester and Birmingham, Leeds and Glasgow. It's all a bit of a worry, the amount of stick that Newcastle's Victorian council has had to take …

However, things did get done; they might have taken a while but they eventually happened.

Parks were finally provided. Leazes Park was the first. It was begun in 1873. It was, and remains a beautiful example of a Victorian park with its lake and terrace, woodland walks and (utterly non-intoxicating) refreshment kiosks. From the start there were bowling greens, croquet lawns and tennis courts. It used to have a bandstand on the upper terrace and when the lake was drained a few years ago as part of the Lottery-funded restoration of the park, it was found to contain a surprising amount of archaeology; alongside the unexpected ARP helmets, an 18th century pornographic medallion, assorted broken toys, a surprising number of shoes and all the usual detritus of such places, there were piles of small, blue glass containers - many were broken and some whole; they were relics of long ago magical summer evenings when the edges of the lake and the surrounding paths were lit by hundreds of candles. In the eyes of the Victorian rulers of the town the whole point of providing such a park was that it should attract the working classes to wholesome and healthy pursuits and promote civilized habits. 'A man walking out with his family among his neighbours of different ranks will naturally be desirous to be properly clothed,' said the government report. Newcastle attempted to reinforce these aims with a formidable list of byelaws to ensure that nothing went wrong:

No *large baskets*
No *vehicles (except prams and invalid carriages)*
No *dogs*
No *bathing*
No *shooting*
No *throwing snowballs*
No *swearing, gambling, begging or drinking*
No *preaching, discussions or religious services*
No *indecently attired persons*

… on pain of 40/- fine.

Between 1878 and 1883 Leazes Park was rapidly followed by Brandling Park, Armstrong Park, Jesmond Dene, Heaton Park and Elswick Park – all of them superb, rich in activities (though no large baskets of course) and with extraordinary variations in their styles and atmosphere - so from being among the last large towns in the country to become involved in the provision of parks, Newcastle was suddenly more richly endowed than almost anywhere else.

In fact, by the later years of the century the council was in pretty full flow and under constant pressure to do even more. There was sanitation and street cleaning, of course, and all the infrastructure and byelaws needed to provide decent housing. Plans for new buildings had to be submitted, checked and stored for future reference. The Police and the Fire Service were council concerns. There were lots of things that made life a bit more fun, a bit more civilized: the parks and libraries and a whole city-wide range of branch libraries. There were the public baths and the museums. For years the city had run the registration of Births, Deaths and Marriages. Pubs had to be licensed. Since 1870 it had been responsible through its School Board for building and running the schools and the city has some excellent ones still in existence – the towering school at the top of Westgate Hill is a terrific example and the absolutely extraordinary splendour of the Ouseburn Schools with their pagoda roofs are among the most memorable in the whole country. Newcastle hadn't yet dipped its council toe into the murky waters of public transport and the tramway system was still privately run; but change was in the air and despite tremendous opposition from some on the council and the local press, they would be council concerns within a few years. Early in the next century the first public housing would be built.

It's a good list. I don't really know how the council compared to similar chaps in other parts of the country; some will have been sharper, others a little bit more tardy but Newcastle Council had certainly come a long way by the end of the century.

One Christmas I was helping out on a gift-wrap booth in a local shopping mall for charity. You know the sort of thing – carefree shoppers buy their Christmas presents and instead of sitting up all night on Christmas Eve, they make a small donation and have the wrapping done for them. The first shopper who came towards me was carrying a three-foot tall fluffy giraffe! It couldn't be done. There was no way the whole of that giraffe could fit into a single neat package so obviously I thrust it into the hands of the girl working beside me. Any man would have done the same.

Writing chapters is like that Giraffe. There are always things that don't fit, things left out when you have wrapped the whole thing up neatly and so it is with me and the 19th century. I have told one story but there are still things I want to say, so this last section is a sort of misshapen bag of 19th century bits and pieces that have been missed out so far. I do apologise.

First of all need to say something about churches because, as I told my father when I was three years old, I'm very interested in churches.

Newcastle has a very impressive crop of 19th century churches and in many cases they have been furnished by talented local craftsmen – in particular the marvellous wood carver and painter Ralph Hedley, who has left terrific interiors all over the city (and the region). There are lots of good churches in fact and I feel a traitor to several of them for not choosing to single them out, but there are three that deserve special mention, partly because they are nice and partly because between them they almost summarise the history of English 19th century church architecture which, in a slender nutshell goes like this:

1. At the beginning of the century church architects usual built in the Gothic style - but not an accurate copy of real medieval Gothic; they took an essentially Georgian building – all rectangular and systematic, rubbed out the classical details and put in Gothic arches and shapes instead.

2. In about 1840 and under the influence of Augustus Welby Pugin, architects began to produce churches and church interiors that were as medieval as they could possibly make them.

3. Towards the end of the century architects got a bit fed up of producing accurate copies and began to experiment with new versions of the Gothic, creating churches that were freer, more personal and eclectic in style than had been possible earlier in the century.

Newcastle can illustrate those three stages to perfection. Firstly there is St Thomas's at Barras Bridge, which was designed by John Dobson in 1827. When Middlebrook wrote his History of Newcastle in 1950 he had no time for this church. He said 'It has little vitality'. He thought it was 'Too badly proportioned to be one of the architect's happiest experiments'. You will discover that he was wrong but understandably so because the style was not at all fashionable at that time. It is Gothic, Georgian Gothic, clearly not medieval but exciting in its way. The exterior is tall and dramatic, the interior a brilliant stage-set of vaulted ceilings and cast iron Gothic shafts. Very, very nice.

Secondly, there is St Mary's Roman Catholic Cathedral, which was designed by the man himself, the originator and main inspiration of pure, accurate 19th century Gothic, A. W. Pugin. He designed it in 1842 at almost exactly the moment that such a style first began to hit the country. So St Mary's was a pioneering building and a big one; it held 1,500 people and was a marvellous statement for the Roman Catholic population, which had been forced for centuries to scuttle around the town looking for places to worship in corners where they wouldn't be too noticeable. They had only recently been freed (emancipated) by the new wave of tolerance and

Some of Newcastle's many spires and steeples. Top: *Jesmond's St George's with its distinctive campanile*. Right: *St Mary's (1928)*. Left: *St Thomas's (1879)*.

reform that had been sweeping the country and in celebration they built themselves a masterpiece. Pugin designed the interior as well and it is wonderfully rich in medieval-style stained glass by William Wailes (from Gateshead!), carved stone altars, angels, carved capitals and encaustic tiles, all creating a perfect atmosphere of the middle ages.

And thirdly there is St George's Church in Jesmond. This is a masterpiece too and an almost perfect illustration of the North-South divide. If St George's was in the South, it would be on everybody's lips; as it is it remains a footnote in national architectural history books. If it was by a famous national name it would be known by everybody but because the people who worked on it were virtually all from Newcastle it doesn't get a mention. Don't get me started.

It was paid for by Charles Mitchell, the ship-building entrepreneur and partner of Lord Armstrong and it stands beside his house, Jesmond Towers, which is also a tremendous 19th century building. It was designed in 1888 by T. R. Spence who is hardly known at all for his architecture. Instead he designed the interiors for Mitchell's ships and he was the secretary of the Newcastle Arts Association. But what he did at St George's reveals that he was a tremendous designer, way ahead of his time. There are Arts and Crafts touches to the building and in places it is almost Art Nouveau, but above all it's tall, noble and eclectic. The vast tower is not an English church tower but an Italian campanile; the interior is among the richest you will ever see. The stained glass … what can I say; the marble, the tiles and mosaics … gosh. The vast majority of craftsmen who worked on this extraordinary building were either born in the North East or they were living and working here so the church stands almost as a manifesto for the cultural power and artistic talent of the city.

And then there are shops. You can't write about Newcastle without mentioning the shopping. It would be like mentioning Ant without Dec.

I was once on the phone to an call centre in Cardiff trying to arrange to pay a bill to John Lewis Stores. The man in Cardiff took the details and then asked me which John Lewis I was dealing with. I said it was the Newcastle store and there was a little pause at the other end of the line and then he said, a little mournfully, 'Oh! It will always be Bainbridges to me'.

It was Bainbridges for a long time before it became part of the John Lewis Group. Emerson Muschamp Bainbridge first opened his draper's shop in Market Street, Newcastle in 1838. By 1841 there were two Bainbridges because Emerson's cousin, Muschamp, had joined the business, which had expanded and now sold furnishings and fashion accessories as well as fabrics; it had a staff of ten. By 1846 the shop had taken over the building next door and added gloves, lace and mantles and by 1849 there were twenty-three separate departments. In 1865 there were over 160 staff and a shop with a frontage five-hundred feet long that stretched back from Market Street as far as the Bigg Market. In 1876 it was rebuilt on four storeys. Emerson died in 1903 but by that time his sons and even his grandsons were running the business, which was among the largest stores in the country; it had over five acres of selling area, a long-established and much vaunted practice of low pricing and clear labelling and a proud certainty that it was the oldest department store in the country. In 1911 its mail-order department was well established and it had a five-line switchboard with twenty-three extensions.

One of the cunning wheezes that helped Bainbridges to grow in those early days was that it was able to attract working-class customers as well as the more obvious middle-class one because it was relatively cheap and always used clear, straightforward price labels, which is good if you don't have all that much money and (like me) you're a bit scared to ask the shop assistant in case they stick to you. I suspect that the working-class shoppers of Victorian Newcastle liked the safe impersonality of a department store. It was a bit like a market; you could wander around it without being bothered.

Pretty soon they were able to wander round Fenwick's as well.

J.J. Fenwick opened a shop selling dresses and fabric and stuff in 1882. He had acquired a doctor's house on Northumberland Street. It was an elegant Georgian house and he spent £181 4s converting it into a shop – a sum you could probably spend nowadays on the same site buying some shoelaces and a couple of birthday cards but in those days it was enough for him to provide the building with a delicately beautiful shop front. A couple of years later his son, Fred, joined the business having trained in Paris at Bon Marche, the world's first department store, and expansion began. Two neighbouring premises were bought and by 1900 the shop was employing two-hundred people. In 1913 the store was rebuilt on its original site. The new build was the present terrific, white faience Edwardian façade on Northumberland Street. It was a veritable palace of shopping, by that date employing four-hundred staff, brilliant at advertising itself and from the start a leader in the art of the striking shop window display.

These two stores are just the most famous and obvious examples of Newcastle's retail success but the clues that the town was destined to become a shoppy sort of place had been there for a long time. There is a direct line from the 16th century merchants, through the proud and spectacular success of the Grainger Market to the vibrant commercial centre of the Victorian years. For centuries Newcastle had been carefully developing itself as the service and cultural capital of the region. It had got into trouble for ignoring the river in its pursuit of the city beautiful and by the second half of the 19th century

shopping was firmly at the heart of the Newcastle experience. I don't know how many shops there were; I have tried and failed to count them but I think that the answer is a lot.

There were certainly a lot of Co-ops.

In 1908 a Board of Trade report noted the 'shopping facilities in Newcastle appear to be good ... the strength of the Co-operative Society which has many branches throughout the city, must be especially mentioned'.

In its early days the co-operative movement was a politically radical movement and was seen by the authorities as a threat to the established order. It was founded by the Rochdale Pioneers in 1843 but five years earlier than that, in 1839, the Chartists in Newcastle had set up 'The North of England Joint Stock Co-operative society of Newcastle,' which acted as a central supplier for several co-op-type stores. They were briefly the first of their type in the country and they were very successful, apparently turning over £1,000 a week. The venture failed though, because of official opposition and because the Chartist leaders were arrested, and nothing else happened in Newcastle until 1861 when the first proper Co-op opened on Nelson Street. It did extremely well, indeed the whole movement took off in a remarkable way so that by 1873 the North Eastern Co-operative society already had:

• Seventy-three shops
• An engine works
• A bank
• A mining company
• A carpet manufactory
• A household furnishing company
• A printing company

By 1893 the Society was known as the Co-operative Wholesale society (CWS) and it was in urgent need of a new headquarters and warehouse so the architects Oliver and Leeson (remember Milburn House) built them Blandford House. It was opened in 1899 and it is one of the finest buildings in the city. It is tall, splendid and Baroque and the Great Hall on the top floor is beautiful

Top left: *Fenwick's on Northumberland Street, 1898.*
Above: *Elswick Co-op, Scotswood Road, 1890.*
Left: *Bainbridges on Market Street, 1912.*

Left: *The Co-operative Society's 'New Offices, Warehouses and Conference Hall' Blandford Square, 1898.*
Below: *The building now houses the Discovery Museum.*

and vibrant. The building now houses the Discovery Museum.

In 1899 the Co-op built yet another exciting and pioneering warehouse down on the Quayside. It's the Malmaison Hotel nowadays and it is the only surviving old building on that part of the river bank but its real claim to fame is that it is probably the oldest surviving reinforced concrete building in the country. It was listed (by my chum Grace) and I recall the shock and disbelief among the other Listed Building people when she told them. Listing a late Victorian, concrete, co-op warehouse seemed a step too far even for fellow conservationists and yet look at it now – the respected centrepiece of a renewed Quayside. It just goes to show that you need to have a bit of vision. (Grace 1: Fellow conservationists 0)

By the time those two splendid buildings were built, Co-op membership in the City was about 20,000 and assuming that that figure represents 20,000 households it means that one third of all the households in the city were members of the Co-op, which probably also means that vast numbers of people will still be able to remember their families divi number and will show a willingness to recite it even when urged, by word and gesture, that nobody else is interested.

By the end of the century the retail business was one of the city's most important employers. In 1881 there were 3,500 people engaged in selling and the numbers increased massively in the next twenty-five years. It still wasn't as many as were employed in the traditional heavy industries, but it wasn't far short and if you add in those working in administrative, business and financial areas, there were vast numbers of people using the city centre. After 1900 the arrival of the electric tram increased the footfall even more to the extent that in 1912 Bainbridges claimed that 2,500 trams a day stopped outside their store. That meant a lot of Geordies were able to get into town, and because wages were relatively high a whole lot of shopping went on. Sadly, not many of the actual shops from those days have survived unaltered but if you press your little nose against the glass of Northern Goldsmiths or Reid's Jewellers on Blackett Street you'll get a sense of the splendours that were available.

A few moments ago I mentioned that Nelson Street was the site of the first Co-op in the city. That shop has long gone and there's no sign of anything from the late 19th century on the street now. One side of it is made up of the Grainger Market, the other just has the façades of its old buildings which were all part of the Grainger plan and now form the wall of the Eldon Square shopping centre, but the mention of it reminded me that I wanted to say something about famous visitors to Newcastle.

Let me explain.

The North-East Co-op was the brainchild and inspiration of Joseph Cowen who was an MP for Newcastle, the owner of the Newcastle Chronicle and a great and unapologetic radical. He came from Blaydon and had done great work there in the cause of improving the welfare of workers. He was quite extreme, even odd at times; for example he used to appear in parliament wearing pitmen's clothes and making speeches in a Geordie dialect but he was also a passionate and active supporter of the various Revolutions and Nationalist movements that were rising all over Europe. He is supposed to have smuggled guns to Italy and Poland in support of their Revolutions and was perhaps personally implicated in a plot to kill Napoleon III in France. He was also a friend of many of the Revolutionary leaders some of whom came to stay with him at his home in Blaydon. I mention these things because on the wall of the building on the corner of Nelson Street and Grainger Street there is a plaque that records how he brought his friends to a bookshop here on this spot in the middle of Newcastle. There was Louis Kossuth who was the leader of the Hungarian Revolution; there was William Lloyd Garrison, one of the greatest radical campaigners in America and there was Garibaldi, the great leader of the Italian Emancipation movement. Garibaldi came in 1854; he arrived in South Shields and stayed a month in the area – in Tynemouth and at Cowen's house in Blaydon. Not only did he not stay in Newcastle, he apparently declined an invitation to dine with the town's dignitaries, but he did create a popular stir. There was a campaign to make a presentation to him; the subscription was a penny a head and they bought him a silver sword that was presented to him with great ceremony by Cowen who made a brilliant speech, which you can still find on the internet, and then Garibaldi accepted the gift with a speech of his own, which ended, 'I thank you from my heart of hearts … whatever vicissitudes of fortune I may hereafter pass through, this handsome sword shall never be drawn by me except in the cause of Liberty.' It was used, though. He recorded in his autobiography that in 1859 he had drawn it against the troops of the Italian Despot.

There were probably lots of famous people who came to Nelson Street because it was the site of a theatre called the Gaiety Theatre, which had started life in 1835 as a music hall and one of the regulars on its stage was Charles Dickens who came six times to perform his dramatic readings. During one performance in 1861 a gas light fell over on the stage – always a danger in the years before electric lights. The original Theatre Royal, which had been demolished by Richard Grainger, had a disaster of that type on February 19th 1820 when the papers reported that. 'This town has been thrown into a state of extreme agitation and distress by a most dreadful accident … A numerous and respectable audience of five-hundred were thrown into the extremes of panic' by an exploding gaslight and though the fire was put out the crowd 'rushed headlong down the stairs where their progress was stopped by a door at the place where the money is taken. There were scenes of horror and distress and the screams were awful and heartrending'.

When the same thing happened to Dickens he managed to stay calm and quell the panic that showed signs of spreading in the audience and there was no disaster.

Dickens liked Newcastle. He liked the place and he liked the people. He thought they were canny but kind. That's what he meant only he put it a touch more impressively, 'Although the people are individually rough', he wrote, 'they are an unusually tender and sympathetic audience'.

Interestingly, Nelly Ternan, the woman with whom he had a long, strange and secret affair was the daughter of the Actor-Manager of the Theatre Royal. He had taken the job in 1838 just after the theatre opened. Nelly, his third daughter was less than one when the family moved here and took rooms in Westgate. His wife, Fanny, was a famous actress as well and the two of them were a great success in Newcastle. The new theatre was as splendid inside as we know it was outside. The stage was huge and £1,000 had been spent on the sort of stock scenery that was needed in those days for the elaborate productions that people liked. There were two entrances – one to the main part of the auditorium where polite society might be found and another that led directly up to a vast gallery where the less polite society (the individually rough ones) tended to go. It cost 6d to get into the gallery and you wanted your money's worth so you tended to get quite a long show. A typical playbill records a performance of *Nicholas Nickleby*, a couple of dances, a song cycle, a farewell address and finally another full play to finish off the evening. As a result the audience were there for some time which can cause all sorts of problems but fortunately those in the seats underneath the gallery were protected from any 'unpleasantnesses' (any unwanted moistness, we might say) because thoughtfully the gallery had been lined with lead to prevent leaks.

Alongside everything else he did, Joseph Cowen also had very strong connections with the theatre and on Westgate Road is Newcastle's other principal theatre, the Tyne Theatre and Opera house, which Cowen founded and paid for in 1867. It was designed for him by a local chap called William Parnell and it is an amazing building, one of only a handful of Grade One listed theatres in the country. It has an almost perfect example of a High Victorian theatre inside and contains, also amazingly, a unique complex of the sort of understage machinery that was needed to satisfy the Victorian craving for spectacular musical entertainments. It includes lifts to allow actors to appear and disappear and it includes the dramatic 'Thunder Roll', a 36lb cannonball installed in 1882 which sadly killed a stage carpenter called Robert Crowther when it broke the

safety net and landed on his head. His ghost walks still. Apparently.

Such machinery was needed for plays like *Pleasure*, an 1888 extravaganza which included an earthquake, or *The Armada*, which came from London and had nine railway wagons of props weighing a total of thirty-two tons. And you will be sorry to have missed *The Prodigal Daughter*, which included a re-enactment of the Grand National with real horses, water jumps and all the trimmings. The winning horse was played by Voluptuary, the actual winner of the 1884 National. I forget the name of the play, which had a character called Lady Gay Spanker. You'll be sorry to have missed that one.

To set you up for a night out like one of those, what you would need would be a swift half in the pub; you might have needed another to recover from the experience afterwards and it won't surprise you to hear that Newcastle wasn't short of places to go to.

I'm going to end this chapter and this look at the 19th century in Newcastle by quoting a paragraph that I wrote myself in an earlier volume called *Grundy's Northern Pride* (available at the occasional good remaindered book shop). It went like this …

Lynn Pearson, who wrote a book about Northumbrian Pubs, records that in 1882, in Newcastle, there were 446 fully licensed houses, 324 beerhouses, thirty-six breweries and seventy-seven off-licences – a total as she says 'of 883 places at which alcohol could be bought'. Ever a woman for a startling statistic, she goes on to tell us that in the late 1870s beer consumption nationally was more than thirty million barrels a year with 'weekly consumption averaging out at over five pints a head for every man woman and child.' Working on the assumption that many children didn't take up their full statistical allowance, that means a lot of chaps were drinking a lot of beer.

In Newcastle at the same time, drinkers drank sixteen pints per week on average!

I suspect that even Newcastle's modern reputation as a party city for binge drinkers is going to find it hard to keep up with that.

Perhaps we'll find out in the next chapter.

Clockwise from top left: 1) *The Pineapple Inn and Hotel, 1850 - part of the Grainger Market building on the junction of Grainger Street and Nun Street. 2) An 1863 flyer for the Temperance Hotel - perhaps it's ironic that it's site is approximately where the Union Rooms stand today. 3) Junction of the Bigg Market and High Bridge, the Beehive Inn, 1899. 4) The Unicorn and the Golden Lion in the Bigg Market, 1889.*

The Twentieth Century

At the beginning of this story, Newcastle was an almost accidental and rather minor settlement on the remotest edges of the Roman Empire. In Saxon days it was the place where all the wonderful developments of that era didn't happen, where no illustrated masterpieces or stone carvings were done and where no great kings lived. It only began to take off as a town when Robert 'Shortstockings' Curthose founded the castle in 1080 AD and it went on through the Norman years to become one of the success stories of the age, rising in about two centuries until it was among the great towns of England. From then on, the rise and rise continued in a relatively unbroken line for hundreds of years, fuelled by a navigable river, coal and a dynamic/determined/arrogant/grasping leadership (*delete as appropriate). In the 19th century the town became a city and good looking as well – its heart transformed by wonderful new buildings on a metropolitan scale. There were still problems of course, inequalities of wealth, health and opportunity on a massive scale but by the end of the century the city had at least begun the process of tackling those and it had successfully made itself the capital and the service centre of an astonishingly inventive region. In Newcastle specifically, and on Tyneside as a whole, things were developed and invented that had a profound effect on the whole world.

I think it's a remarkable story. In 1950, S. Middlebrook M.A, the senior history master at the Royal Grammar School Newcastle upon Tyne wrote an extraordinarily good book about it called, *Newcastle upon Tyne: Its Growth and Achievement*. He stopped before 1914, having decided that it would be unwise for him to continue into the 20th century because he felt it was so much more difficult to get a proper perspective on things you have lived through yourself, but he did end his book on a pretty hopeful note, suggesting that Newcastle's centuries of growth might keep going into the future. This is what he wrote:

'...the towns in which we live, with rare or partial exception, are chaotic, grimy and ugly, and the sense of local community that was once their strength has been almost completely destroyed by over-rapid growth. We know now that we can change all this. We can make the town both efficient and lovely ... we can do more still; we can turn it once more into a living community. A new spirit is already astir. The first steps forward have been taken. Unless mankind misuses the immense power that modern science and modern industry have put into its hand, the people of Newcastle can face the future in good heart. The Newcastle which has

Stage one of the construction of the 'new' Tyne Bridge, 16th December 1927.

(Steve Brock Photography)

Top: *Suffragettes on Northumberland Street, 1912.*
Above: *Councillor Hazel Stephenson (centre) and Councillor
Linda Wright (following), respectively made Lord Mayor of
Newcastle and Sheriff of Newcastle in 2016.*

*passed through so many periods of critical transition can do so
again but only, one feels, if the vigorous and vivid sense of
community which informed the small walled borough of earlier
days can be recreated in a unified Tyneside.'*

Well … there's bold. Did we do it? Have we made the town
efficient and lovely? Do we have a vivid sense of community and
do we live in a unified Tyneside? Answers on a postcard please.

There have been many, many changes to Newcastle in the
hundred years since Middlebrook decided to close his story, and
even the quickest glance, the merest peep, will reveal that some of
them have been good, some of them have been distressingly bad
and some, maybe even most, have wallowed around in the middle
between those extremes.

I am going to start with a change that I think has made an
undoubted improvement in the lives that people live.

I have to warn you that if you don't agree with me I will weep
brokenly because I'm going to start with the impressive
improvements that have happened in the lives of fifty per cent of
the population.

I'm going to start with women.

Just before writing this chapter I met the Lord Mayor of
Newcastle who's a very nice lady called Hazel Stephenson. She's
the 19th female Mayor in the history of the city and she's been a
councillor for quite a long time, representing Benwell and
Scotswood since 1999. I met her Mum as well, who is an
Alderman so the women in their family have not only been
involved in local politics for years and years but they've reached
the very top of the local political tree. Meanwhile in a Parliament
in far-off London, two of the three MPs representing the city are
women. At least half of the doctors I know are women and we're
never surprised to find a woman in any sort of business. How
much of a change is that?

Because, until this chapter started, there weren't a lot of women
in this book. Among the very few I've found time to mention,
most, I'm afraid, have been assigned very stereotypical roles; there
have been 'Cyprian Nymphs' behaving nymphily in the dark
chares of the Quayside or nice middle-class girls being allowed
half-price tickets to the Assembly room concerts, presumably to
make sure there was something to attract the men. Just

occasionally there have been a few tougher cookies in evidence – the market women hauling sides of beef around the riverside markets were certainly tough enough and so was Bessie Surtees leaping out of windows to elope with the man she loved. The working-class women who formed self-help societies in the late 1700s and the wife and daughters of Humanus who banned sugar from the house in protest at the slave trade were taking active political decisions. There were others, like Miss Deer, the first female member of the Lit and Phil, who was one of the first women in the country to become a member of a learned society. Women were pushing back the social limitations of their lives. Others, of course, were not in a position to push against restrictions, their aim was to survive. Richard Grainger's mother's job, like hundreds of thousands of others, was to keep her family alive, fed and educated and she achieved it with heroic splendour. The elderly women who ran dame schools had an even simpler drive – they had to find a way to keep themselves alive in a world where nobody else would help.

I could, I should have mentioned others, not by name because I don't know the names but they were there, being radicals and Chartists, occasionally even starting Trade Unions but in the main, for most of our history, women have been more or less invisible. If you go into an old graveyard you will see that a man could be what he liked; he could be a doctor or a master mariner, a blacksmith or a farmer, any one of hundreds of titles that defined who he was, but women have been restricted by history into only two; they could be wives or they could be daughters.

However, towards the end of the 19th century that situation was beginning to change. There were schoolmistresses and nurses; occasionally you come across women who had a different non-traditional sort of female job. In St John's church, next to the monument to Richard Grainger and his wife, there's a wall monument to a church caretaker.

In Memoriam
Dorothy Hall Bennett
For many years the faithful
And highly respected caretaker of this church
RIP
1895
Erected by public subscription

By that time, by 1895, women were beginning to fight their way into a broader range of jobs. The first women doctors had been trained by then; though they had to go abroad to get the experience they needed before fighting for acceptance in English society. The first one to arrive in Newcastle was called Ethel Williams. In 1906 she opened a practice on Ellison Place in the centre of town but within a couple of years had moved to Jesmond. She is reputed to have been the first woman to have driven a car, not only in Newcastle but in the North of England. In 1917 she founded the Northern Women's Hospital on the site where the Nuffield Hospital is now. For a while, before the war she was joined by another early and redoubtable woman doctor called Dr Ethel Bentham and the two of them were important members of the Newcastle suffragettes.

The UK was relatively late in giving women the vote. The Isle of Man, New Zealand, Australia and the USA all enfranchised women before the end of the 19th century but in Britain women had been totally ignored and they had got pretty fed up with it.

The first suffragettes were the National Society of Women's Suffrage Societies (NSWSS) which had been founded in 1897. This is the group that the Ethels joined. On the whole they believed in a constitutional approach to reform, though Ethel Williams did go a step further down the path of civil disobedience when she refused to pay her taxes. Mainly, though, they held meetings and handed out leaflets and were generally fairly polite in their protests. They listened to speeches on the Town Moor and marched with banners through the town - Ethel Williams' beautifully designed suffragette banner still exists and is one of the treasures of the collection in Newcastle University Library. Rather engagingly the members of the NSWSS held their meetings in the evenings in Fenwicks Tea Room, which is as good a place to plan a revolution as any. I've seen many a shifty character there, disguised in Fenwicks French frocks, plotting the downfall of society as we know it over furtive cups of tea.

In 1906 the more militant group, the Women's Social and Political Union, the followers of Emmeline and Christabel Pankhurst, took a more dramatic line; they decided that politeness wasn't achieving anything and engaged in lots of pretty violent activity. There were plenty of members of this group in Newcastle as well and because they were mainly middle class (working-class women were usually too busy surviving to get involved in politics, though posher members with large kitchens were encouraged to make them available to allow the servants to organise meetings as well) their attacks mainly took place in middle-class areas. Telegraph wires were cut in

Kenton; the pavilion and bowls house in Heaton Park were burnt down. In the centre of town the Barras Bridge Post Office and the Moot Hall were attacked with incendiary devices. They attacked Gosforth Golf Club and from where I'm sitting now, typing these words, I could, with a decent arm and a following breeze, heave a brick though the windows of the Globe Theatre in Gosforth as they did in 1913.

Remarkable times and remarkable women - but their protests came to an end in the face of the First World War when quite suddenly, instead of fighting against society, women had to step into the breach to help it survive. From the start of the war men were answering the call and signing up in vast numbers; Armstrong's factory alone lost 2,000 workers who had enlisted and the situation got more critical in 1915 when unmarried men between seventeen and forty-two became eligible for conscription, so there was nothing to do but allow women to work in all sorts of jobs, including heavy engineering jobs and shipbuilding, which had been completely closed to them before. Suddenly the public transport systems were being run by women and the shipyards too; there were female welders and most of all, female munitions workers. By 1915 there was a desperate shortage of munitions and an equally desperate shortage of people to make them so by the end of the war ninety per cent of all munitions workers were women. Armstrongs employed women from all different backgrounds to make their guns and their shells.

They didn't pay them a lot, of course. The female workers were described as 'dilutees' and paid less than the men. Is that a surprise to you? Almost inevitably the sudden employment of women raised all of the issues that we are still faffing on about today, 100 years later. Equal pay was an

Female workers meet King George V and Queen Mary, Tyneside, June 1917.

issue and the work/family balance; working hours, morality, health and safety – they were all up for discussion just like they all are today …

But whatever problems there might have been, it seems clear that the women involved took to the life with tremendous enthusiasm. Maureen Calcott (I keep coming back to her) quotes a lady, a twenty-five year old from Gateshead called Ruth Dodds who described the laughter among the women at work. It was 'full of talk and fun'. Of course it was hard physical work but 'one forgets colds and all else in the intense excitement of the work'. She talked about the excitement of getting paid and said 'I hold my head much higher now I know I am worth something'.

For most women the excitement ended when the war ended. As soon as the men came back, the women were paid off … and it hurt. Ruth Dodds went on to work for her family's printing works on the Quayside for a while but mourned because she had to hand that job back to her brother when he wanted it. And that was a common situation. One of the most extraordinary examples of it was Charles Parsons' daughter, Rachel, who was another of those prodigiously talented and pioneering women of the Edwardian Age. She was one of the first three women ever to study Mechanical Science at university and, along with her mother, she founded the Women's Engineering Society in Britain. She was a member of the Royal

Institution of Naval Architects and possessed a Master Mariner's Certificate. She was a leading member of the National Council of Women and in 1914, when her brother enlisted, she took over his job as a Director of her father's works, Parsons' Marine Turbine Company in Heaton. Sadly, in 1918, her brother was killed, the war ended and her father, in his grief, insisted that she give up the job. She never forgave him. She never spoke to him again. In 1920, along with her mother and eight other women, she set up an all-women engineering company called 'Atalanta' which lasted until 1928 but was wound up and her life spiralled off into increasingly bizarre and tragic directions until 1956, when she was living more or less as a recluse in a country house at Newmarket, supposedly protected by an extraordinary burglar alarm she had invented herself using trip wires attached to shotguns. The alarm worked. She was never burgled … but she was murdered by one of her former employees.

So the opportunities provided by the war didn't lead directly or automatically to new, working lives for women – but the atmosphere and the law were changing. Women over thirty (provided they had a bit of property behind them) got the vote in 1918 and were allowed to stand for parliament. In 1928 all women over twenty-one got the vote. Our Ethels remained thoroughly excellent role models. Ethel Bentham went into politics and, after a number of attempts, was elected as a labour MP in 1929. Ethel Williams retired in 1924 and passed on her practice to Dr Mona MacNaughton who, with her (female) partner, Dr Blackledge, eventually brought my wife into the world and guided her (and her mother and sister and lots of other Jesmond women) though all the slings and arrows that flesh is heir to.

Through the 1920s and 1930s the number of jobs for women increased a bit but mainly in those areas that seemed somehow appropriate – shop work and food manufacture, dress making and stuff like that. In Newcastle most of the industrial jobs were in heavy industries which weren't deemed suitable for woman until yet another war opened the factory gates once again. This time women were conscripted into war work and encouraged to go into industry or agriculture. The mother of a friend of mine became a caulker at Swan Hunters and was driven deaf by the experience – and once again the job, however hard it might have been, seemed liberating from 'the restrictions of oppressive home life'.

Since then, well you know the story as well as me. More and more women began to go out to work; fewer and fewer were driven to give up once they got married; more and more jobs and positions began to be made available to women. The situation isn't perfect of course. There may have been nineteen female mayors so far but the council still hasn't had a female leader, there's still a shortage of women in the top jobs, all the old dilemmas about work and family and unequal pay continue to be unresolved but the change has been astonishing and of course these new freedoms have become available to others too. Gay and Lesbian groups, those with disabilities, diverse ethnic groups have all found levels of acceptance that would have seemed laughably unlikely on Tyneside before the First World War. Newcastle University was the only institution in the country to honour Martin Luther King, Mohammed Ali came to the city amid ecstatic acclaim, Nelson Mandela was given the freedom of the city and his name is engraved on the walls of the Civic Centre as an Honorary Freeman of the city. Of course these levels of tolerance and acceptance sometimes get stretched and can sometimes seem tenuous – but it is still a marvellous change that has occurred.

Hats off to the 20th century …

Ah but, there are other aspects of the 20th century that have not been so satisfactory and I am talking now about what has happened to Newcastle's fabled industrial greatness.

Given all of that astonishing level of achievement that I recorded a couple of chapters ago, all of that brilliantly inventive Victorian shipbuilding, mechanical engineering, munitions, electrics, light, Newcastle probably felt that it was set fair to do equally well in the next century and for the first couple of decades there weren't really any signs that it wouldn't, but eventually the 20th century seemed to wear them all down until there was virtually nothing left. For various reasons, by the end of the century the coal was gone, there was no more shipbuilding, the electrical industry had disappeared, hydraulics had gone and there were hardly any armaments left. There was no glass industry and no potteries. There was no metal industry. A few mechanical engineering firms clung on but they seemed like small fry by comparison to what was here before.

Take Armstrong's as an example. What did the 20th century do to them? Well they were undoubtedly boosted by the massive demand for armaments and ships during both of the World Wars, but from the beginning of the century they seem to have had worries that their traditional products (and their traditional base) weren't going to be enough, so like any prudent set of managers they decided to diversify.

First of all they moved into cars. In 1904 they bought a London car maker called Wilson-Pilcher and moved production to Newcastle. For a while everything was not only hunky but also reasonably dory. In the Discovery Museum there's a beautiful example of what they built. It's called 'The Challenge' and it's a vision of brass, leather and polished wood dating from 1911 – it had the reputation of being a smooth and comfy ride and being especially good at going up hills, which is exactly what you would have wanted to do if you had been its Edwardian owner – it looks a dream of the open road – Toad of Toad Hall would have loved it.

By 1913 Armstrongs had become plane manufacturers as well. The company was asked to move into plane production by the War Office and they converted what had been the Grandstand of the old Town Moor race course into a factory. They laid out an aerodrome on the Duke's Moor and went on, after a few false starts, to build 1,075 assorted planes for the British Army by 1918.

But in the 1920s things began to change. They merged the plane division with a company called J.D. Siddeley, called it Armstrong-Siddeley and moved production down south. That business later became Hawker-Siddeley, was bought by Rolls Royce and then by BAE Systems and of course had nothing more to do with Newcastle or Armstrong's. Much the same happened with the cars, which also merged with Siddeley, moved to Coventry and became lost to Newcastle

I look at this process as a complete outsider. I'm a man with no background in business or economics, I wasn't even very good at managing my own pocket money, but I feel such a sense of hopelessness about it all. It feels as if they had lost the will to keep going. They joined with Vickers in 1927 and like a fading film star failed to get top billing in the new company. The once majestic Armstrong's didn't turn into Armstrong Vickers; they became Vickers Armstrong instead. Vickers shareholders got sixty-six per cent of the company while Armstrong's only got a third.

And of course it went on and on and on. They made locomotives for a while – and then they didn't. They continued to make armaments and tanks and then they didn't even do that. In 1979 the works closed down and in 1982 the buildings were demolished.

In 1913 Armstrong-Whitworth took over a skating rink on the Town Moor near Grandstand Road, here BE2c aeroplanes are being built.

Armstrongs are of course, just an example; the same happened to everybody else so that the town is filled with the ghosts of former products. I do my shopping at Sainsbury's in Heaton, on the site of the old Cremona Toffee factory. I don't drink Newcastle Brown Ale, invented in the town in 1927, but if I did it would have to be brought to me from Tadcaster where it is now made. I have stood in front of the sanitary pottery made by Adamsez so many times but I'll never stand in front of a new one because it has gone, closed down, not in Newcastle of course but in Northern Ireland where it moved decades ago … and now that I have become dyspeptic with frustration, where do I get the Liver Salts to make me better? Not in Newcastle any more but from some multinational conglomeration a million light years away.

Do I sound cross? I'm not cross really, just a bit sad. I can't see that there are any individuals to blame (except perhaps a certain handbag wielding Prime Minister who put the boot into the fading survivors of the old industrial greatness in the 1980s). The loss was really caused by forces far beyond the boundaries of Newcastle. I'm going to list a few:

• In the Treaty of Versailles at the end of WWI the German navy was given away, a casual move that had the unexpected effect of producing a glut of ships in the world so the bottom fell out of the North-eastern market. The appalling recession in Germany meant that there was no domestic market for German coal – so they exported it cheaply, not to here, but to places like Scandinavia which had been key British customers.

• Britain (and the rest of the world) also passed through two massive recessions – one in the late 1920s and one in the 1980s. In the recession that started in 1929 Newcastle survived a bit better and emerged from recession a little earlier than other parts of Tyneside because it had the strength of its service sector and the quality of its shopping to keep it warm, but it was still a devastating experience here as it was elsewhere. The 1980s were just as bad from an industrial and employment point of view and to prove it here are three rather revealing Newcastle statistics from that time (though I assume that the figures were much the same everywhere else as well).

1979-81:	Nineteen per cent of Newcastle factory jobs lost
1981:	Unemployment was 21.8 per cent
1991:	Unemployment was 22. percent

• The rest of the world was catching up. The trouble with being clever and a trendsetter (not that I know anything about that personally) is a bit like being the fastest gun in the west – there's always some eager young cowpoke desperate to steal your crown and that's what happened to Newcastle (and Tyneside) (and Britain as a whole) in the 20th century. Others had found out how to do it - so suddenly the shipbuilders of Japan, Korea and even Sweden were sailing into the lead; the electrical baton which we had invented was seized by everybody else and we were left behind. It takes a lot of energy to stay in the lead generation after generation and we lost some of our energy.

• We didn't come up with enough new ideas and we relied too much on the things we had made before.

• But … but, but, but, but! All of those explanations are big global explanations and sometimes you can take comfort from the fact that it was happening to everybody else as well, but you can't help feeling that the managers, the owners and the shareholders of our local firms let go a bit easily. Here's a quote from the historian Oliver Lendrum:

'The alacrity with which the region's economic elite were willing to transfer resources from the local industrial sector to the metropolitan and global financial markets helped in the erosion of the city's great industrial economy.'

Humph!

• And finally – there were people, many people, who wanted us to leave the old grimy, fading industrial past behind and leap bravely into a new world, to turn Newcastle into something sharper, cleaner and sleeker. They included the exceedingly famous and influential T Dan Smith.

Thomas Daniel Smith had been born in Wallsend in 1915 to a working-class family. He grew up with very left-wing ideas and in the 30s was a member of the Independent Labour Party and the Communist Party. In the war he had organised strikes among Newcastle apprentices and then, in 1950, he moved into more conventional politics and got elected to the Council. With his left-wing and working-class background it's not surprising that he took a particular interest in housing and by 1958 he was in charge of housing on the council. Two years later he'd moved on and was in charge of the council itself, a position he held for five years until 1965 and which he used to drive forward extraordinary changes to the city.

Before I start to talk about those changes I'll have to confront the fact that many readers (always assuming there are many readers. Worry, worry, worry) will have two immediate reactions when facing the stories of T Dan and the 60s. Ever since he was gaoled for corruption in the 1970s because of his involvement with the unspeakable architect, John Poulson, there has been a widespread belief that he was corrupt from the start. The BBC drama, *Our Friends in the North* painted a picture of his fictional counterpart as a slick, dark and cynical man, ripping up cities for his own ends.

I don't know whether that's true but there's no doubt that he was a controversial and rather contradictory figure. He was a believer in social justice and equality but sent his children to private school and lived a flamboyant and lavish lifestyle. He was the leader of a labour council but owned a whole stable of other businesses from Joinery to PR. He clearly had terrific power. He had the ear of Westminster politicians and behaved like he was the boss of the city. You would not have been surprised to see him on Northumberland Street wearing a Stetson and riding a white horse like some legendary US city boss man; instead he had to make do with a Mark 10 Jag and the number plate DAN 68. He seems to have been charming but he was ruthless too – and especially ruthless in his determination to do something about the city's dingy image …

… which he did. His years in power made or started vast changes to Newcastle; changes that remain controversial fifty years later. They fall into two groups: there were huge changes to Newcastle housing and there were even bigger changes to the city centre. I'm going to deal with the housing first.

Friends in the North? T Dan Smith, 1965

I left the development of housing in the last chapter on a pretty optimistic note – a world of efficient, if noisy toilets, increasing privacy and generous accommodation which, for the first time had been provided for ordinary people. The situation was far from ideal, you might recall, with many still lacking inside loos and baths, but it was a step in the right direction.

The council, of course, still hadn't built any houses themselves but shortly after 1900 they began to put that right. The first council houses were built in Walkerville in 1906. They weren't terraces or Tyneside flats like the private developers were putting up, they were 'cottage homes' – nice little brick cottages with gardens and twisty-bendy streets which look as different from the terraces as you could imagine. They were (and are) very successful and the city went on to build thousands of similar ones after the war. In 1919, the Pendower Estate, just off the West Road in Benwell, was the first. It was designed by C and B Dick (my favourite firm!) and almost 100 years later it has a sort of mature prettiness that you might really expect to find in the country; and there's the High Heaton estate, which was put up in the 1930s by R.G. Roberts, the excellent Borough Architect. He designed really pretty Arts and Crafts style houses in bright red brick with red-tiled roofs and often red tiles hung on the upper walls and gables. They are as nice as any council houses I have ever seen. Altogether, by the end of the 1930s, the council had built 5,500 houses, all nice, all with little gardens, laid out along pretty streets with a positively suburban feel and fine privet hedges. They were a million miles, or possibly two million miles, from the hideous overcrowding and neglect that had been the norm in the fever districts a century earlier.

It was all very exciting but sadly, at the same time elsewhere in the city, something much nastier was happening and I was an unsuspecting witness to it.

My very first visits to Newcastle were in the 1950s when I was a little boy. On several occasions my big sister brought me over from Carlisle on the train for a day out. Our needs were simple. She wanted to go to C & As, I wanted to watch cartoons at the News Cinema and we both wanted to go to Carricks for lunch; so that's what we did. I mention these trips because the view from the train as we came towards Newcastle astounded and fascinated me. I was enthralled by the endless rows of narrow and steeply-sloping terraces on the western edge of the city, in what I now know were Scotswood, Benwell and Elswick. I had never seen anything like them; Carlisle was an industrial city too and I had grown up in a terraced house (I've never lived in anything else) but these were darker and more intense and on a scale that I could hardly believe. They were the one thing about Newcastle (apart from cartoons and Carricks) which I talked about when I got home so I was surprised and even disappointed when I came back ten years later in 1965, on my way to college in Durham, to find that they had disappeared.

They had been demolished as slums, of course, along with the similar terraces in Byker at the opposite end of the city and along with hundreds of thousands of similar houses in towns elsewhere in the country.

It's a horrible word 'slum'.

We know what it means. A slum is overpopulated and squalid. The houses are substandard with poor or no sanitation, clean water, law and order. Most places that get called slums were never planned, they just happened in a chaotic and informal way but the word can also include proper, professionally built houses which have been neglected and come down in the world.

So were these suburbs of Newcastle really slums? I ask because they were all built in the later 1800s as part of that massive building boom that I have already greeted

Next page, clockwise from top left: 1) *First listed in the directories in 1908, Roberts Street, Scotswood.* 2) *Post-war programme of slum clearance, Newcastle City Council Department of Enviromnental Health, 1955.* 3) *Cruddas Park, 1966.* 4) *Lancaster Street in 1970, Westgate Court and Todds Nook Flats loom in the background.*

with enthusiasm. If you look at photographs of them, taken in the 1950s, well, there were certainly some which had some of the characteristics of slums. There are houses which look terribly run down, toilets are in the back yard and the only bath is hanging on the yard wall. One lady called Pat Rogerson, who lived in a Tyneside Flat in Walker in the 50s, wrote about the chore of bath nights which were always on a Friday. The tin bath had to be brought in from the yard and placed in front of the fire. The water was heated and carried in kettles and pans to the bath and the family then took it in turn, kids first, Mam next, and Dad last of all. Her family shared a toilet (a nettie) with three other families and each family took it in turns to provide a candle that might keep the temperature above freezing on winter nights. The whole family shared a single bedroom. There were still thousands of families whose homes were like that in the 50s and lots more that weren't much better. Most of them were rented from private landlords who had done little or no maintenance for almost half a century and most of them were home to people who were too poor to make many improvements themselves.

Outsiders, and especially outsiders who had an official interest in such things, were convinced that they were slums that needed to go. The *Guardian* said in 1962 that Scotswood 'has a desolation that matches the worst that Liverpool, Birmingham, Manchester or Leeds can show in the way of slums' and the people responsible in Newcastle had no doubt at all that the slums had to go.

And yet looking at photographs of them now, photographs taken of Scotswood by the local photographer Jimmy Forsyth in the 50s seem to show houses which look rather like mine and there were people at the time, including many people who actually lived there who were not so sure they were beyond the pale; Pat Rogerson followed up her account of the hardships of toilets and baths with this:

'The back lane was our playground and social meeting place for mothers. There were always mothers standing at the door

Sycamore and Suffolk Street, 1961.

to their yard watching us and gossiping with their neighbours'

The literature and folk memory of Newcastle is full of community stuff like that. One lady I was talking to blamed modern social problems and youth vandalism on the disappearance of the back lanes and the outside toilets or netties, 'There's nowt for them to dee nowadays. In them days you could gan nettie lowping' which I take to mean running along the backyard walls lowping from toilet to toilet. You wouldn't need the tele if you could do that. And when the netties had all been lowped you could drop your penka doon the cundy or play football and cricket until you had the skill to help England win the world cup.

It's a paradox that we keep loving the memory of such places and there were clearly people who loved them at the time. The Finnish photographer Sirrka Liisa Kontinen arrived in Newcastle and settled in Byker just before it was demolished. From the start she loved it:

The vision began; from the hill, sweeping down along the steep cobbled streets with row upon row of terraced flats into the town … the streets of Byker, serene in the morning sun with smoking chimney pots. I was put under a spell that was to last ten years; after that there were no women to stand in the doorways, no dogs to doze on the pavements and no streets to run down the hill.

Sirrka's photographs create an elegiac picture of a community just before it was bricked up and became just 'deaf and dumb facades of empty streets'. She wrote about the moment her neighbour …

'Mrs Potter, born, bred and widowed in a street as old as herself, kindly closed her door on the man who came to sell her a wonderful future elsewhere.
'Thank you hinny, but I belong here'

So there was a sadness and a sense of loss among many at the demolition of the 'slums', but for those in charge there was no choice. In 1960, T Dan and the council had appointed a planning officer called Wilfrid Burns. He led what was one of the first planning departments in the country and he was going to go on to great things. After a few years in Newcastle he first of all became the president of the Royal Town Planning Institute. The following year (1968) he became the country's top planner, the Chief Planner at the ministry of Housing and Local government. By 1971 he became the Deputy Secretary at the Department of the Environment. He got a CBE and finally, in 1980 he became Sir Wilf … not a bad career trajectory for a man who could write this:

'In a huge city, it is a fairly common observation that the dwellers in a slum are almost a separate race of people, with different values, aspirations and ways of living … One result of slum clearance is that a

Elswick - slum clearance, 1970.

considerable movement of people takes place over long distances with devastating effect on the social groupings built up over the years but one might argue this is a good thing when we are dealing with people who have no initiative or civic pride. The task, surely, is to break up such groupings even though the people seem to be satisfied with their miserable environment.'

I have to admit that I had never read that extract from Wilfrid Burns's autobiography until I was thinking about what to say in this final chapter and I was wild with indignation when I read it. I have known so many people who grew up in those environments who don't fit his descriptions in any way including one key friend whose sense of initiative and civic pride is as profound as anyone I know. For several days I became a Wilfrid Burns bore but I shouldn't have been surprised because the whole country, all of the councils and the Government, the architects and the building industry felt that the only solution to the housing problems of the age were to start again and build upwards, buildings that reflected a new age; technical innovation was what they wanted. They wanted to swoosh away the stagnant world of the past, breathe new life and energy into local authorities and all over the country there was a new breed of politicians whose aim was to reinvigorate their councils.

I have a faded, torn and ragged old photograph on the desk in front of me that I tore out of a copy of The Architect's Journal back in the early 1960s. It shows a row of three multi-storey blocks of flats in Shieldfield. They are towering over a long terrace of Victorian houses called Falconer Street. You can see

Top: *Byker back lane, 1970s.* Middle: *Ralph Erskine's Architects took over a shop on Raby Street to consult with Byker residents.* Left: *A view along Byker Wall to Newcastle, late 70s.*

almost exactly the same view today, looking across the central motorway from the end of Ellison Place; both types of buildings have survived in their original form. The caption at the bottom of the photo reads:

In contrast with the old-fashioned and dingy buildings of yester-year we illustrate here the modern way of living that comes from modern design and constructional methods.

T Dan could have written that. His maiden speech when he became leader of the council went … 'I don't feel that Newcastle City Council has much to be proud of. It is a hundred years since it did anything and I mean to change that!' So he did and there's no doubt that he pulled the whole council with him There was a sort of revolutionary, reforming zeal about him. His aim was to create 'a metropolis fit for the people who lived there'.

He started with Cruddas Park in 1958 and in no time at all a great block of old terraces along Scotswood Road had been replaced by two twelve-storey blocks and eight fifteen-storey blocks, 980 flats in fairly basic blocks with pretty countryside names like 'Sycamore' and 'Beech'. By the standards of the day they weren't particularly advanced – the council already owned the plans of towers that had been designed some years earlier, which meant that they were relatively cheap and building could start quickly. They had electric heating and underfloor heating in the lounge, which they needed because with single glazing they weren't very well insulated. They were a bit short of parking places as well – six spaces per block, which was deemed to be about right at the time. On more conventional council estates there was space allowed for one car for every ten houses! Nobody expected council tenants to be able to afford cars. The first residents were there by summer 1962 and the estate was officially opened by Hugh Gaitskell, the Deputy Leader of the Labour Party, which was a bit of a coup for the city and he was clearly impressed. On the whole the residents liked them too. Those with views over the river were delighted and only the families with young children

expressed the doubts that became as common as clichés a few years later, that there was nowhere for children to go and nothing to do. At a stroke the old 'eyesore' of Scotswood Road had been erased by a bright new symbol of modernity. Newcastle had joined the modern world. As far as I can recall and as far as I have read, nobody cast much doubt on the process and it went on fast. There was a taller, sleeker and more exciting tower added at Cruddas Park in 1968 and quite a lot of others can be found dotted around the town. I should have tried to find out how many – indeed I stood on Cow Hill at the top corner of the Town Moor and tried to count them all but I either gave up (typical of the man) or have forgotten the answer (even more typical of the man), but there were quite a lot. I could see the three on Westgate Hill and the ones I mentioned in Shieldfield. Heaton has several and there's a smashing example in Jesmond Vale. Quite a lot then, which you might find surprising because the enthusiasm for them didn't and last all that long before problems of decay, vandalism and unpopularity, the psychological effects of isolation and the lack of any sense of community gave many of them an unattractive reputation and we have see hundreds of such schemes being blown up on the tele; but in fact almost all of Newcastle's 60s towers have survived … and not just survived …they have all been sharpened up, the entrances made more attractive and much more secure, the heating and insulation has been improved. They have been re-clad in newer and more durable materials and the landscaping, which tended to be very much an afterthought originally, has been given proper consideration. They have been, in fact, properly looked after.

Cruddas Park has seen more changes than most. Half of the towers have been demolished and the others given radical makeovers so that they look extremely sharp. One of them is exclusively for older people and the others for private buyers. It's not called Cruddas Park anymore, the new residents chose the name Riverside

Dene which would have pleased me more if the estate had been near the river and if there had been a dene, but the flats themselves are very impressive and there was a flock of thrushes under the trees and on the grass between the towers when I last went there; it made the names 'Beech' and 'Sycamore' seem more appropriate.

But however much they have been improved and despite the valuable role they still play in housing the city, it is hard not to be pleased that tower blocks went out of fashion as council houses. Even as they were being built there were murmurings of change. My house is an example. I bought it in 1970 when the building societies were very doubtful about lending money to buy a terraced house even in posh Gosforth. I only got it because I promised to pay back the loan in twenty-five years instead of the more normal forty, because I had a twenty-five per cent deposit and because it cost about twopence. But by the end of the 70s that situation had changed and people had begun to realise the economic sense of restoring old properties instead of replacing them. They had also discovered the popularity of traditional forms and materials. People like houses … and on the whole that's what more recent council housing has been.

Before all of this happened though and about the time that T Dan was falling from grace, Newcastle began one more gigantic and hugely experimental housing scheme. The demolition of the old terraces in Byker had been first proposed in 1960 and in 1964 the council had agreed to a complete redevelopment. In 1968 the job was given to the architect Ralph Erskine, who had been working on housing schemes in Sweden since before the War. Swedish architecture at that time had the reputation of being modern but very humane, very idealistic and Erskine's approach to Byker reflected that.

What he built looked extraordinary and still does but it had really sensible, rational explanations behind it. At the time there was a proposal to build a motorway through Byker towards the coast so he built a long,

snaking wall of flats to protect the development from the noise of traffic. He had already used that technique when protecting a new village in the Arctic from the worst effects of the weather. In Byker about half of the properties in the scheme were flats built into the wall, the rest were low rise buildings and individual houses sheltered behind it. It sounds quite simple and sensible but in fact it doesn't look like that, it's positively wild. The wall is a riot of multi-coloured brickwork on the outside and varies from three to twelve storeys high. On the inside there's even more colour – brightly painted wooden balconies and all sorts of over-the-top details make it a visual delight, like something in Barcelona or North Africa. The low rise houses are just as bright and varied and all of these colours were among the choices made by the original residents …

… because that was the other remarkable feature of the scheme – from the start the residents were kept firmly informed about what was happening and invited to take part in the decision. Ralph Erskine had taken over an old undertaker's shop as his local office and as a drop-in centre. The aim was to retain the powerful sense of community that Wilfrid Burns didn't believe in. The properties were built and occupied 250 units at a time with each block containing a local shop and community facilities and about forty per cent of the new residents were people who had moved from the old Byker terraces – a much higher proportion than happened in more conventional schemes.

Wherever possible existing buildings like schools, churches pubs and swimming baths were retained as part of the scheme and there were plans to create other community facilities but unfortunately the plan was never completed. In 1981 Mrs Thatcher pulled the plug on public housing and it all ground to a halt. Isn't that an amazing thing?

Nevertheless what is there remains astounding and beautiful to visit. It has achieved a National and International reputation. It has been listed and received

Civic Trust Awards. From Harvard University in America it was given the punchily titled 'Veronica Rudge Green prize for Urban Design'. It has been reviewed in thousands of articles and hundreds of books, almost always in terms of the highest praise. Inevitably locals are a bit more mixed in their responses – some of them love it, some of them loathe it but now, almost forty years later it still looks superb, which is amazing considering the amount of planting and painted woodwork that needs to be maintained, what one writer has called 'the vulnerability of the detail'. Like the tower blocks – it's been well looked after.

Meanwhile, back in the centre of town even more contentious things were happening. T Dan Smith and his head Planner wanted to replace the dirty old industrial image with a shiny world of stylish new architecture. Unfortunately they have tended in the public imagination to get rather pilloried for what they created and they have come to be seen as the vandals at the gate instead of the builders of the city. At least part of the problem has been that T Dan is stuck in people's minds with the notion that he wanted to turn Newcastle into 'the Brasilia of the North' which is such a ludicrous idea that I can't believe he ever said it – I rather suspect that someone else said it and it became attached to him.

The problem is that the real Brasilia was built from scratch on a virgin site hundreds of miles from existing towns and was the product of one man's imagination at one time. It is a vision of architectural purity, gorgeous buildings with vast spaces round about them. It looks good in photos but I bet it is a rubbish place to live in or visit. It doesn't have any messy bits or variety. You wouldn't be able to pop down to the shops for the milk or sneak round the back of anywhere to find your favourite little oojah or whatsit. The glory of Newcastle is that it is exactly the opposite of that. It is messy, packed with variety and vitality. There are endless juxtapositions of one period against another. It has been growing and changing for over a thousand years. You'd have to knock it all down and start again to turn it into Brasilia.

Colourful sections of the Byker Estate.

(Dr Tom Yellowley)

(Alan Morgan)

Aha! I hear you say, nodding sagely, but that's what they wanted to do and if they'd had their evil way for a bit longer that's what they would have done. But they wouldn't. T Dan believed in conservation. He was a definitely a bit more cavalier than we would be nowadays about knocking down old buildings that were in his way but so were most people in those days, so some things were definitely lost that should never have been demolished – two sides of Eldon Square, for example, and the Royal Arcade on Pilgrim Street, but the vast majority of Grainger's legacy was left untouched and that was true of the really old buildings down on the Quayside and the splendid Victorian and Edwardian palaces in the Business district. No! He wasn't concerned to get rid of all that was old and replace it with new; his aim was to mingle old and new together in ways that made sure that the modern world wasn't forgotten. The comparison he made wasn't with Brasilia but with Renaissance cities like Florence or Milan or Venice.

So, what was the plan?

First of all he wanted to deal with the traffic. Newcastle's traffic was notoriously awful. The A1 came across the Tyne Bridge, up Pilgrim and Northumberland Street and out via the Town Moor and Gosforth. East-West traffic crossed it all over the place and the result was chaos so the first thing they wanted was to get the through traffic out of the town centre and that led to the building of the Central Motorway. Now I know the Central Motorway has been in receipt of a certain amount of criticism down the years. Some find it frankly terrifying; a friend of my mother drove over from Carlisle, found herself on the Central Motorway, found a way off it and went home never to return. Others have criticised its route as being too close to the city centre, restricting its freedom to expand – but that was the original plan. It was meant to be a bit like a medieval moat wrapped around the central core and protecting it from invasion and damage of an automotive nature. There was supposed to be a matching road on the west side of the centre but that was never built; but the existing one seems to me to work even after all of these years. It gets busy, of course, but I've driven through lots of worse towns. My experience, and you will laugh at my pitiful, small-minded ETA mentality, but having travelled along the central motorway on my way to and from work twice a day for 20 years I found that, except on the most catastrophic days, those days when churchyards yawn and hell itself breathes out contagion to this world, it would take me twelve minutes from being caught in the first traffic jam, to get to the Tyne Bridge. That's bearable. Just. So I give a sort of half tick to the through traffic part of the 1960s plan.

The second thing they wanted to do was also traffic related. They wanted to find way of keeping cars and people separate – another thing that was shockingly difficult to do in Newcastle in those days.

Northumberland Street, for example was beyond belief. As well as being a major through route it was also the busiest shopping street in Northern England and possibly, it has been suggested, in the solar system. You might recall that annual horror show which replayed in the town each December - 'Christmas at Burton's Corner!' it was called, a time when even the pedestrian traffic stopped dead as people ran out of places to put their feet. I have wept at Burton's Corner on the Saturday before Christmas. At one stage they put up two revolting pedestrian bridges to allow people to cross Northumberland Street without fear of death but they merely made the pavements worse at each side so the plan included a very necessary wheeze to separate people and cars. It was decided that cars were going to go underneath and people on top. – except in places like the Swan House roundabout where the reverse was the case and led to the most extraordinary of subterranean journeys down two steep flights of stairs and through two slightly unsettling tunnels. One of the flights of stairs has never once been known to be free from the smell of urine and for many years the end of one of the tunnels

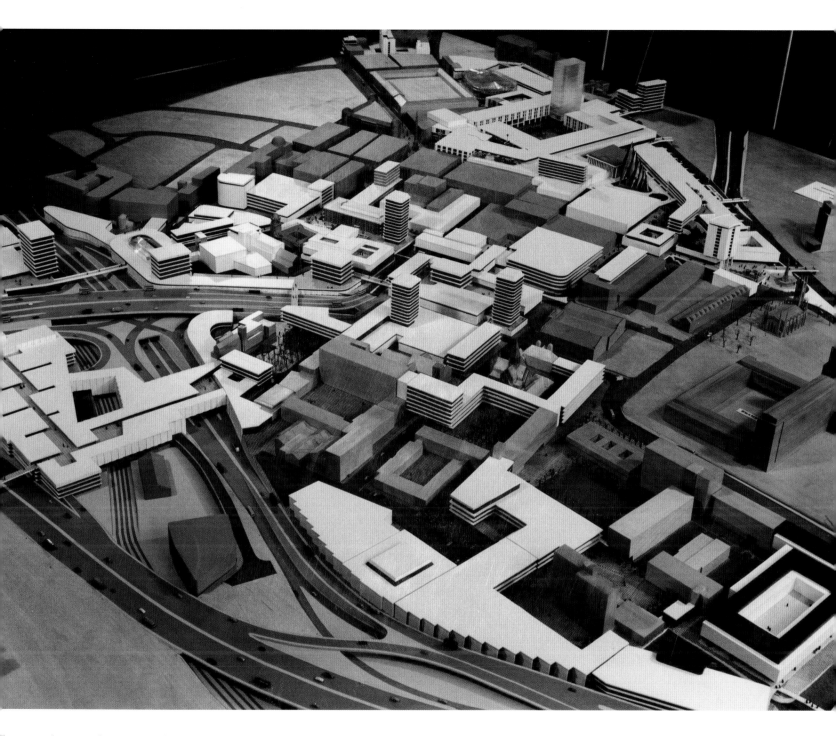

...bitious plans made in 1966 show what our city could have looked like. Some features such as Eldon Square Shopping Centre, the Civic Centre ...the Central Motorway were constructed. But the model also shows several multi-storey buildings that were not built and a motorway running east/west directly under the City.

was always blocked by a lake of unknowable depth whenever it rained. I was there once when the lake was about twenty-five feet long and washed against the walls at both sides of the tunnel, blocking it completely. Some people just marched through. Others pitifully attempted to jump it but it was far too long to be leapt over except by Bob Beamon on top form so they landed well before the middle; others minced across with their trouser hems delicately lifted up in the hope that it was only an inch or two deep (it wasn't). Others gave up.

The more normal form of vertical separation has never worked much better. It was meant to include most of the town centre with all the main streets and buildings reachable from walkways at first floor level. Can you imagine how vile and how bland that would have been? But of course you can; you can recall the dozens of other towns where a similar approach was adopted. But in Newcastle, fortunately (fortunately, fortunately) the only bits built were around the library and over John Dobson Street. The streets underneath were (until improvements very recently) entirely bleak and unpleasant, the walkway above were and remain little better. You find yourself on high concrete paths in the sky, narrow and slightly claustrophobic with exciting but unnerving views down to the cars roaring beneath you. Obviously there were intended to be lots more of these but, thank goodness the scheme was never finished so now we have the slightly manic and inconsequential effect of incomplete roads and walkways soaring out into infinity.

This area was intended to be a sort of 'Cultural Quarter'. There was a new library and should have been a new or extended art gallery; the elevated 'plazas' or 'piazzas' should have been peaceful traffic free places for cultural activity and exchange. Bewick Court, the tower

block that towers towerily above John Dobson Street was to be an exemplar of contemporary urban living. It just didn't work. The problem is that the architecture wasn't good enough, neither the buildings themselves nor the public spaces around them. It always felt bleak and unfinished for the very good reason that it was always bleak and unfinished.

It's not that they didn't try with the architecture. They brought in the top men. The library, for example, was designed by Sir Basil Spence whose Coventry Cathedral remains one of the best-loved 20th century buildings in Britain. His library doesn't … because it has been pulled down; his other contribution to the plan, the All Saints Office Precinct between the Tyne bridge and the church, still stands and though it has never found a full use or a full place in the affections of the city it does at least remain one of the few places where the original vision of concrete walkways and contemporary buildings woven into the fabric of the old town can still be experienced – if you can get past the lake at the underpass to reach it.

Swan House is another disappointment. It was designed by Sir Robert Matthews, one of the most eminent post-war architects. He did the Royal Festival Hall on the South Bank for example, which is a gorgeous place; unfortunately his Swan House is not. It's not rubbish as a design, in fact the facades are quite monumental and exciting; it's just in a rubbish place, cutting the town off from the glories of the Tyne Bridge and leaving Pilgrim Street … I was going to say 'high and dry' but in fact it has been left low and wet like a sort of substandard car drain. For half a century and more it has failed to gain or regain any of the sense of place that it could so easily have had – especially considering the quality of many of the buildings on it.

Next Page, clockwise from top left: 1) *The junction of Northumberland Street and New Bridge Street with 'Cook's Corner' in the background (now Pearl House and 'Five Guys' Burgers. The footbridge seperated pedestrians from what was then traffic on the A1 (1968) 2) A model of what Haymarket might have looked like, with raised pedestrian decks and submerged dual carridgeways (1966). 3) Swan House in 1991. 4) Work at Central Motorway near Trafalgar Street 1973*

So … Oh Lord, there are so many things to regret about the 1960s plan and the way it was carried out and there were other things that should have been in the plan but weren't. The river and the Quayside, for example, were almost abandoned areas at the time. I took a group of newly retired doctors for a walk recently and met them beside the Millennium Bridge. They had all trained at Newcastle University in the early 60s and none of them, except the organiser who had settled here, had returned to the city in the intervening years. Because of where we were I asked them what memories they had of the Quayside. They had none. They had studied at the university for six years but could not muster a single memory of the river between them because at that time it was in a dire condition, polluted and ignored. I recall the story of a boy who fell into the river and died. He didn't drown, apparently, he died of chemical poisoning. There used to be, somewhere near the High Level, a building that contained a tank and engine which could pump vast quantities of oxygen into the water when the salmon were due to run, in an attempt to make it possible for them to get through the pollution of Newcastle.

Clockwise from top left:
1) *Newcastle in 1973, much of the city centre has been demolished to make way for Eldon Square Shopping Centre.*
2) *This aerial view shows Newcastle in 1977 with the shopping centre complete.*
3) *Recent renovations to Eldon Square Shopping Centre and changes to the 'hippy green' have made it a more vibrant communal space.*
4) *Indoor shopping: places to sit and have an ice cream, 1978.*
5) *The former Green Market was closed and demolished to make way for Eldon Square South, a new mall with a Debenhams department store as the main tenant. Intu Eldon Square South opened on 16th February 2010 where other new tenants include an Apple iStore, making it the UK's largest city centre shopping complex, a title previously held by Manchester Arndale Centre.*

(Dr Tom Yellowley)

Dear, dear, dear.

I need to mention some good things otherwise you are going to be reinforced in your prejudice against T Dan and his dreams because what happened in those days wasn't a disaster. If it had been a disaster the town wouldn't be the one we live in today. Let me start with the university district, for example. There were calls at the time to move the university out to Gosforth. Lots and lots of other towns, confronted with new or growing universities, moved them out to suburban sites or even to rural campuses but TDS did the opposite – he not only encouraged the University to stay and expand within the heart of the city but he also founded The Poly (now the University of Northumbria) as a sibling on the opposite side of the road, making a creative area on a huge scale, filled with students who spill out onto the main streets and filled with new and creative architecture. That was a brilliant decision to come out of such a contentious plan and one which still has a profound effect on the mood and the feel of the city; where the Cultural Quarter was underwhelming, the idea for an Educational Quarter was quite the opposite. Newcastle University, contained on its vast island site, has created a superb campus, a magnificent melange of buildings and styles from every decade of the last 120 years; and Northumbria, starting from scratch, has done much the same. People who have not walked along Northumberland Road beyond the City Hall in recent times should do so now to see what a university can do with a hotchpotch of available buildings and a bit of encouragement.

If the architecture had all been a disaster we wouldn't have had the Civic Centre we have today – a beautiful building. You might want to try to come up with the name of a better 20th century set of Civic Buildings in the country. There are some really good Edwardian town halls, of course – Colchester springs to mind or Cardiff, but it's hard to come up with one that combines unmistakably modern lines with real beauty. Its tower is noble, the council chamber strong and sculptural, the central courtyard peaceful and among the most attractive public spaces in the whole city, the interior rich in 20th Century art.

And finally if the plan had been a disaster we wouldn't have had the Eldon Square Shopping Centre. I feel almost like a naughty boy saying this because people interested in architecture aren't supposed to like shopping centres and many writers still bemoan the fact that the centre of Newcastle is given away to a vast, bland shopping centre – but not me. It was the largest shopping centre in Europe when it was built and well ahead of its time. It may not have been great to look at from outside (though I do remember a professor of architecture at the University writing that the Eldon Square facades were 'a worthy successor to the noble tradition of Dobson and Grainger) but it has worked ever since. You will remember that for at least two-hundred years, Newcastle had been doggedly pursuing its aim to be the service capital of the region and Eldon Square cemented that position. It has gradually, over the years, got to be a nicer place. When it was first built it was essentially a vast box with a few doorways and almost entirely blank walls around the outside; but more recently it has been persuaded or allowed to make itself more a part of the fabric of the city. So the blank brick arches around Old Eldon Square are now bright with windows and cafes. On Percy Street and Clayton Street East, where formerly there were blank facades, there are now entrances, shops and cafes so that the mall shares in and adds to the energy the streets.

And finally, finally, the principles of the plan, even where they were crude and naïve have been retained and refined. Our grasp of sleek contemporary architecture has become better and much less contentious. The new City Library is brighter, lighter and more uplifting than the 1960s version and the town is increasingly littered with new buildings that people love instead of hate. There are historic towns where the aim is (and maybe should be) to keep the historic atmosphere pure, but Newcastle has never been one of those and increasingly we are willing to mingle the old and new.

The river has been brought into the equation and made beautifully clean; the Quayside (and of course the Gateshead side of the river) have been turned into a place of national pride and international reputation. In districts like Grainger Town we have shown real restoration skills. And we have even taken on board the old T Dan separation of cars and pedestrians – we just do it better now. I was walking up Grainger Street a while ago towards the Monument and an elderly gentleman in a car drew up beside me, wound down his window and said, 'Excuse me, but how the bloody hell does one get out of this town?' It turned out that he was an officer in the Territorial Army or something and hadn't been in Newcastle since the late 1960s. He was expecting to drive round the Monument, up Northumberland Street and off towards Alnwick where he lived. I offered to set him on the right road in exchange for a lift to Gosforth where, as you know, I live.

At the beginning of this chapter I quoted S. Tomlinson's optimistic vision of what the 20th century would do for the city and asked the question, 'Have we done it? Have we made Newcastle efficient and lovely? Do we have a vivid sense of community?'

I think we have. More or less, sometimes, it depends where you look. I think the town is vibrant without being brash; I think it's feisty and tough in appearance but with lots of beauty. I think it is diverse in every way, a remarkable mixture of old and new building and old and new people. We have had to re-invent ourselves, of course, and the great industrial giant of former times has become something quite different, but on the whole I think we are quite comfortable with that we have turned into (except when we're not).

A spanking new Civic Centre, 1968.

Mayors and Freemen: the Unbroken Chain

In 2016, when I was writing this book, two important groups in Newcastle had a good claim to be celebrating their 800th anniversary.

The Office of the Mayor and the Freemen of the City both claim to have come into being in 1216 AD, which was a significant date because, and I want you to note this very carefully, it was the year after 1215 …

I don't know whether you recall 1215, but it was a very good year for the development of democracy and local government and a pretty bad year for Kings called John. In 1215 King John was in trouble, his country was filled with discontent, teetering on the brink of open revolt and he himself was desperately short of everything you could mention – cash, friends, ideas, clean socks and he was forced to make concessions. He was forced to sign the Magna Carta, item 13 of which says this:
'The City of London shall enjoy all its ancient liberties and free customs. We also grant that all other cities, boroughs, towns and ports shall enjoy all their liberties and free customs.'

In London and across the country, 'Ancient liberties and free customs' was taken to mean the freedom to become Freemen, to make their own choices and to select their own leaders like they had way back in the olden day before the Norman Conquest, and towns lost no time in grabbing their new/old rights. The City of London dates its first elected mayor from the very same year as Magna Carta, and the following year, in 1216, it seems that Newcastle (and Bristol) followed suit. A year later Southampton joined the club and gradually over the rest of the century other (less ambitious) towns did the same.

So the men of Newcastle were given the freedom to choose and elect their own leader, which was a very big deal.

The word 'Mayor' wasn't new. It had first appeared as a title in London in 1189 when a man called Henry Fitz Ailwyn was described as the mayor. A bit later, sometime before 1200, Winchester had a mayor as well and early in the 1200s one or two other major towns began to get a top official who was called 'the mayor' but none of them was a mayor of the sort that appeared in Newcastle after the signing of Magna Carta.

All towns already had head honchos of course. They were usually called the Shirereeve (or Sheriff). From the point of view of ambitious towns, the irritating thing about them was that they weren't chosen by the locals but were appointed to their jobs by the King who was always the ultimate Lord of the Manor. The Norman kings in the 12th century were just like central government today and every century in between; they liked to keep as much control in London as they possibly could so the Sheriffs were entirely the king's men, responsible for collecting the king's taxes and keeping order in the king's name. Those first mayors in London and Winchester and Oxford and so on might have had a new title but they still had the old job – they were still the king's man – but the changes that were forced on King John in 1215 put paid to all that. Suddenly, the residents of towns had a new freedom – they were no longer completely controlled by central government and had been allowed to make a few steps in the direction of independent local power– they could select their own mayor.

And that's what they did in 1216 AD.

There are lots of Newcastle mayors in this book. The first one, the one who was elected in 1216, was called Adam son of Richard though you may prefer to call him Adam Richardson, which is a reassuringly modern and ordinary sort of name; lots of his successors, however, turned out to be far from ordinary – they were a pretty interesting bunch. One of them was murdered by the burgesses of his town; one of them tried to kill a Prior of Tynemouth and another added his name to the list of those agreeing to kill a king. Yet another sailed down the river with his chums and fellow councillors and burnt down North Shields which was (I think we could all agree) something that he shouldn't have done. At least one of them was killed in battle and another proved to be such a hero in a different battle that the king presented him with a magnificent sword that could be borne in front of his successors forever. One heroic mayor failed to save the town from capture by the Scots – but he made a pretty good fist of trying. In the face of overwhelming odds he nobly rejected surrender and wrote defiantly to his attackers that 'we declare to the world that we keep the town for the use of his majesty ' and in return, the king gave the town its motto: *Fortiter Defendit Triumphans* which translates as 'Triumph by Brave Defence. '

As for the men who elected these interesting mayors, you'll not be surprised to know that 'independent' didn't really mean 'democratic' or that the title of 'Freeman' didn't apply to everybody in the town. In the Middle Ages the Freemen who ruled the town of Newcastle were a small group of rich chaps, all members of the powerful Guilds in the town and mainly members of the oldest and most powerful Guild of all, The Merchant Adventurers. The first mayors were all chosen from among their chums and a small group of families ruled the town for ages. The Scotts were dominant in the 1250s and 60s; they provided three Nicholases and one Peter as mayors before they faded a bit and were superseded by the Carliol family. In those days there was no restriction about the length or number of terms you could serve and a really successful or determined mayor could stay in post for ages. Richard Emeldon, for example, was mayor on eighteen occasions in the early 1300s before he was killed leading twenty-eight men-at-arms and thirty-one light horsemen to support the king at the Battle of Homildon Hill near Berwick.

His death lead to one of the great crises in the history of Newcastle's mayors because in the election that followed there were two candidates determined to replace him. One of them called John of Denton was actually elected and declared mayor by the poshest Freemen, the ones from the most important guilds (you can tell that they were the posh ones because they were known as 'the former electors' and sometimes 'the greater brethren') but he was accused of being corrupt by the slightly less posh Freemen from the next rung down the Guild ladder ('the lesser brethren') and as a result there were riots and massive civic disorder. John of Denton was put in prison and starved to death, his killers were executed – it was all just a touch more dramatic than the battles that rock the council chamber in the Civic Centre these days and it was all a bit too much for the king, who imposed a new voting system on the town. It was fiendishly complicated and I have, I'm afraid, rather taken the mickey out of it elsewhere in the book.

Triumph by Brave Defence

Left: This painted wooden Coat of Arms hung in the old Town Hall, when the Hall was demolised it was moved to the Swimming Pool on Northumberland Road. It is now hung on the sixth floor of City Library in July 2016. *Centre:* From Brand's *History and Antiquties of Newcastle Upon Tyne. Right:* A postcard from 1902 featuring the Coat of Arms.

The City's Coat of Arms was in use as long ago as the fourteenth century but was not made official by the College of Arms until 1954.

The castle motif goes back to when the town took its name from the 'New Castle' built by order of Robert Curthose in 1080 and a castle was shown on the twelfth century common seal. The earliest surviving example of the three silver castles on a red shield, dates from about 1400, it is in the window on the north side of the Chancel in St John's Church. The castle motif is repeated in the crest which is a golden lion atop a silver castle. He is holding the golden staff of St. George's pennon. The castle stands upon a wreath of red and white leaves above a fifteenth century style helmet. The supporters, two mythical sea-horses shaded in green with gold manes, fins and tails, are a reminder that Newcastle is a seaport. Both the supporters and crest were added to the shield by grant of William Flower, Norroy King of Arms, in 1575.

So ... not a perfect system but a powerful one and to be elected mayor was really something. He presided over the town's courts, he controlled the meetings of the corporation, he wore spiffing bright red robes lined with sable fur (it's imitation fur now in these politically correct days), he presided over civic banquets and could command the town band to perform for him; bigwigs had to be presented to him and unless they were the king they had to be nice to him because then, as now, only the monarch took precedence over him. Of course in Newcastle, as it happens, there were quite a lot of monarchs available to bow down before which must have been exciting. For a couple of centuries the town was thick with them. Sometimes they had come up on stag weekends but mainly they were on their way to biff the Scots. Once there were even two kings at the same time so you can imagine the pride in the fluttering mayoral breast on that occasion.

Some of the early mayors were pretty impressive. Robert Rhodes the richest of them all, and the man who left the greatest lasting visible impact on the town gets a substantial mention elsewhere but another, William Bishopdale, deserves more than a glance because he was both typical and extraordinary. He was an MP for the town five times and he was mayor for two extended terms.

He was born in Newcastle and he was a typical Freeman. He had made a fortune out of trading in wool and tallow to the extent that he owned more property than you have shaken a hot stick at in a month of Sundays. He had nine different estates in North Yorkshire – not counting 'parts of Richmondshire '. He did just as well in Newcastle where he owned 'numerous shops and tenements. ' A host of marriages all brought extra holdings into his bulging portfolio and you can call me a cynic if you like, but it may not have harmed his bank balance that he had lots of official jobs as well. He was on lots of royal commissions and he was the Customs Officer for Newcastle and also, whatever this means, the Deputy Butler of the Port. There are even suggestions later in his career that he had 'an unhappy fall from grace' (whoever Grace was) because of accusations of corruption in the management of the town. All of these things, the good things and, sadly, the bad, are quite typical of the behaviour of the medieval mayors and their brethren on the corporation but there was another side to him that was more unusual and that was his interest in the defence of the realm. His involvement with the port and the export trade clearly made him concerned about the safety of the seas and in 1387 he built a ship 'a large ship, a barge and a balinger of war arrayed and equipped for the safe passage and return of fishmongers, merchants and other the king's lieges at sea. 'He built a warship in fact; nowadays we might call it a fisheries protection vessel, to patrol the approaches to the Tyne. The following year he took an active role in the Battle of Otterburn.

In 1388 the Earl Douglas led a Scottish attack as far as Durham. There was skirmishing around the walls of Newcastle but then the Scots withdrew up the A697 past the airport towards the Border, pursued, not only by Harry Hotspur but also by William Bishopdale. In the battle Douglas was killed, Hotspur was captured and the English were defeated, but William must have done alright because in 1391 Richard II presented him with a magnificent sword that could be carried in procession before all the mayors of Newcastle through the centuries. You can see it still, if you blag your way into the Mayor's Silver Gallery in the Civic Centre. It's in the gold cabinet and has a magnificent scabbard with a pommel and guard in beautifully chased metal. Beside it is another item of similar age called 'the cap of maintenance', which was worn by the official sword bearer. It is made of grey squirrel fur lined with red velvet and shaped rather like an upside-down hat box – a bizarre, rather alien shape that I have been fascinated by in 15th century paintings but never come across in real life.

In the gold cabinet there's also the Great Mace.

A mace is a sort of club with a long shaft and a heavy bit at the end. For centuries and centuries maces have been used as weapons but also as ceremonial symbols of state and power. You've probably noticed the Great Mace of England resting on the despatch box in Parliament when the Prime Minister is shouting at the leader of the opposition. Newcastle's Great Mace was made in 1687 and is said to be the largest one made in England since the Reformation. It is massively impressive, silver gilt, 4ft 11ins long and magnificently decorated. It used to be carried in front of the mayor by the Water Bailiff because it symbolised the mayor's role as the President of the Court of Admiralty on the Tyne. Newcastle had claimed the River Tyne as its own early in the medieval period and, as you will see later in this book, expended a great deal of energy (and violence) over the centuries to maintain its claim. It was to stifle opposition to Newcastle's monopoly of the river that Mayor Nicholas Scott burned down North Shields in 1267 and other mayors encouraged their roughnecks (Freemen or councillors we might call them) to pull down the Bishop of Durham's quays at Gateshead. So Newcastle had claimed the river for centuries but in 1605 the mayor was granted a new role as President of the Court of Admiralty, which meant that he was responsible for maintaining maritime law on the river.

Well, this was exciting because it meant that he had to have an official barge in which he could carry out his duties. At first he was preceded by a symbolic oar when he was busy on Admiralty Court business but who would want an oar when he could have a huge mace carried by a Water Bailiff? Certainly not the mayor of Newcastle.

Presumably there were court cases to be presided over at which the mace would be on display but the main ceremonial event of the Admiralty Court year was barge day, Ascension Day, the fortieth day of Easter, when the mayor, the rest of the court jury, who were all members of the ruling elite, and the Brethren of Trinity House would sail from end to end of their bit of the river, from Tynemouth to the tide stone at Heddon-on-the-Wall, which marked (and still marks) the tidal limit of the river and the upstream point of Newcastle's jurisdiction. Their job was to inspect all the quays and jetties to make sure they were in good condition. I call it a job but really it seems to have been a good fun day out. The river was always crowded with vessels, barges and wherries, little pleasure boats, but the stars of the show were the Mayor's barge and the Trinity House barge. There is a terrific painting in the Mansion House by a painter called Wilson Hepple, which imagines the event as it might have looked in 1771. The barges are below the old medieval bridge and the bank of the river is lined with splendid merchant houses and the original Mansion House, which used to stand on The Close. The river gleams and the Cathedral tower, the castle keep and the tower of old All Saints stand out against a beautiful sky. The barges have low prows and towering sterns on which the dignitaries stand, the mace bearer is on the prow and eight beautifully dressed keelmen man the oars. It's like a cross between a Canaletto and a painting by Turner and Newcastle and its ceremonies look like a perfect image of ancient power and splendour.

The ceremony continued into the 19th century and the old barges were replaced with new ones. There is an early photograph that shows top-hatted mayors and things

The Great Mace.

A deed dated 20th February 1483 gifting land in Hebburn by Richard and Isabel Lylborn to Robert Byrgham in Newcastle (Novi Castri Super Tynam) – the document records 'because our seals are unknown to most people, we have procured the seal of the office of Mayor of the town of Newcastle aforesaid to be affixed' (seals were used instead of signatures to authenticate documents). (Reproduced by kind permission of the Chapter of Durham Cathedral)

Bottom left: *Barge Day, 1903.*
Bottom Right: *By Ralph Heldey, 1891.*

standing on the roofs of richly decorated Victorian launches still being rowed by buffed up keelmen in straw boaters and white trousers. Tens of thousands of people turned out for the day with the river banks lined with carriages and fashionably dressed spectators.

I read an account of the Mayor's barge party arriving at Heddon-on-the-Wall in 1818. They had to walk the last bit of the route because the river was low but they were all very jolly and there were musicians all around them making the scene as festive as possible. Traditionally when the Tide Stone had been claimed by the mayor he would kiss the prettiest girl in the village and give her a golden sovereign but on this occasion there was no pretty girl – just the 'Harbour Master, Mr Ostle, an individual of considerable proportions'

climbing on the stone with a wine glass in his hand, and an elderly lady from a nearby cottage cadging wine off the mayor and getting unsuitably sloshed.

By 1818 Newcastle had had a mayor for over 600 years. They had pretty well all been rich chaps. They had been drawn from a limited group of probably no more than about thirty families who had sort of reshuffled the title between them over the years. Virtually every one of them had also been an MP for the town and they had all been elected (in a roundabout and bizarre way) by a smallish band of their chums and families and social equals. They remained very powerful. In 1827, according to Mackenzie's history, the mayors were head of a corporation of about eighty-eight officers. They had a state coach and a state barge and were able to live in the

Above: *A statue of John Marley on Northumberland Street.*
Left: *Lord Mayor of Newcastle, Councillor Hazel Stephenson shows off a replica of the sword presented in 1391 Richard II.*

absolutely splendid Mansion House on the banks of the river. They had a salary of £2,000 per annum, which was better than a kick in the pants.

The system they ruled was full of holes and some of them coped with it better than others. Some of them panicked and became repressive in the face of difficulties; others showed an awareness of the sufferings of the poor.

The electorate were an unrepresentative group and the mayors they chose a mixed bunch, but the town they ruled did pretty well out of those 600 years. It had grown from nothing to become one of the great towns of England but it was about to enter into one of the greatest periods of change in its history.

In 1835 the world of Newcastle's mayors changed entirely and the Freemen even more. Following the Great Reform Act of 1832 the new Parliament passed the Municipal Corporations Act, which abolished all the old unrepresentative corporations that had ruled towns since the Middle Ages and replaced them with new councils that had to be properly elected for a fixed term with mayors who could only serve for one year after being elected by the rest of the councillors.

The Freemen lost their old political power when the new system was introduced but they survived to keep going the role they still perform today – as guardians of the City's open spaces and in particular the glorious and extensive acres of the Town Moor. The earliest charters of the Norman town had declared that the Freemen of the City had possessed grazing rights on the Moor since 'time immemorial' and they possess them still, protecting them for the rest of the population.

The world of mayors changed too. Before 1835 almost all of them had been MPs as well; since 1835 only two have. The lists of early mayors are dotted with 'sirs' and the vast majority of them bear the names of well-known landed families; since 1835 most of the mayors have come from much less elevated backgrounds - though there have been exceptions. At first a lot of them were still well-to-do people, industrialists and business men, a smattering of professional men like doctors and surgeons.

A couple of them were seriously famous or became so later. William Armstrong, the great North East industrialist, inventor and entrepreneur was mayor in 1850. Isaac Lowthian Bell had already risen from humble origins in Cumberland to become a successful ironmaster on Tyneside before he became mayor in 1854, but his rise and rise was going to be inexorable until he was among the most powerful and successful industrialists in the country.

Others were still well off but less famous. John Fitzgerald was a successful local brewer, George Lunn the owner of a shipping company. Some of them were philanthropists. William Haswell Stevenson not only paid for a number of branch libraries around the city but he also paid for the extraordinarily realistic statue of Queen Victoria outside the cathedral, a wonderful figure that gazes oddly off into the distance towards the station so that the Queen doesn't have to have her back either to the cathedral or to the Town Hall, which used to stand opposite each other. Arthur Munro Sullivan who was Lord Mayor in 1918 was another ship-owner and another philanthropist. He gave a fortune towards the establishment of the medical and dental schools at Armstrong College, the future university in Newcastle, and eventually left his exquisite house in Jesmond to be the city's future Mansion House.

You might have noticed that I snuck the phrase 'Lord

ROGER THORNTON

H.M. JUDGES CARRIAGE AT MANSION HOUSE, NEWCASTLE

NEWCASTLE UPON TYNE, ss.

YOU swear, That you shall from henceforth hold with our Sovereign Lord ___ the King's Majesty that now is, and with his Heirs and Succeffors, Kings and Queens of *Great Britain*, against all Perfons, to live and to die, and maintain the Peace and all the Franchifes of this Town of *Newcastle upon Tyne*, and be obedient to the MAYOR, ALDERMEN, SHERIFF, and all other the Officers of the fame, and their Counfel keep; and no Man's Goods avow for yours, unlefs he be as free as yourfelf, and of the fame Franchife: And you shall obferve and keep to the beft of your Power, all lawful Ordinances made by common Confent, on High Court-days; and all other Things you shall do that belong to a FREEMAN of the faid Town.

So help you GOD.

___ of *Edward Humble Hoffman* ___ was this 25 Day of *July* ___ in the Year of our Lord God 1775 admitted a Free Burgefs of this Corporation, before the *Worfhipful Charles Atkinson Efquire* ___ and ftands charged with a Musket for the Defence thereof.

Mayor' into that last paragraph and I did so because, in 1906 the role of 'mayor' in Newcastle was elevated to 'Lord Mayor', one of only twenty-five cities in the country to receive that honour. It seems a little bit ironic to me because in the 20th century the job has increasingly been given to chaps and of course chapesses from less lordly and more ordinary backgrounds.

So far as chapesses are concerned there have now been nineteen female Lord Mayors since Violet Hardisty Graham first took on the role in 1952 and introduced not only a new gender into the job but also the unexpected delight of finding Lord Mayors with interesting and unusual middle names. I noted with pleasure that the recent mayor David Slesenger has 'Serge' as his middle name, but my favourite discovery was that Theresa Russell, Lord Mayor in 1965, and a famous and fascinating figure in Newcastle political circles for 50 years, was actually called Theresa Science Russell.

I think it's good to have mayors called Serge and Science, but I think it's also good to have mayors called 'Madge' or' Doris'. Madge Elaine Graham was Lord Mayor in 1971 and Doris Starkey in 1978 – those are good names – ordinary, reliable names. If Madge and Doris can get to the top, I can't help thinking, there's not a lot wrong with the system.

As I was growing up I never met a mayor and any I saw were posed in dignified situations like royalty. But now that I'm old, older, getting on, more mature I seem to have met quite a few and I find that I like them. I gave a talk a few years ago and the Mayors of all five Tyne and Wear boroughs turned up at it. They didn't come just to listen to me, though they were very polite and nice, they came because they had decided to have what they described as a 'chains night out' – a bit of a chat, a couple of glasses of wine and a pizza - just nice and ordinary. I

sat in front of a former Lord Mayor on the bus the other day. She didn't spot me because she was having a bit of a laugh with her granddaughter. I often share events with mayors these days so I have had lots of opportunities to observe them in their natural habitat and it seems to me that there has been an extraordinary change since the early days of mayors.

It's not that their role has changed particularly. They are still the first citizen of the city; they still speak on behalf Newcastle and its community. In the city nobody has precedence over them except the monarch and occasionally in special circumstances, the Lord Lieutenant. They need to show diplomacy, welcoming visitors to the city and promoting its qualities and community. There are still specific tasks like signing legal documents and chairing council meetings. The sense of ancient ceremony still holds sway. All Mayor's Parlours are places of unexpected historical delight, filled with official gifts and memorials of long past visits, but Newcastle's 800 years of history has created an extraordinary wealth of memories. The office door is framed by 18th century carriage lamps from the Mayor's coach, which are alight whenever the Lord Mayor is in the room. The Silver Gallery, which forms a sort of antechamber, is awash with treasure like the swords and mace I mentioned before. There's a silver spade used by the Prince and Princess of Wales in 1884 to plant a tree at the opening of Jesmond Dene park, a cup awarded to the feeder of the best fat ox in the city's Fat Stock show in 1920, a fruit stand from Gelsenkirchen and a silver model of a Viking longship given by the people of Bergen. There is a silver cup that throws an extraordinary sidelight on the First World War –it was awarded to the battalion winning the highest number of points at a Brigade Sports Day held just behind the trenches in December 1917. There are items associated with famous

Previous page, clockwise from top left: 1) *Roger Thornton immortalised in a statue above a shop on Northumberland Street.* 2) *With the Great Mace, George Harkus, Mayor 1898-99.* 3) *Carriage at the Mansion House (the second one at Ellison Place)* 4) *The Oath of the Freeman states that the person being admitted to the 'Free Burgesses' or Freemen stands* 'charged with a musket for the defence thereof'. Centre) *The musket.* 5) *Reassuringly ordinary, Lord Mayor Alderman Madge Elaine Graham, 1971.* 6) *The 'Mayor making' ceremony of Lord Mayor, Doris Alma Starkey, 1978.*

local men – a goblet given by his workers to Robert Stephenson and a wonderful silver soup tureen presented to Admiral Collingwood in recognition of his great service to his country – and there are artefacts associated with the people and groups who have been made honorary Freemen of the City; the ship's bell of HMS *Newcastle* is engraved inside with the names of all the families of the sailors and the accompanying certificate gives the ship's company 'the privilege, honour and distinction of marching through the City on all ceremonial occasions with bayonets fixed, drums beating and colours flying.'

It is all fantastic stuff, entertaining, informative and moving. Downstairs, in the Banqueting Hall, the walls are inscribed with the names of every mayor since 1216 and all of the Honorary Freemen as well – people like Baden Powell, William Gladstone, Jackie Milburn, Nelson Mandela and Bob Geldof. When you put all of this pomp and splendour together it makes a fascinating picture of ancient tradition.

So the Mayors still do the same job and from outside it doesn't look as if it's changed a lot – but they do it differently. I've seen them in schools, sitting on tiny little chairs or making speeches in church halls. I have seen them being sweet and kind to the candidates at prizegivings and while handing out the certificates at award ceremonies. They arrive in a splendid car, wearing the chain of office which has two eighteen-carat gold chains, sixty inches in length, with a gold medallion engraved with the Arms of the city; it was made in 1821 and must weigh a ton and be worth a fortune so they turn up at these event with all the dignity of their role around their necks, conveying a sense of something special to the occasion; but then … and this is a lovely thing I'm talking about … then they undermine the formality by being nice and friendly and ordinary.

I bet Roger Thornton never did that for the ordinary people of his town nor even Adam son of Richard, however reassuringly modern and ordinary his name might have seemed.

Modern Newcastle, clockwise from top left: 1) *The atrium at Newcastle City Library,* 2) *The Tyne Bridge and Gateshead Quays.* 3) *Swan House Roundabout* 4) *St James's Park.* 5) *Newcastle University's Devonshire Building.* (*All images: Dr Tom Yellowley*)

Index

Newcastle's Quayside and the Gateshead Millenium Bridge.

Grey Street and Grainger Street from Grey's Monument, 2016.

(Steve Brock Photography).

FINIS.

ffortiter defendit

triumphans.